There Must Be
YOU

Dear Jay,

Having you with us at St. Matthias was a wonderful gift. Thank you for your music, your heart, and your help. I hope our friendship doesn't end here.

Here's to _you_ journey!

much love,

Rivu Adams

Feb. 2022

There Must Be

YOU

Leonard Swidler's Journey
to Faith and Dialogue

RIVER ADAMS

RESOURCE *Publications* · Eugene, Oregon

THERE MUST BE YOU
Leonard Swidler's Journey to Faith and Dialogue

Resource Publications
An Imprint of Wipf and Stock Publishers
199 W. 8th Ave., Suite 3
Eugene, OR 97401

www.wipfandstock.com

ISBN 13: 978-1-4982-0213-8

Manufactured in the U.S.A.   09/26/2014

To Mom, always my first and most faithful reader.

At the same time that we are earnest to explore and learn all things, we require that all things be mysterious and unexplorable . . .
—HENRY DAVID THOREAU, *WALDEN.*

All streams flow into the sea,

yet the sea is never full.

—ECCLESIASTES 1:7

Table of Contents

Preface

I love deadlines. I love the whooshing noise they make as they go by.
—Douglas Adams, *The Salmon of Doubt*

He steps out of the elevator across from my little apartment, where I stand at the open door. A triumphant grin reigns over his face, and he lifts up his arms to the ceiling, filling the space of the hallway with all of his gangly and laughing nearly-six-foot stature. This is Len Swidler in full glory. "Ah! I am on time!"

In fact, he is not. He is ten minutes late, but by Len's standards he is early. Whenever he's due to come to my door, I usually expect him between 20 and 50 minutes after. That's if he shows up on the right day.

Today is a Saturday in December of 2012, and we've planned to have dinner at 6 o'clock and talk about this book—one of our first real, detailed conversations. Yesterday, exactly at six, my phone rang.

"Hello? Len?"

"I'll be there in 5 minutes!"

"You'll be where?"

"At your house!"

I digested this for a second. "Len. Today is Friday. We are meeting on Saturday, remember? I am busy today, and I told you I couldn't do it. We agreed to meet tomorrow. Saturday. Remember?"

Phone static in my ear sounded like the chaos of that moment, then his voice came back. "Right! I remember! So where was I supposed to go tonight?"

"I don't know."

"I made an appointment to meet with somebody tonight, instead."

"Did you write it down somewhere? Try to pull over and look."

"Right, right. I'll figure it out. I have Chinese food!"

"Awww . . ."

"I'll put it in the fridge, and we'll eat it tomorrow."

It is now Saturday, and Len is back. The epitome of an absent-minded professor. I lift my eyes to the bag of Chinese he is holding in his upraised hand.

I've been his colleague at the *Journal of Ecumenical Studies* and the Dialogue Institute for six years, his student for five, and his friend for—it's hard to say—maybe from the beginning. I was raised in Soviet Russia, in a culture of punctuality and responsibility, and for six years I've scolded him for his perpetual lateness—nagged and mocked and rolled my eyes—but as we go inside, fill our plates, and carve out some space at my tiny kitchen table, I think to myself, *Waiting a while is a small price to pay for having him here after all.*

We eat and talk—about the book and about his life, going on tangents and telling stories, plunging into discussions, as we are wont to do. He talks of the students from the Middle East coming to study dialogue in Philly, and of the future of the church. He talks of his trip around the world many years ago, of the tremendous minds and hearts he has encountered, the giants of humanity he calls "friends," the revelations of faith, reason, and love that made him who he is. He recalls times of hardship that would make another shudder, and he laughs. He is turning 84 in a couple of weeks.

He was there for the Depression, for World War II, for Vatican II, for the Civil Rights movement, for D-Day, and for Dorothy Day—small steps and giant leaps. He worked in Tübingen with Hans Küng and Joseph Ratzinger, whom Len calls "Joe"—and again he laughs. I rest my chin in my hands, listening, and egg foo young is going cold on my plate.

"You know," he says, "people often tell me, 'Dialogue is nice, but it's just drawing room entertainment.' I hear it a lot." He shakes his head.

I know dialogue is more to Len than that. I've heard his stories. I know where he's been.

In early October of 2000, Len Swidler stood on a hilly road's stretch behind Skopje in Macedonia, shoulder to shoulder with his long-time comrade and co-editor Paul Mojzes, and listened to the choking patter of gunshots from below. Five hundred yards down the highway, cement barriers were blocking the way, and beyond them smoke billowed up in odd, diseased patterns throughout the valley. Not the fires of home—the fires of war.

No one seemed to be able to tell them who was shooting at whom exactly, only that Slavic Macedonians—Orthodox Christians by religion—were fighting ethnic Albanian Muslim separatists. Civil war was brewing in the country.

Len and Paul had come to Macedonia at the invitation of its president, Boris Trajkovski. He called them a few months before, as they were holding their Abrahamic Trialogue in Indonesia: a meeting of Jewish, Muslim, and Christian international scholars. "Our traveling show," Len calls it. President Trajkovski got Paul on the phone at the presidential palace in Jakarta and said, "We are on the brink of civil war. Our religions are being part of the problem. Bring your Trialogue here, help. Please. We need you."

Orthodox Christians make up the majority of Macedonia's population, and Albanian Muslims are a significant minority at about 25 percent. There are also Catholic and Protestant minorities and some Jews. Boris Trajkovski himself was a Methodist Protestant with education in law and theology, newly elected to the presidency in 1999. He inherited a country torn by economic strife and ethno-cultural and religious conflict, immersed in the boiling-hot and bitter soup that used to be Yugoslavia.

Bringing the Trialogue to Macedonia wasn't an easy feat. It took the efforts of the U.S. Institute for Peace, two trips to Skopje, and a grant from George Soros. The leadership of the two major religions were reluctant to participate, especially the Orthodox Metropolitan. "He didn't want public debate with a shmuck coming from the outside," Len explains. "And he didn't want dialogue with the Muslims."

Still, in October, more than two hundred people came together in a great hall, many of them local clergy, and Len's Trialogue. President Trajkovski opened with a speech, Prince Hassan of Jordan sent his personal delegate to read the lecture he'd written for the occasion, the deans of the Orthodox and Muslim theological seminaries spoke. It was contentious, it was aggressive, and day passed after day. They kept plugging at it and talking. Prof. Mojzes spoke Serbian and conducted a lot of conversation with the local clergy. They took the whole cohort to one seminary and the other, where the deans addressed each other's flocks. Then something happened.

Literally at the eleventh hour—at 11 o'clock in the evening on the last day before closing—the Orthodox Metropolitan issued an invitation to the leadership, Macedonian and foreign, for a banquet at his home. The main dish was cold turkey.

"It's like a transformation came over the Orthodox leadership. A great conversion experience." Len smiles with the satisfaction of a cat that just found the sour cream.

"What do you think prompted his conversion?"

"We assumed it was all kinds of positive talk from his clergy. Remember, we got fifty local clergy to come regularly and participate. They were talking from the floor, it was not just the podium dialogue. I think this upwelling from below persuaded him he should ride this horse. But whatever the reason, it was a last-minute decision—we'd had a farewell banquet at 6 PM that day."

They didn't get to sleep much that night. By the wee hours in the morning, after a marathon of debate and cold turkey, they formulated three commitments to announce at the closing day's press conference:

- The leaders of the five religious communities would meet twice a year, just to talk, under the aegis of the president of the country;

- The Interreligious Cooperation Council would be set up immediately, to exist 365 days a year, with a member from each community, to collaborate among themselves, with the university, and with the parliament;

- There would be collaboration between the faculty and student bodies of the Orthodox Christian and Muslim seminaries.

The Macedonian Trialogue of 2000 did not prevent violence in Macedonia. Hostilities broke out openly in January 2001 between separatists and the state, and there were battles and casualties, although compared to the wars on their neighbors' territories these could be called mild. Dozens of lives were lost.

A meeting of two hundred people cannot solve all problems. Language rights, borders, and ethnic tensions did not disappear in Macedonia—even religious conflict, of course, lives on many levels and far outside of Skopje—but Len and Paul went back twice, a year later, and the commitments were being observed. They brought more money from the U.S. Institute for Peace to train Christian and Muslim representatives who would go out into communities and talk with clergy there. Two hundred people in a room did not stop a war, but they did what the President asked them to do: The religious leadership was no longer a problem, and organized religions used their agency to band together for peace.

Len stretches on his chair, his expansive figure making my kitchen feel tinier than ever, his feet touching the stove, hands behind his head, and I can see a seam coming apart under the arm of his thirty-year-old sweater. He never seems to care what he wears.

"There is still so much to do!" he says, and in the swirls of his eyes I discern the future of international conferences, workshops, grand dialogue initiatives, shelves and shelves of new books, and the breathtaking form of his church, with roots in the earth and steeples in the heavens—bright and unblemished, full of love, and open to all—though Mass in it will never start on time.

"You know," he says, lingering on the thought, "I think, I am going to be very reluctant to die."

I chuckle. And then, beginning a mental pattern, I make a note to myself: *This is going in the book.*

And, finally, I take out my pencil.

Acknowledgments

Writing a book, like climbing a mountain, is a long and treacherous endeavor, sometimes exasperating, sometimes lonely and painfully tiring—and always, always beautiful. It is easy to fall to your death, especially as you get close to the summit, so I'd like to give a few grateful nods to the people who caught me, led me, and helped me up.

First, to Len Swidler himself, for being who he is: an inspiration and a friend, on occasion a good-natured flake, but in any case, an agreeable subject. To the many people who gave interviews and lent me their perspectives, whether they made it into the book or not. Everyone's voice was helpful. To Nancy Krody, the managing editor of the *Journal of Ecumenical Studies*, who managed and edited through this whole disordered process and went above the call of her duty, at times on very short notice. To Laura Ferris, who, when I begged her for urgent notes, read this manuscript on the airplane and then patiently answered question after question. To my family, who valiantly let me work in peace, even when the pressing questions of what's for dinner were burning their tongues. And, of course, to my mother, who has always been the first to love everything I do. Never my best critic, she's always been the best at understanding what I mean.

Introduction

Since his college years Leonard Swidler has had two goals in life: to become an intellectual and to become a saint. You want to laugh now, and I, too, couldn't hide a snigger when I heard him say it the first fifteen times, but he was dead serious in this pursuit, and in a way, though the word "saint" has certainly changed and acquired new meaning over the years, it still has never left him. He is now eighty-five years old, and if you ask the many thousands of people around the world who know his name whether he has achieved his goals, their answers will differ: He is hailed as a visionary of peace and dialogue, and he is denounced as the enemy of true faith. If you ask Len himself, his answers are likely to differ as well. Catch him in a pensive mood, and you will hear a reflection on the meaning of sainthood. Catch him in a playful moment, and see him shake his head and laugh. "I'm still working on that second one," he'll say.

I've also wondered about this phrase. He repeats it quite a lot. Could he be serious? He has spent his life developing, promoting, and leading interreligious dialogue. Did he find his road to intellectualism in it? His road to sainthood? And is it childish even to think in these terms?

It took my studying the whole portrait of the man to understand how dialogue, faith, and intellectual inquiry fit together in his mind and in his life—and, once I did, I better understood how they fit together in the world. To Len, reality itself is dialogical. I'd like to sketch that portrait for you now. And at the end of the book, I will tell you why I believe that, when we talk about dialogue, faith, and intellectual inquiry in Len Swidler's life, we are not talking about three different things but one—one and the same.

What to expect from this book

This is not an exhaustive biography. When a century from now experts look for a definitive source of all things Swidler—names, places, and events, arranged chronologically on a timeline—this will not be it. I rather tell the story of Len's search for himself and for his place in the world—and of the place he's found. He's traveled a long road, but for Len all things—war, Antisemitism, religion—have come together and brought him to his life's cause: dialogue. This story will meander sometimes back and forth in time, and sideways into considerations of our own choosing, Len's and mine.

The structure of this book is a little unusual in that it contains three somewhat distinct genres intertwined with each other throughout. Mainly, the progression of Len's life will be traced in the chapters. You will read there about his remarkable international and interfaith family, his quest to become a priest and the devastating loss of vocation, his graduate school days sparkling with adventure and the adventures of world travel, the discoveries of spirit he found with his students in Philly and on the other side of the world, his friendships with the giants of the church, and his life's work.

Every so often, I will step briefly out of Len's story into "historical interludes" that venture into the roots of the world that made him who he is. These segments bring forth the people and places he has encountered along the way and give voice to his times, because in many ways the history of Len is the history of the twentieth century, and, after all, the history of us all is that of humanity. In "historical interludes," more than in the chapters' main text, you will hear my voice, taking up on occasion the issues of ethics, politics, and controversy. This is where I'll think out loud about the world, and when you wish to make an argument, it will be with me.

And then you will hear Len's voice directly. All throughout the book he will be present in quotes and in conversation with me. Within the body of the chapters, you will see short bits of our interviews moving the story along, where Len's personality and gentle humor sparkle so that I didn't want to change a word. Between chapters, separate sections titled "Talking to Len" will take us often away from events and into the realm of Len's reflections, convictions, findings, and faith journey. A few of the interviews are with people who know Len in unique and interesting ways, and their names will be indicated at the top of each interview, but then the participants are identified by their initials. You will see that *LS* always stands for "Leonard Swidler" and *RA* for "River Adams."

"Talking to Len" sections are not dialogue, at least not formal dialogue. They are excerpts from months and months of couch talk in Len's living room about the things we all ponder, struggle with, and are shaped by—the questions that grow into wisdom in the diligent seekers' gardens. It's about faith of many kinds, exploration, flying and falling, and, most of all, discovery. My roles in these conversations are mixed. I am his student and his friend, and I am his oral historian and biographer, and I am sometimes a challenger of his views, digging for something more or other. There is a freedom in this format but also limitation. I tried deliberately to direct our conversation as little as possible, and so it roams away at times from its starting topic, and it is more natural this way and more interesting, but it also means that I might leave an issue before Len gives me an answer that satisfies. No question of depth, of course, can be mined to its fullest, so I leave it to you to decide, to pursue, and to persuade.

I have omitted many events from Len's life in this book because, if I hadn't, his eighty-five-year-long Odyssey would have produced a multi-volume series, and because his journey has been driven less by events and more by evolution. Still, to make sense of the journey, some facts are needed as guideposts.

Brief facts about Len Swidler

Leonard Swidler was born on January 6, 1929, in Sioux City, Iowa, and grew up in Green Bay, Wisconsin. His father, Samuel Swidler, had come to America as a Jewish immigrant from Ukraine, eventually to become a Christian and an American citizen. His mother, Josephine Marie Reed Swidler, was a Catholic from an Irish family. He had two younger siblings: brother Jack and sister Sandi. All through his childhood and college years, Leonard's nickname was Leo.

From 1946 to 1950, Leo attended St. Norbert College in De Pere, Wisconsin, where he first became involved in a Catholic Reform group, and right after graduation he entered the Norbertine Order as a novice but was found to be excessively serious and asked to leave shortly before the taking of vows in 1952. "I got kicked out of the monastery for being too pious," he often says.

From 1952 to 1954, Leo was preparing for parish ministry at St. Paul Seminary in St. Paul, Minnesota but left, this time of his own accord, before ordination and started his graduate studies from scratch out in the world. In 1955 he earned a Master's degree from Marquette University and in 1961, a PhD from the University of Wisconsin—both in history. To write his dissertation, he received a grant from the German government and lived in Tübingen and Munich from 1957 to 1960. He returned, having been introduced to Protestant-Catholic dialogue and having become, to his knowledge, the first Catholic layperson in modern times to earn a degree in theology.

In 1957, Leonard married Arlene Anderson, who preferred "Len" to "Leo," and together they had two daughters, Carmel and Eva. Arlene, who was a feminist Catholic scholar, writer, and editor, collaborated with Len on many projects throughout their married life and, by his admission, inspired him both in theory and in practice. In the early 1990s, she began showing symptoms of Alzheimer's disease and eventually passed away at home in 2008. He has one granddaughter.

In 1960, Len took a teaching position at Duquesne University in Pittsburgh, Pennsylvania, and there he lived through the Second Vatican Council and founded his first major organization: the *Journal of Ecumenical Studies*. Soon *JES* would become a flagship publication in the field of ecumenical and interreligious dialogue. In 1966, he and his family moved to Philadelphia so Len could begin work at Temple University, where he is teaching to this day.

Since that time, he has founded multiple organizations and initiatives, most notably the Dialogue Institute (1978), International Scholars' Abrahamic Trialogue (1978), and the Association for the Rights of Catholics in the Church (1980). He has written or edited eighty books and over two hundred articles. He travels the world to organize, to lead, and to lecture, to seed local groups, to garner support, and to start conversations.

He is most widely known for his thunderously controversial 1971 article with a self-explanatory title "Jesus Was a Feminist" and for his 1983 editorial in *JES* that flew around the world and into dozens of languages, taking on a life of its own: "Dialogue Decalogue: Ground Rules for Interreligious Dialogue."

Brief facts about River Adams

River Adams is the pen name of your humble author. I have known Leonard Swidler since 2006, when *JES* needed help with the book review section and I first met its founding editor. I soon became his doctoral student and then, without realizing quite when, his friend.

Len and I have a few surprising things in common. Similar to his father, I am a Russian Jew, and my family and I left my homeland when the collapsing economy of the dying Soviet Union raised a swell of Antisemitism so mighty that it almost swallowed us whole. Samuel Swidler came to America a fifteen-year-old immigrant. I came in 1991 a nineteen-year-old refugee.

I was a classical pianist in Russia and share with Len his love of music, but a wrist trauma shortly after the move to America ended my first career. I was raised an atheist child in an atheist world—not at all like Len—and yet, much like him, I found myself searching intensely for the meaning of life and the reasons for suffering, and I found the most profound questions in the wisdom traditions of the world, in the field of religious studies. I became a theologian, began to teach and to write, and practiced Zen Buddhism and dialogue, but my friendship with Len rose to a new level of spiritual sharing in 2010, when a conversion experience of an unending kind—the embrace with the Divine—created out of me a Catholic Christian mystic. When people ask me what happened, I often say that I ran into Jesus. It's as good an answer as any.

Shortly after my baptism, I entered into discernment of religious life, and Len and I have had countless hours of musing and cogitating about it.

PROLOGUE

In the City of Neighborhoods: Philadelphia

Philadelphia was the first city to foresee the advantages of a Federal constitution and oatmeal as a breakfast food.

—Christopher Morley, *Travels in Philadelphia*

We live in Philadelphia, Len and I—a city of history proud and painful, a city of neighborhoods: South Philly with its bustling Italian market that mixes the smells of fish and custard, with its local dive bars where everybody knows your name; West Philly with its honking din and Ethiopian and Moroccan restaurants and mind-wrenching pot holes; and the sprawling Northeast, where Russian, Jewish, Georgian, and Uzbek shops and eateries still bear signs in native tongues, and where older immigrants can still be identified by their old-world clothes and the ineffable mannerism of their gaits.

This is Philadelphia. Here Len has had a home since 1966. From here, he flies away to his innumerable conferences and workshops in Jordan and Kurdistan, to teach summer courses in China, and to give talks on dialogue in Washington DC. And here he comes back, and on his way from the airport crosses the bridge at the confluence of the Schuylkill and Delaware Rivers, past the shipyard, where an oil refinery washes a wave of foul odors through the car, and the tallest smoke stack reigns over a

1

dystopic landscape, spewing into the sky a conical mass of steam that merges with the clouds like a bizarre, backwards tornado.

This is Philadelphia, a city we love despite itself and like despite ourselves. Olde City is now just another neighborhood here. Independence Hall still stands, and the Liberty Bell still hangs, cracks and all, behind thick glass. Red-brick walls and buckled alleys, it is the place that still exhales the air of the first capital and of colonial America. At the City Tavern, a costumed, eighteenth-century-looking server will seat you at a solid wood table to the sound of a colonial harp and offer you some West Indies pepperpot soup or a flaky lobster pie in a pewter casserole, a selection of very out-of-style drinks, and an opportunity to turn off your cell phone so you might feel almost a little bit as if you were actually in the past—unless you go to the bathroom, look out the window, or pay with a credit card.

A few blocks south is South Street, the haven of a bohemian and an urban weirdo, a screaming, bursting bottleneck of foodstuffs and trinkets for every language, palette, and taste. A few blocks north, Chinatown floats through time permeated by spice and color, where the phoenix and the dragon peer from the Friendship Gate all the way to our sister-city Tianjin. Toward the west, William Penn watches over our scurryings from the top of City Hall, his head bowed, the Treaty of Friendship in his hand, as if he were ready to step off and intervene any second should we get it really wrong. Over him, skyscrapers are crowding more and more, a forest of reflective glass, glare, and whimsical, angular shapes. Modern sculptures guard the doors.

This is Center City, where we do our business and keep our art. Concert halls and museums live here along the Ben Franklin Parkway and the Avenue of the Arts, and on hot days children splash with deafening squeals in the enormous fountain on Logan Square.

All of this is Philadelphia. Len Swidler has a small corner house at the end of a row in a neighborhood that still bears the remnants of its Jewish roots. "When we moved in here," Len says, "except the neighbors across the street and us, everyone around was Jewish!" Now the crowd is a lot more diverse, and you will see faces of every color, but a Jewish deli on the corner and a bakery with a Hebrew sign advertising Bar Mitzvah cakes betray the past with a bit of nostalgia.

Len's house is shady and old, crammed with books, mementoes, and artifacts. An office in an addition to the side is covered by piles of unsorted papers, and one shudders to think what treasures lie buried in those mounds. Three bedrooms are upstairs, and there's always somebody living or staying there: a doctoral student from Azerbaijan or a visiting former student from Kurdistan who can't afford a hotel.

For the last five years, Per Faaland and his daughter Rakel have been occupying two of the bedrooms. This house has seen Rakel grow from a round-eyed little girl into a tall swan of a pre-teen with raven-black hair and the beginnings of a feminine presence, and the unkempt profile of an old academic's dwelling now gets regularly interrupted by slumber-party sleeping bags on the living room floor, late-night TV, a hamster traveling from the second floor to the basement, and the sound of children's voices.

I remember when Per appeared at Temple's Department of Religion in the fall of 2008. He was a thin and scruffy-looking fellow, badly shaven, with salt-and-pepper hair sticking out freely in longish, unruly locks, and a beaming, infectious grin that reigned upon his face, announcing the enthusiasm of a seeker starting out on a new road. I have gotten used to it now, but back then especially stunning was his laugh: a sudden torrent of such volume and force, such fantastic modulation of frequencies, that it was an entity in itself let loose by Per's joy, booming and overpowering, and, when finally over, left a trace after it in the air for seconds.

Before Temple, Per was living in Florida, teaching at a small college, and dreaming of a doctorate to be a scholar and a church leader. He looked for just the right place, and an interview with Len cemented his decision, but he and Rakel arrived in early summer armed with nothing but admission, a scholarship, a stipend, and a couple of months to create a settled life, and Len was the only person they knew in Philly.

They stayed with him for a week, then he said to Per, "You know, if you want, you can just stay here."

"I thought about it—for about a minute," Per told me. "And then I said, 'That sounds awesome!'"

TALKING TO PER FAALAND

(On sincerity, Christian proselytization, and getting ticked off at Len—and, of course, on dialogue)

RA Per, are you paying rent to live at the house?

PF No. I take out the trash, I do dishes. My sense is that Len has, kind of, discovered where and how he can have the most positive effect and is wholesale devoting himself in that direction. It involves, you know, everything from his career choices to his social life to his house to his free time. Len is just driving toward what makes the most good—and I think he'll be driving to his dying breath. I can objectively say that there's no person on this planet who has more substantially supported me in being a second-career aspiring scholar and activist, and we don't see the same way on lots of issues.

RA   Where do you disagree?

PF   Well, one difference is in how we approach dialogue.

Now, we start out in common: we both come at it from a Christian base—our white male American Christian one. Still, my sense is that Len is consciously stepping into what I think he would call a "humanist perspective," away from his Christian starting point. He becomes a Christianized humanist and then has aspirations for the world. I do not step out of mine, so, you know, when I participate in dialogue, I do so as an open Christian. I don't mean he is being insincere; I mean he can distinguish himself by his Catholic heritage, yet he stands as a humanist, in his life, now.

RA   Not proselytizing?

PF   Right. Neither is he testifying.

RA   And you are testifying?

PF   Yeah, and I *am* proselytizing. In some ways I look a little less humble because I am inviting people to receive Jesus. I look a little *more* humble because I admit I'm not really sure where the other paths lead, while Len affirms something like what John Hick says: "I know where the other paths lead: to the same place." So I don't know who wins the humility contest.

RA   Do you feel that proselytization is an integral, necessary aspect of being a Christian?

PF   [*smiles*] I think that proselytization is a necessary aspect of people with mouths.

RA   You've only known Len for about five years, but you both work *and* live with him, so you have a perspective few people do.

PF   Right. I've observed people get ticked off with Len, in social and professional and community settings, and the one thing I can say is that they are getting ticked off at the real Len. Because he really is *that way.* I never observe insincerity in him. He sits in his chair in his undershirt at the house as he is, just the way he sits with people at the faculty meeting in a suit and tie.

RA   Len in a suit? He wears a corduroy jacket with three holes in it.

PF   [*laughs with abandon, throwing back his head and shaking the walls*] Yes, right! But he'll say the same thing there as he will at home. And so it's the real deal. Yeah.

    The thing about Len, I think, is that there is an organic consistency between his life and his teaching. He lives his life to make a positive impact—lets people stay at his house, drives a twenty-year-old car, spends his time to do good—and his teaching is dialogue.

    People get ticked off about his behavior: like, he is always late. And they react to his teaching: like, "What do you mean, this is the Dialogue Decalogue?" Or, "Who are you to create a global ethic?" But it's all sincere on his part, so the response that his life and his teaching and his reactions inspire is the response of dialogue. How does the Decalogue need to be changed? What happens to the Ethic? His response is talking about it. He is late again? His response is talking about it.

RA   Not everything can be helped by talking about it, though—or can it?

PF   No, but the response is dialogue. What we really want to do when he is four hours late or when he presumes to know the universal ethic is to engage in conversation. He may be pushing his legacy into directions other than where he's led it deliberately, but his is a pretty influential voice in instigating a conversation.

RA   Whether we start out yelling at him or inquiring of him, he starts a discussion.

PF   Yeah, and it's not that he invented this, but he continues to be a pretty significant promoter of it in word and deed.

RA   Is Len quintessential dialogue?

PF   Well, okay. There is a critique that he isn't always. That he does teaching and not always learning. That he is not listening. A number of people out there feel this way, and I think the critique has teeth, so it should be clear where I fall on it: While Len may not *be* dialogue, he does inspire it.

TALKING TO LEN

(On Christian Humanism)

RA   Len, what about proselytizing in dialogue?

LS   It depends on what one precisely means by "proselytizing." I am inviting my listener to consider the possible veracity of my statements. At the same time, I at least want to be open to other positions and evidence. In that sense one wants to avoid the term "proselytizing."

RA   Are you first and foremost a Humanist?

LS   A particular kind of one. I find the most attractive form of being human expressed in Jesus and to a significant extent in the community of his followers, but I no longer, let's say, naively start out with the assumption that Christianity is the embodiment of what it is to be a good human being. I am open to such embodiment taking place on the basis of other starting points than Jesus and Christianity.

RA   You have your unique Catholic Christian worldview to contribute in dialogue, but you choose mostly to leave it aside when you approach dialogue.

LS   I don't want to put others off in conversation. I want to find grounds that would be humanly common, so to speak, and from there proceed to dialogue. I started out as a Catholic Christian, but experience with other ways of understanding and living life came along to me, and I gradually moved to this more, let's call it, "basically dialogic stance," because I want to speak to all people not just fellow Christians.

RA   Yet the dialogue you try to facilitate and engage in is between Muslims, Hindus, Christians . . . They are not simply humans, although we are all, of course, humans. So after recognizing common ground, do you assume your Christian viewpoint as your partners express theirs?

LS   At times, yes. At times, no. I use the vocabulary that makes sense to all human beings, and the whole notion of humanism looms very large. I don't look upon this as any kind of "watering down." Jesus—Yeshua in the original Aramaic—speaks to us today, to me at any rate, specifically as a human being, not as a Christian or a Catholic.

Yet, I do have very profound appreciation for Catholicism: its emphasis on the goodness of matter and on the value of the beautiful, its fostering of intellectual life in the most intense fashion. These are not exclusively Catholic contributions to humanity, but I see them here exemplified in a paradigmatic manner, which is one of the reasons I will not abandon my embrace of Jesus and Christianity and of Catholicism—and why I am very disappointed at times when these values seem betrayed by the fellows in my community. Now, the same reason leads me to a sort of quiet exhilaration at the behavior of Pope Francis. He won't make profound changes in doctrine, but if he lives long enough, he will change the orientation of Catholicism toward Yeshua-like ways. I hope he lives as long as Leo XIII—and me too.

PART I

At the Source of the River

After him, the deluge came!

HE WAS BORN AT the start of the tumultuous year 1929, on January 6. Only a few months after, the roaring twenties would come to a screaming end with the Dow Jones' peak on September 3rd and then crash into the dark decade of the Great Depression by the end of October. Len Swidler, of course, doesn't remember any of that. He is a child of the Depression.

"I am like Louis XIV!" He laughs. "*Apres moi la deluge!*"

He doesn't remember the shock or the despair of jobless America, and he took his own family's struggle to survive for granted the way we accept the conditions of our lives as children; it was just how the world was. His world had long lines of sullen men spilling out of a building near his house in Green Bay, men waiting for free bread and canned foods. Len's parents never stood in that line, but what they ate at home was probably the same: canned tomato soup, canned salmon, bread . . .

"It's strange: canned salmon was one of the cheapest things you could buy in those days!" He laughs again. "So we had a lot of salmon loaf! And for a time I remember Dad bringing home these sweet rolls called 'Long Johns.' I thought they were really scrumptious!"

That must have been when Samuel Swidler worked the early morning shift (4 to 11 AM) driving a delivery van for Glickman's Bakery in Green Bay. This, too, Len remembers—his father changing jobs—and only now, as an adult, quite understands what it meant: unemployment, a struggle to survive.

Len leans back on the couch cushions when he talks about Dad and slides his hands under his head, rolls his eyes up under the bushy eyebrows, and I recognize a familiar expression on his face: respect that borders on reverence, flowing and mixing with nostalgia. Longing. It's love. It's a bit different from the absolute tenderness I see when he mentions his mother, but the admiration in his voice is the same.

CHAPTER 1

Of Cabbages, Kings, and the American Dream: Len's father

. . . it's no use going back to yesterday, because I was a different person then.

—LEWIS CARROLL, *ALICE'S ADVENTURES IN WONDERLAND*

SAMUEL SWIDLER AND JOSEPHINE Marie Reed were a perfect example of the American "melting pot": an ethnic and religious odd couple. She was an Irish American Catholic, and he was a Ukrainian Jew who had crossed the ocean as a fifteen-year-old boy in 1912 the old-fashioned way—on a boat—fleeing either pogroms or an impending draft into the czarist army, possibly both. He made this journey alone, a teenager, from his hometown of Kamenetz-Podolsky across Eastern Europe to the German port city of Bremerhaven, on a transport ship crowded with immigrants to Philadelphia, then on to Chicago, to connect with what Len calls "some shirt-tail relatives."

Len knows little of this voyage or of his father's first years in America, but one story became a family tale, passed down the generations. It appears that Samuel traveled through Europe by way of Austria and on some occasion, somehow, was selected to escort a young woman to a ball at the Emperor's Palace in Vienna. He described to his son time and time again the lavish ballroom with elegantly dressed couples milling about, the extravagant arrival of Kaiser Franz Josef and wife, and the dancing that ensued.

Many years later, in 1972, when Len, now possessed of his own wife and two daughters, was spending a sabbatical year in Tübingen, Samuel came to visit them, and the girls peppered Grandpa with questions. As the story of the Emperor's ball came spilling out in sparkling detail, Len thought his habitual thought: It seemed to sound more spectacular every time it was told. Pop could really spin a good yarn. But then, the following spring, the family finally made it to Vienna—and, of course, took a tour of the Schönbrunn Palace. One step into the grand ballroom took their breath away, and they stopped. They looked at each other. In an awed chorus, they half-whispered half-sang, "He was really here!"

The grand ballroom had not changed much in sixty years.

Still, despite his "royal connections," all of his adult life Sam Swidler worked as an activist for labor unions and for the Democrat Party and strongly supported Franklin Delano Roosevelt. More than that, in his early twenties, once World War I had ended, he returned to Europe to organize for the legendary international labor movement whose heritage is claimed the world over by disparate crusades from the Bolshevik Revolution in Russia to some of the American business trade unionism: the Industrial Workers of the World.

historical interlude

After their founding at the Industrial Congress in Chicago in June of 1905, the Wobblies (a nickname, the origin of which even the Wobblies cannot find) have been engaged in a radical struggle for the working class across trade and national boundaries. "One Big Union" they call themselves. Their motto is *"An injury to one is an injury to all"*; their most powerful weapon is the general strike, and they do not advocate for fair wages. Their ultimate goal is the abolishment of the wage system altogether, for they can't imagine an employer-employee relationship that's actually fair: free, just, mutually respectful, not oppressive. They grow from the roots of socialist and anarchist parties and philosophies of equality and fraternity—and they are smaller now, but they are still around.

It has not been an easy history for the Wobblies, especially the early years, while they were most active and workers' rights were in their infancy. This history is full of martyrs, lynched and framed for crimes and executed, leadership serving prison terms or fleeing the country. It's full of strikes and fights, collateral damage, internal schisms, their own over-reaction, and public misperception. From its iconic *Little Red Songbook* (1919), the IWW website quotes on its "History" page:

> "Yaas," said the farmer reflectively, "all the I.W.W. fellers I've met seemed to be pretty decent lads, but them 'alleged I.W.W.'s' must be holy frights."[1]

At the time Samuel Swidler was engaged with the Wobblies, they must have been at near peak strength, though the reports of their numbers vary wildly from source to source: Daniel Saros estimates the IWW to have reached its largest membership in 1923 with forty thousand members,[2] but a contemporary report from 1917 quotes this many members already at the founding assembly and claims that the IWW had a paid-up membership of sixty thousand in January of 1917, with three hundred thousand cards issued.[3]

end interlude

Len doesn't know how long Samuel persisted in his efforts for the Wobblies, but he thinks it wasn't long—and the One Big Union eventually declined in numbers and lost much of its prominence on the world stage through a series of red scares, another world war, and the evolution of less radical labor movements and more moderate management practices. It has seen a degree of revival in recent decades, now that America struggles with a crisis of capitalism, but Samuel's son is not part of it.

Len has not inherited his father's particular battle for labor reform. He does not agree with everything the IWW stands for. He did, however, pay attention to the priorities of his father's heart—the thirst for social justice that pushed Samuel to his work and his convictions—and, in his own way, Len inherited the cause: equality, fraternity, social justice. It is this cause that would propel him into Catholic reform, into founding the Association for the Rights of Catholics in the Church, and into devoting his life, ultimately, to dialogue.

---

1 "The IWW Little Red Songbook."

2 Saros, *Labor, Industry, and Regulation,* 63.

3 Vincent St. John, *The I.W.W.,* "The I.W.W. at Present," para. 2.

"Dad's support of unions and the Democrat Party helped shape the way I grew up," he says, "during the Great Depression, World War II, and after."

Talking to Per Faaland

PF   I hosted a bunch of revolutionary Occupiers for a book club, and Len joined us; we had dinner together. These are people who have radically different opinions from his and come from radically different generations from his—bless them, Laura Levitt would be too far right—and Len was right in there, appreciating them and their idealism and the change they might make in the world he wouldn't live to see. What touched my heart is how Len really got who they were while acknowledging that they were a world apart from him, yet there was a common quest to make a better world.

Somehow I don't think that Len has found it. It's not that "if we just memorize the Dialogue Decalogue, there'll be world peace," no. But I think he has sincerely sought it, and therein lies the example. When I encounter conversations like that book club, I think Len sees that too—that his answers will not be those of tomorrow, that they are a stone on the path, and the next generation is rising up, and he is laying down some more stones.

Samuel was what I would comfortably call a polyglot; he spoke Russian, Ukrainian, Polish, and German. In Yiddish, he *schmoozed* through the streets of Green Bay with such gregariousness that a two-block walk seemed endless to Leo, who was little, purposeless, and bored with adult conversation. As a Jewish man, Samuel could read Hebrew, and his irreverent son, then a look-down-your-nose-at-your-parents young novice at a Norbertine abbey, once tested that skill by opening a *Biblia Hebraica* before his father's face.

His English was impeccable—perfect grammar, without a trace of an accent.

"I remember." Len's features soften, almost smudge, as if he's shifted just out of phase with our time. "Dad took great pride in speaking correct English, and he'd often grump about American-born kids and mimic them: 'dese, dose, dem . . .'"

Still, Samuel Swidler's gift for languages did not save him from hardship during the Depression, though it might have helped at times. Trying job after job, he sold pianos in the Polish community on the south side of Milwaukee and for a time sold insurance, drove an early-morning delivery van, and drained a swamp around Bay Beach on the edge of Green Bay. This last engagement was with the Works Progress Administration, or WPA—an immense New Deal agency that gave jobs to millions of the unemployed between 1935 and 1943 building roads, parks, bridges, and the like: mostly unskilled labor but also artists and musicians. Nicknamed "We Poke Along" by the "impudent" kids of Len's generation (his word not mine), in truth, WPA became a saving grace for many an American family in the most desperate economic decade of the twentieth century.

historical interlude

On Valentine's Day, 1930, a Fox Theater opened on Washington Street in Green Bay amid great pomp and circumstance. Its imposing, though, perhaps, unimaginative, form rose up from the ground at the start of the Depression like a hope of better things to come, and thousands-strong crowds waited at the doors to fill its inner sanctum adorned in the intricate, "Spanish atmospheric" style: textured plaster, gold-leaf columns, and gilded cherubs.

The Fox did not weather the Depression, declaring bankruptcy in 1933, but in its place the Bay Theater soon opened and, with its 2,200 seats, became the largest movie house in town and a perpetual landmark. It persisted through the war and its aftermath, the countercultural sixties and the bell-bottomed seventies, all the way to 1998, when it turned into the Meyer Theater—the name that still reigns over Washington Street. A transition into a triplex cinema, decades ago, had stripped the building's inner space of its original décor, but the Meyer's volunteers came in and crawled the walls to restore its former glory, to paint the ceiling midnight-blue, and to install fiber-optic lighting for an illusion of a starry sky overhead.

The stage at 117 South Washington has felt the feet of Lawrence Welk, Liberace, Nat King Cole, Louis Armstrong, and Johnny Cash.

end interlude

In Len Swidler's memory, a miniscule Karamel Korn shop is latching on to the wall of The Bay Theater, and next to it stands the Bay Beauty Shop, a women's hair salon run by Len's mother. She had made her living with a mastery of haircut, perm, and color for many years, and in the late thirties Samuel went to a beautician school to join his wife in the family business, to use his thorough work ethic and what Len calls "European charm." Little Leo, too, helped out at the shop during the summer, sweeping up and picking bobby pins out of cut hair.

When the family moved out of Green Bay into its suburb Allouez in 1946, they sold the shop and opened what would now be a "beauty parlor" in the basement of their new house, the first and only one they ever owned. Len still remembers himself with a pick in his hand, digging out the space under the front of the house—just him and a hired day worker—carving a beauty parlor out of rock-hard clay.

He was seventeen that summer, just out of high school, and working some resort job as a delivery boy in his pick-up truck. Until the needs of the family business pulled him away, he was spending his time driving and bellowing Irving Berlin out into the judgment-free Wisconsin air.

The farmhouse was old, with a barn in the back and a cow tethered to a little transparent apple tree, biding its time and fertilizing the roots for the sweet tanginess of the autumn fruit. "Terrific apples!" Len says for the third time.

Adjacent to the property, the doomsday apparition of the State Reformatory blocked out the sun with its somber, dark grey stone, heavy bars over the first story, and the fine grill that made upper-floor windows look blind and despairing. Two human-height eagles framed the massive front entrance. Guards lived in a row of modest homes across the street.

"We never locked our door," Len says. "We figured, if someone escaped from there, they wouldn't hang around the neighbors."

The Reformatory is still there, gloom and all, but the house is not. Len, Jack, and Sandi held on to those few acres on Riverside Drive until the late eighties, after their father's death, and then sold them to a home for Alzheimer's patients. The house was razed and replaced by an expansive ranch-style complex that seems perpetually ready for a brochure photo shoot. Only one familiar thing remains: among manicured lawns and curly bushes, the apple tree still stands, now an imposing juicy cloud of red-speckled green.

Samuel did not work at the new shop. For the first time in a stretch, he found a long-term job at a paper mill in De Pere, a neighboring town on the Fox River—a town that would hold fast for years to the Swidler family.

De Pere is consummate Wisconsin, and paper is its consummate industry till this day. Over two decades before the incorporation of the Village and seven months before the Territory of Wisconsin was itself created by the Congress, three entrepreneurs were given authority "to erect a dam across the Fox River at the Rapids De Peres for the purpose of erecting mills or any other industry to make use of the water power."[4] This was September 1835, the birth of the Fox River Hydraulic Company. Around it, towns soon started to spring up as people poured in for opportunities to work and own land and to cut timber of white pine, oak, and maple that filled the boundless forests along the river.

The Village of De Pere, incorporated in 1857, by the mid-1940s counted probably in the vicinity of seven thousand residents and boasted, among other things, several paper mills, a trucking company, a tuberculosis sanatorium, a finger-shaking nearness to the Green Bay Packers, and the nationally known St. Norbert College, founded and run, unsurprisingly, by the priests of the Norbertine order. At this college Leonard would get his education. This order he would dream of joining in a vowed life. At one of these mills Samuel would spend the rest of his working days, past his wife's death in 1962, and would stick with it—or so it appeared to his children—through thick and thin. Len recalled in his later reflections: "Dad would write letters once in a while, and it was a kind of joke among us kids . . . that Dad's letters often said that he 'went on longer hours,' but he never seemed to go on shorter hours, so we had the impression that after a while he must have been working 200-hour weeks!"[5]

Len is missing most of the details of his father's early life, and he is missing them terribly. This is often the case for the children of immigrants: parts of their "first" lives can be too painful for parents to recall, other parts impossible to explain to their American offspring. Len's mind holds scattered shreds of information, a few stories—even those probably distorted by the haze of years.

He recalls that Samuel was the oldest child of a Russian nobleman's estate manager. Of course, the October Revolution of 1917 eliminated

4 Legislative Council of the Territory of Michigan, cited by Milquet, "De Pere sesquicentennial," para. 1 in "De Pere's Incorporation."

5 Swidler, "A Life in Dialogue," section "Pre-Beginnings," para. 15.

both noblemen and private estates, so people like the Swidlers ended up in a variety of places and professions. My own grandfather came from exactly the same background and, after the revolution, joined the Party and worked as a community organizer and died a communist of deepest conviction, but, because his family had done well for a wealthy man, his lack of proletarian heritage always haunted him and caused him both hardship and heartache. Naturally, many remained in the rural areas where they'd grown roots and continued in the agricultural trade that had been theirs for generations. Ukraine and the Volga regions were the country's bread basket.

Len recalls stories of the Ukrainian blizzards, so long and abundant sometimes that the family would dig a tunnel from the house to the barn to milk the cows. He has an image of his grandmother's kitchen with a samovar always hot and the tea brewing—a neighborhood's gathering place. Samuel and his mother wrote to each other for as long as the letters kept coming from the Soviet side. They stopped suddenly in the early thirties, during the difficult times in the USSR: repressions, starvation, and the blossom of Stalin's cult of personality—the dark and hungry times.

historical interlude

In 1906, Russian peasants were given the right to acquire plots of land, essentially on mortgage, by paying from their surplus product, and, as always happens, very quickly and for a great variety of reasons some became more successful than others. Between 1918 and 1929, the creators of post-revolutionary Marxist-Leninist ideology divided all peasants in the Soviet Union into four categories: landless farm hands (hired laborers), poor peasants (who couldn't make enough from their tiny plots to make ends meet), mid-income farmers (who just made ends meet and tended to have perhaps one cow per family), and *kulaks* (who had more land and higher incomes than average). The first two categories were considered to be allies of the Revolution almost on the par with the proletariat, the third to be unreliable, and *kulaks* to be a class enemy.

With the goal of the regime having early become to achieve nationwide, large-scale industrialized agricultural production, for a decade all farmers were encouraged—and pressured—to join collective farms, but, by the end of the 1920s, the Party leadership lost patience. The large and most fertile regions of the country along the Volga, in Ukraine and

North Caucasus, became areas of "total collectivization," and on January 30, 1930, a government decree directed local enforcers to eliminate the *kulaks* as a class. It was this order, initiated and edited by Stalin himself, that unleashed the disaster in Soviet history that took away millions of lives and seeded in their place resentment, paranoia, and never-ending grudges. In English, we call it "dekulakization."

Local executives came to the homes of the *kulak* families: anyone who owned more than eight acres of land or more livestock than someone judged sufficient; anyone who employed hired hands; anyone who traded surplus grain, rented land or equipment, gave out loans with interest; anyone openly engaged in church organizing; anyone who resisted giving the lion's share of his grain to the state for its strategic reserve. Sometimes they came for those who didn't have much land—or anything else—because each region had a quota of *kulaks* to dispose of. Or because somebody with power had an antipathy. Or just because.

The *kulaks'* property was confiscated. Some—judged the most dangerous terrorists—were arrested and sent to the camps or executed. Some resisted and were shot. The rest were deported with their families to the yet-uncultivated wilderness: the northern parts of Russia, the Urals, Siberia, Kazakhstan, or just the outskirts of their own regions. In order to start a new life from nothing, in a strange, harsh environment, a family of farmers each was allowed to keep five hundred rubles.

We can only estimate the number of victims, but it seems that almost three million people were "resettled" by 1933. Maybe half a million died resisting arrest, on the way to their exile, and in exile: from disease and malnutrition.

After two or three years, Moscow discontinued mass deportations from the villages, but the damage had been done. Rural Russia and Ukraine had lost so much human power to dekulakization and to young people running to the cities from collectivization that already in 1931 there weren't enough people to weed the sown grain and even fewer people to harvest it. The next year, things got worse. What helping hands arrived from the cities in an emergency effort made barely a scratch in the enormous expanses of rolling amber waves. Between 20 and 40 percent of the grain rotted in the fields. Bread became scarce, then nonexistent. Starving animals died or had to be slaughtered. There was no meat, no milk, and no eggs. What precious little remained went to feed the cities and the strategic reserve.

The famine of 1932–33 is one of the four worst in Russian history as it is recorded, but it is the only one not caused by a drought. With the worst horror having swept through rural Ukraine, the Volga region, and Kazakhstan in 1933, it affected all of the USSR and robbed it, by the latest official estimates, of over seven million lives,[6] but not before reducing people to cannibalism and forever killing all hope for trust in the system, in one's government, or in the idea of socialism—for many, too many.

The famine of 1932–33 was a human-caused catastrophe that is brought up next to the Killing Fields and the Holocaust. The hatred it birthed is still birthing theories and pitting nations against each other. Some say it was done on purpose by Stalin's party to exterminate, specifically, the Ukrainian people. Others say, no. I say, no. Yet it was done, brought about by the hands of the Soviet regime, as a consequence of its agrarian policy and fast industrialization. It was, you might say, a "felony famine": an unpremeditated tragedy that was the inevitable result of the Party's premeditated brutality and short-sightedness in the villages, its betrayal of the peasants, its ghastly mutilation of its own communist ideals. In that, it was a crime as sure as if each victim of the famine had been strangled by human hands.

end interlude

We don't know what became of the Swidler family in the USSR. Much was happening in the 1930s besides dekulakization and starvation. People lived and moved and died. Nationalist and anti-Western sentiment grew by leaps and bounds, and, amid pervasive paranoia of "foreign agents," many families who had relatives abroad (like mine) chose that time to sever their connections for safety's sake. Even among those who were "resettled" and those who were caught up in the worst of the famine, the majority survived to tell about it.

A number of families (like mine) restored their ties thirty years later, when the Iron Curtain fell and opened the flow of air, of culture, and of care packages to and from the West. The Swidlers never did, and the reasons are likely to remain a mystery to Len. World War II had swept through the USSR in the intervening time, killing over twenty million on and off the front lines. Post-war famine added to the count. By the 1960s Thaw, much had changed in the Soviet Union: generations turned over,

6 *Postanovlenie GD FS RF #262-5 GD.*

addresses were lost. But to Len, whose last news of his father's family came from the thirties, their disappearance is forever associated with the murder of peasants in Ukraine, and it is this particular grief he carries with him, and this particular grudge.

Len likes to say that he is "a product of *Abie's Irish Rose*"—an NBC comedy radio show that ran from 1942 to 1944. Based on Anne Nichols's blockbuster Broadway play from the twenties, the show followed the new-lyweds Abie and Rosemary Levy: he an Orthodox Jew and she an Irish Catholic, who had eloped despite their family's objections. Mutual disgust of the in-laws subsided after Rosemary delivered twins on Christmas Day, but a comedy would not be comedy without some bickering, and so the interethnic and interreligious bunch proceeded to entertain its American audience, which occasionally included little Leo Swidler from Wisconsin.

Samuel and Josephine seem to have worked out their cultural differ-ences very well: Leo was raised in the Catholic tradition but was deeply aware of his Jewish roots. His father eventually engaged with Christian-ity so intimately that he underwent instruction by a Norbertine priest and was baptized into the Catholic Church. Still, much like the fictional Levys, the Swidlers did not avoid bumps in the road: the road to extended family. One of Len's early memories is of roaring verbal battles between Samuel and Josephine's older sister Eva that raged on Sunday afternoons in their home. Barely of school age, Leo did not then understand the sub-ject of the controversy, but he remembered enough to recall it later, and then he understood. Judging by the little Len now recalls of the content of those fights, the time was the second half of the 1930s, and the subject, Father Charles Coughlin and Christian Antisemitism.

Leo's Aunt Eva was a divorcee with a son, Leo's cousin Bob, but be-fore marriage she'd taken a shot at religious life and spent some time in a convent. Although her vocation as a nun obviously did not work out, she retained a sort of piety one might call overt and stereotypical—or was, in Len's words, "quite devout." Around her neck, with great pride, she wore a locket that contained what was supposed to be a piece of "the true cross"—according to legend, the cross on which Jesus had died—and believed that, if all its little bits were to be brought together, they would constitute a small forest. Len calls her "clerically oriented." The word of the clergy to Eva was truth and law.

historical interlude

Father Coughlin was an Irish Catholic priest, originally of the Basilian Fathers in Canada, who had left the order and by the mid-1920s was serving a small parish in Royal Oak, Michigan. When in 1926 the Ku Klux Klan burned a cross on the grounds of his church, Father Coughlin went on local radio with a weekly hour-long address. CBS picked up his program four years later; the popularity of the talented broadcaster grew, and soon he became known nationwide as "the radio priest."

With the advent of the Depression, Coughlin's broadcasts shifted from religious to social and ideological topics, and, bursting with opinions and already possessed of a hefty following, he began to wield increasing political power. He founded his own national network, hooked up to thirty-six radio stations. His audience reached at its peak in the mid-1930s in the tens of millions. More mail arrived at his office in the mid-thirties than arrived at the White House, and tens of thousands of letters poured into Congress at his say-so. This audience, at first, he actively pumped up to stand against socialism, for Roosevelt, and for his New Deal, coining two famous slogans: "Roosevelt or Ruin" and "The New Deal Is Christ's Deal." Twice he testified before Congress: in 1930 as a prominent anti-communist, and in 1934 in support of Roosevelt's policies.

This, however, is when his support ran out. Later in 1934, Father Coughlin seemed to make a radical turn and began to denounce the very president he'd just endorsed. His broadcasts were now peppered with attacks on "money changers" and called for the nationalization of the Federal Reserve and "necessary" industries, guarantees of employment and income for workers, redistribution of wealth through tax reform, and increased government control over the country's assets. In the face of mounting pressure from the Roosevelt administration and the church to tone down his rhetoric, Coughlin pushed back, calling FDR a "tool of Wall Street" and eventually "anti-God," and ramping up his vitriol against free-market capitalism. As years passed, his views were becoming more and more nationalistic, even isolationist. He founded the National Union for Social Justice, a workers' rights organization, and later a political party that tried but failed to unseat the incumbent Roosevelt in 1936. In a historical blink of an eye, this ardent proponent of the New Deal turned into an extreme nationalist with socialist leanings.

Yet, this must not have been the fire that fueled the rage of Sunday afternoon combat at the Swidlers' house. Samuel may have accepted to various degrees the premises of nationalism or socialism, but he could not have tolerated what sounded increasingly like Charles Coughlin's National Socialism.

After the elections of 1936, Father Coughlin's Antisemitism blossomed steadily and unmistakably. He openly denied it, but the "international bankers" ruining America and robbing the workers, in his portraiture, clearly sported yarmulkes and hefty noses. In 1938, his rotogravure magazine *Social Justice* reprinted the fraudulent and rabidly antisemitic *Protocols of the Elders of Zion*: an "account" of the Jewish conspiracy to take over the world. In the world of Charles Coughlin, the Jews were both the corrupting hand of modern capitalism and the force behind Russian Bolshevism. After *Kristallnacht,* he implied to his huge audience that the persecutions of Jews in Germany were a well-deserved payback for the repressions of Christians in Soviet Russia.

If Father Coughlin meant to keep his admiration for European fascism a secret, it was the worst-kept secret on the radio. He sounded like Joseph Goebbels. One of his biographers, Donald Warren, finds evidence that at the end of the thirties Coughlin was indirectly receiving funds from sources in the Nazi government.[7]

One can only speculate how Samuel Swidler must have felt seeing the glimpses of Hitlerism on the face of his wife's sister, every Sunday, after her weekly dose of *The Hour of Power*. One can imagine what he would have thought hearing from his own family the words that would befit a Nazi ideologue. Eva's argument must have been little beyond, "If Father said so, it must be true!" How many others like her spewed hatred that wasn't theirs onto unwary heads of innocent bystanders?

Still, the march of the Radio Priest did come to an end. After his post-*Kristallnacht* speech on November 20, 1938, radio stations began refusing to air his broadcasts. The pressure both from the state and from the church had been mounting already for a couple of years. He had trouble obtaining a broadcaster's permit, so, as his radio show was withering into nothing, he poured all his passion and hope into the magazine, *Social Justice.*

It was eventually Pearl Harbor that put an end to his last outlet, as well. Coughlin's vehement opposition to the entry of the United States into World War II had been a controversial issue before, but after December 7, 1941, he began to sound like an enemy sympathizer. The Attorney General of the United States informed the archbishop of Detroit that

---

7 Warren, *Radio Priest*, 235–244.

his famous wayward priest had two options: a revocation of the magazine's mailing privileges and a possible trial on charges of sedition, or
finally quieting down.

Thus it happened that in early May of 1942 Father Charles Coughlin, once possibly the most powerful voice in America—certainly the
loudest—was ordered by his superior in the church to retire from public
life and confine himself to his duties as a parish pastor. *Social Justice* died
silently as *The Hour of Power* had done before it, and their creator spent
the rest of his considerably long life in relative peace, much of it at the
Shrine of the Little Flower, inspiring and agitating his modest flock. He
died in 1979 at the age of eighty-eight, having seen the destruction of
European fascism and the resurgence of neo-fascism, civil rights, social
programs, and run-away American capitalism, many wars started by
U.S. interventionism, and many, many Jews at the steering wheel of this
uneasy world.[8]

end interlude

Len believes that it was the type of "nativist" talk Coughlin and others
of his kind propagated before the war that pushed his mother to insist
that Samuel finally apply for American citizenship in 1940—apparently
something he had never done in all the years he had lived in the United
States. She was afraid some law would be passed to get her husband deported back to war-torn Europe, into the fires of the Holocaust, from
which a Jewish man was almost certain never to return.

Len doesn't know why his father had not completed his citizenship
process before, but he remembers how proud Samuel was once it was
done. "We kids got a lot of talk about how fortunate we were to live in
the 'land of the free,'" he recalls. "That has stuck in my heart ever since."

Another thing Len doesn't know is what moved his father to become a Christian. He knows only that it happened five years later in 1945,
when Leo was sixteen, and remembers vaguely the announcement that
Dad had been instructed in the faith and baptized by Father Killeen, the
principal of Central Catholic High, where Len was a student.

The school stood two blocks from the family's house, and the priests
lived another two blocks away, at St. Willebrod's Parish. It must have been

---

8 For a summary of Charles Coughlin's life story and for a list of resources, see
Ketchaver, "Father Charles E. Coughlin."

Christmas of 1945 when young Leo helped his father bring evergreen trees to the sanctuary and set up colored lights to be cast upon them, but he remembers nothing else of Samuel's involvement with the parish. Still, he recalls vividly the change in his Sundays between his childhood time and the high-school days, now that Dad was a Christian. Samuel had come to church before on occasion with his wife, little Leo, and even younger Jack, but when the time came for communion, he stayed behind in the pew. Len knows that more than once he'd asked his mother why. He also knows that, whatever her answer, he had not understood it. Now, things were different.

From the farmhouse in Allouez, where they'd moved in the summer of 1946, the boys would accompany Samuel every morning at what felt like "breathtaking pace" down Riverside Drive to Mass at the McCormick home for the elderly. Eventually, Samuel became an acolyte and spent regular time visiting the sick at hospitals and nursing homes with a series of local parish priests, bringing the bed-ridden Holy Communion. It sticks in Len's mind, though the source of the story is anybody's guess, that some of the older folks then would say they liked "Father Sam" better than the parish priest.

"It's probably because Dad would stop and schmooze with them." Len's smile takes on a bit of mischief as it usually does when he uses his limited but choice Yiddish vocabulary.

RA   Have you any ideas as to how your father arrived at the decision to be baptized?

LS   Very unfortunately, I really don't know much more about it than I already said. This is another one of those many questions that I wish I had had the wit to ask then.

RA   You never talked about it, even when you were a novice at a religious order, and your abbot was the very priest who had baptized him? Weren't you curious?

LS   I began to pursue my interior life, I guess, when I got into college and into a Reform Catholicism group, and then I was so focused on those ideas and activities that in a way my father was quite incidental in my life, emotionally and otherwise. I would say, kind of, "shame on me."

When I think about it now, it's amazing how little self-awareness I had in high school. Maybe it's true of most people. What today occurs to me as really important and interesting to ask of my father and of myself, never really occurred to me then, and I never knew anybody who would have had that mentality, who would have stimulated me to pose such questions.

I deal with eighteen-year-olds now in the classroom, and I do ask them, and they respond, obviously never having had questions like that put to them before.

Talking to Len

(On self-awareness, dog consciousness, and sufficient reason)

RA   Len, let me take you out of the timeline of your life for a moment. You've struggled with the question of God's existence, and we'll talk more about it, but you say that you now find the principle of Sufficient Reason convincing in proving the existence of God. Can you explain?

LS   Well, everything that I learn about the way reality works—I'm thinking now especially of our so-called scientific knowledge—just boggles the mind. I see how incredibly interlocked it all is and how everything works in such precise ways, and it seems impossible, at least to my intellect, to think this could all result from pure chance. So the answer suggests itself automatically to me that there must be some incredible, knowing Entity (though "entity" is not a good word) that could think up all these un-believable things and rules. This fantastic universe must have minimally an equally fantastic source. And since, so far as we know, this fantastic universe finds its apex in the self-knowing and responsible beings called humans, in this regard Genesis hit the nail on the head by calling humans "*Imago Dei.*" So God must be a *Du*: YOU.

RA   You make a principal distinction between knowledge and belief—the provable and not—and according to your views, this is a belief.

LS   Yes, I have to say so. Logically, I cannot exclude the contrary, but it sort of seems like a ninety-nine-to-one chance. You'd have to be a betting person to go against those odds. Pascal had it right. All of that morphs into the questions of what's "on the other side" of the grave, which of course is the fundamental question that creates all religions. The difference between my dog, now dead, and me is that we are both going to die, but he didn't know it, and I do. And so we automatically go into a "limit question": Mommy, what happens to Daddy after he dies?

RA   Okay, let me ask you this: How do you know that your dog doesn't know he is going to die?

LS   Of course. That's the question people like you always want to ask.

RA   People like me?

LS   Who want to push the question further. And the answer is not very satisfying: All the evidence we have of my dog's self-consciousness doesn't suggest such awareness. We don't have the means of communicating, so I may not have put the question to him in a way he understood, but all indications are that there is no self-consciousness.

RA   But you'll agree we are learning more and more about how much we don't understand about animals and even plants. You just mentioned the vastness of this world's complexity we are barely beginning to discover. Do you think our realization of how much we don't know should prompt some humility in our statements about, say, other species' capacities?

LS   Dogs have been doing what they're doing for thousands of years, while humans have been making progress.

RA   But that's human-defined progress, no?

LS   We have no other definition, but monkeys don't change, and humans do.

RA   That's debatable, but let's say it's true. Why is change a measure of self-awareness?

LS　In this case, changes have occurred in humans and included self-awareness. We are aware now of what we were unaware of in the past. It's a vast improvement, closer to the goal.

RA　Could some animals have achieved their own, relatively stable state of self-awareness earlier than we have and so not needed drastic changes in the same time frame as humans?

LS　That's thinkable, but there is no evidence to indicate this.

RA　Hearing you say that the universe finds its apex in humanity, one might think you are quite married to your anthropocentrism, even speciesism.

LS　Yup. I think that's what the evidence indicates—until either other evidence or other lines of thought become persuasive.

CHAPTER 2

Chubby the Dog

The misery of keeping a dog is his dying so soon; but, to be sure, if he lived for fifty years, and then died—what would become of me?
—Sir Walter Scott

CHUBBY WAS WHAT LEN calls a "thoroughbred mongrel": furry, white and brown, he cared as much about propriety as he did about ancestry. Play was the thing for him, and kids were the company, especially rife with hilarity when they showed up in Chubby's kingdom wearing winter caps, which he could grab and carry away to almost everyone's delight.

"He knew how to play." Len's eyes grow misty behind a thin fog of nostalgia.

Chubby was Leo's dog. Since his early puppy consciousness, he was Leo's dog, and he spent many of his days at the window of whatever house the family occupied at the time, waiting for his Leo, ready at the first sight of the familiar gait to tear up the floor and, at the door still beginning to open, to spill over his ecstasy in the usual doggy ways, leaving his human unstable on his feet, covered with tongued, vigorous wetness, and unstoppably smiling. Chubby lived with Leo all of his sixteen-year-long life, grew with him, breathed with him, frolicked and grieved with him, went with him on the coveted fishing trips with Dad.

Those trips—fishing and camping in summertime, for weeks at a time—were the highlight of the year and an inviolable prerogative of male bonding for Samuel and his sons. Leo and Jack—well, at least we know it's true for Leo—cherished every day out in the woods, in their tent on a lake in northern Wisconsin, and the family slowly improved their camping equipment with cots and air mattresses, a camp stove, an ice chest, and a gas lantern. From the age of nine to fifteen, Leo was in Scouts. Samuel became the Scout Master of his troop, and, like any Scout, the boy couldn't wait to learn all about outdoor living, edible berries, lean-to shelters, and making dinner on a stone heated in the fire. I can only imagine that his younger brother adored everything about it with an even greater passion: Not only was it fun, but Leo was doing it!

The drama that seared itself into Len's life story happened on one such trip, an early one, when he was maybe eight or nine. Jack, of course, was still too young to go.

The fishing had been good and early that day, and by nine o'clock Dad went back to the cabin to shave, leaving his boy at the pier with a rod to try for more. Standing on the wooden edge, little Leo held the bait two inches above the water and watched it sway. The lake sparkled and flowed underneath: changing, depthless, elusive, trance-like . . .

In the next moment of brutal awareness, the cold hit Leo in the face, and he was sinking—panic, flailing, and chopped-up breath—one second, and another. He made it to a soaked pier support and clutched its mossy, desperate safety with all his eight-year-old might, nothing else in existence, nothing penetrating his shock but the relentless barking overhead. He was not alone.

Chubby knew what was wrong. Chubby couldn't save Leo, but he knew who could. Chubby ran to the cabin, and Chubby barked, deafeningly, continuously, until the man in the cabin understood.

When Dad got to the pier, Leo was still glued to the support, and no amount of reasoning would make him release his transitory shelter to take his father's hand. Through hazy half-stupor, he kept repeating only, "I won't let go! I won't let go! I won't let go!"

I wondered, as I heard this story told, if Leo Swidler, age eight, had been holding on so to a pier support or to life itself—or both.

It finally occurred to Samuel to focus his son's attention.

"Where is your rod?" he shouted.

"Over there."

"Where? Point it out!"

"Over there."

"Point it out! Where is it?"

And in an instant he grabbed the child by the outstretched arm and pulled him out of the water, onto the warm wood of the pier, under Chubby's bathing tongue. It wasn't maybe that close a brush with death—except, but for the dog, it could have been.

Chubby died a peaceful death while Leo was at St. Norbert College. Rest in peace, Chubby, and someday we'll see you.

CHAPTER 3

Dialogue in Utero

*We know to handle loaded shotguns with care, but do not wish to
know that the same must be done for a word. A word can kill, and
can do evil worse than death.*

—LEO TOLSTOY, *PATH OF LIFE*

WHEN LEONARD SWIDLER STARTED down the path of dialogue in 1957,
the term still barely existed, and yet, if anyone had been born for it, it was
the half-Jewish, half-Catholic Len.

"I was doing dialogue *in utero!*" He sniggers.

Listening to his father and Aunt Eva battle it out over Christian
Antisemitism, he thought, in a half-conscious fashion of a child, of reconciliation and compatibility of difference and of the primacy of love.
As a graduate student, he fell spellbound at the University of Wisconsin
for the lectures of George Mosse, a German Jew who'd escaped from the
Nazis in the thirties. Mosse's course on Modern European Cultural History brought Len to his dissertation on the *Una Sancta* movement, and
that, to Germany, where he'd become involved in Catholic-Protestant
conversation before Vatican II ever opened the floodgates of ecumenical
and interreligious benevolence of the church, dammed up for decades by
the stone wall of doctrine, fear, and resentment.

All the work he's ever done—on church reform, Christology, or feminism, in teaching and organizing—is, for him, about dialogue. About what dialogue is and what it means.

It's more than talking. It's talking, all right—but in the "dialogue craze" of recent decades the word has been thrown around so much that Len started feeling misunderstood. With Ashok Gangadean and Howard Perlmutter, he came up with a term: "deep-dialogue." Still a convergence and conversation, deep-dialogue hints at a more profound experience than an exchange of words: a life-transforming experience, a coming together of people, communities, entities to learn and to change—and to enrich the world with their interaction.

This would take shape by 1990, but all through the seventies and eighties, he thought and he wrote, turning things in his mind this way and that, and the theoretical framework of dialogue poured into form and molded, year after year. "It was all incubating," he says.

It started in '83 as an editorial in *JES* on some rules of dialogue. Then another version of it, and another. Ten guiding principles of dialogic encounters. He named them the "Dialogue Decalogue," and they went viral—translated into thirty or forty languages and reproduced out of count around the planet—before they landed in 1990 in what would become his best-known book, *After the Absolute*. It was the fruit of two decades of birthing and the first of a litter-like barrage: between 1990 and 1992, he put out a dozen books on dialogue. And it established a weight-bearing pillar of his worldview and of his field.

"There were people who were working at the same time," Len says, "and we were working together. And others were thinking about it from their own perspectives, like David Bohm from the point of view of physics. The point is, clearly this idea's time had arrived, and I was one of the many worker ants in this part of the hill."

If you ask Len to explain his theory of dialogue, he will begin with an aphorism. He'll shrug his shoulders and throw his hands in the air and offer up this: "Nobody knows everything about anything!" And let it hang. This means that all claims of absolute truth are false. All statements are incomplete. This means that we all can learn from each other, and it has only little to do with an inability of any person to learn all there is to learn. Len is talking about the very principle of existence, and our awareness that all knowledge is interpreted, for him, is the heart and soul of the era in which we live: modernity. Of it he is a faithful son.

On a historical scale, it has not been very long since the Enlightenment sparked the beginning of modernity, but we've come so far, so fast in its rapidly speeding-up train that we've almost forgotten what it was like before, and we started to take it for granted and became bored with it and even resentful, as children do with a strong parent. We struck out looking for a new era to play with—"post-modern" we call it—and thanked it for the very qualities of diversity, pluralism, and relationality that modernity had birthed. Yet it was, through a couple hundred years of a thoroughly modern process, not only our understanding of science that changed, not just our approach to religion or our concept of an individual; through all of that, modernity changed our very conception of Truth.

We used to think of truth as a universal, unchanging kind of entity—a thing out there that you might know or not, speak or not, hide or reveal. Truth used to be something complete and eternal, and only a degree of wrongness separated us from it, some more than others. Then, modernity brought natural and social sciences into our world, personal freedoms and the debate on human rights, travel and mixed communities, information technology, linguistics, hermeneutics, and quantum physics—and the world began to change.

Modernity dug into history with a magnifying glass and discovered not one objective narrative but as many histories as there were narratives, and we wondered if history were not, after all, subjective. Scheler, Gadamer, Ricoeur, and Wittgenstein wrote their philosophy, and we found that truth varied with context, time, and culture. It depended on the questions we asked of our reality and the answers we wanted to hear. It took shape in accordance with the languages we spoke: beautiful, colorful, never complete.

Len is passionate about this. "With this new and irreversible understanding of the meaning of truth, the critical thinker has undergone a radical Copernican turn," he wrote in *After the Absolute*.[9] All knowledge is limited; all knowledge is interpreted. No knowledge, therefore, is a passive reception of what is but is a back-and-forth process of mutuality between reality and the knower, forming and reforming and sent back into being to be known by others. Physics calls this "the observer effect." Sociology speaks of intentionality of knowledge. History speaks of multiple "histories." For Len, this leads inevitably and urgently to dialogue: of discipline with discipline, of religion with religion, of culture with

---

9 Swidler, *After the Absolute*, 11.

culture—and between us, of person with person, of me with you. Besides any pursuit of peace, the pursuit of Truth demands it.

The Dialogue Decalogue has become a staple of the field. I went to a Christian-Muslim dialogue in Austria once—three weeks in a gorgeous Benedictine monastery in Altenburg, forty-six people from seventeen countries, seminars on religion and human rights law—and an Indonesian Muslim presenter was teaching Len's Decalogue. He's re-thought a bit of wording since the eighties and some organization. People have taken up an issue with the commandment-like title that invokes the authority of the Bible, but the principles haven't essentially changed. From *After the Absolute* and the many later incarnations, I paraphrase them like this:

1. *Come with a desire to learn, not just to teach.*

2. *Dialogue both within your group and with those outside it.*

3. *Be sincere in your desire to seek truth together, and start out believing in others' sincerity.*

4. *Start with the points of agreement, then engage controversy.*

5. *No tradition is perfect. Be careful not to compare ideals with practice but practice with practice and ideals with ideals.*

6. *Self-identify for mutual recognition. Describe your experience of your tradition for other participants, and let them do the same.*

7. *Do not let your preconceptions obscure the other's points. Keep reconsidering.*

8. *Be conscious of power dynamics in your encounter. Value everyone's contribution.*

9. *Be willing to critique yourself and your own tradition as you seek the truth.*

10. *Try to see your dialogue partner's point of view, even for a moment.*

Talking to Len

(On women, friends, and women friends)

LS   I had a series of "peak experiences" traveling around the world, in 1983. Since then, there's been an openness in my heart, and experiences come accordingly. I just got a phone call from Uli Kortsch. We are very close and share very much, and in a strange way it's the same with Pat Burke. A new friend in my life is Marcus Bingenheimer; in some ways we are like this [*crosses his fingers to indicate an impasse*], but we sympathetically vibrate on a number of issues. Maybe it has to do with music. And there are a number of women I feel very at home with—and you are number one! [*Pokes me and laughs.*] Don't put it in the book.

RA   Oh, that's going in the book!

LS   It goes back to that trip around the world. It's about the meaning of life and how it relates to people.

RA   Why do you separate your friends by gender?

LS   I feel closer to women.

RA   You loved your mother very much.

LS   That could be the mother of all reasons.

RA   So far you only named one. Let me hear more.

LS   I feel very close to Filo Hirota, a Sister of the Mercedarians, who is in Rome—she's been elected the head of Mercedarians. I met her thirty years ago during this sabbatical trip around the world, in New Delhi. There was a gathering there of theology types, a traveling conference on Catholicism in non-Catholic countries, and I went and said, "How can I join in on some of this stuff?" They said, "No problem." Filo was already there, and we rented a *tuk-tuk*—this kind of tricycle—and, with another guy, Vietnamese, saw the city. We took a long train ride to the Taj Mahal. It was overnight, very slow, so we had several hours of quiet conversation about the meaning of life and such topics and quickly found that we were in many ways sort of soul-mates.

That was in the fall of '83. They met again and then again: in Manila, in Tokyo, in Rome . . . They showed cities to each other and talked and argued, she arranged for Len to lecture in Japan on Catholic Reform, and he got her involved in his Trialogue initiative. She came to visit and stayed in the Swidlers' house. "Oh," she said, "You have Seven-Eleven stores in the U.S. also?"

Filo Hirota, only a few years younger than Len, looks like a remastering of her own photographs from thirty years ago: shapely, with black, now-short hair, she hasn't changed much but for a bit of gray. "Comely," says Len. Raised in Tokyo, she left her hometown during the bombing raids and learned English from American movies playing in occupied Japan. Then she came to Kansas—on scholarship to a Catholic college—and discovered Christianity. Her baptism broke her father's heart, but one cannot betray one's nature, and she followed her call all the way to the leadership role in the Mercedarian order.

LS   Filo is a very thoughtful person, very deeply committed to social justice. She listens to another person very intently, like a client-centered therapist. And not shy about alcohol! I'll be stopping to visit her and get her a duty-free bottle of Chivas Regal.

RA   So you'll have wine and she'll have scotch whiskey?

LS   No, she'll have four whiskeys, and I'll have one! She can hold liquor very well, and she drinks only on specific occasions. For her it's like: this is the time to drink and be merry! She took me to see the Vatican Nuncio, an archbishop, in Japan, and we were in his palace—what do you call it?

RA   A mansion?

LS   His mansion in Tokyo, and we were drinking the wine. Shoot, the two of them would drink four times as much as me! We were having a very enjoyable time, and then they say, "Let's go eat." Well, fine. We walk to an Italian place four blocks away, he is not wearing his robes, and the person there goes, "Ah! Monsegniore!" In Italian. We order food and drink some more, then they get seriously into something about the Catholic Church in Japan, and she says, "You've got to do this and that!" And the archbishop is taking notes like a novice from mother superior. I'm thinking, *This gal really knows what she's talking about.* And he is a very smart guy in general—and also knows what a gem he's got.

Filo is a very close friend. I can share all kinds of things with her. I suspect, being the big boss, she doesn't have too many close friends. She didn't want this, but she allowed herself to be elected and then reelected as part of a "trio" that runs the show from Rome for the Mercedarians. She is always on a plane, spends two-thirds of her time outside of Rome, visiting Sisters. Her trio is "Lincoln's cabinet of rivals," difficult to work with. So I am a listening ear.

CHAPTER 4

Samuel's Irish Rose: Len's mother

Thou art thy mother's glass . . .

—WILLIAM SHAKESPEARE, SONNET 3

HER PORTRAIT HANGS ABOVE the piano in Len Swidler's living room. Though barely medium-size and of subdued, sepia-touched tones that reveal its age, the photograph is somehow prominent in the room, among the other pictures and paintings that cover the walls. Unobtrusively, it draws the eye.

In it, Josephine Marie Reed Swidler is in her forties, not so much a beautiful as a handsome woman with a short hairdo, wearing a simple but elegant suit. She stands, resting one arm on a fireplace mantle in the Swidlers' house in Green Bay, in a pose of dignity and patience, with a hint of fatigue, and her face and her entire figure exude such poise and self-possession, such easy yet solemn peace that, each time I have stood before this portrait, I found it hard to move away. Knowing nothing else about the woman in the photograph, I would have thought she'd had command of strength and wisdom and that she'd known suffering.

It appears that both are true, certainly in her eldest son's memories.

The only facts Len possesses about his mother's life, besides her Irish background, are these: She was one of fifteen children; she once worked at a chicken factory, plucking feathers; and she met her children's father in the 1920s, when Samuel was selling insurance. Starting at least with her married life, though, Josephine was a hairdresser, and her little beauty shop at the top of a long outside wooden stair is one of Len's earliest memories.

This was in Cumberland, a pretty tiny town in western Wisconsin, where the Swidlers had moved from Iowa when Leo was not even two and which they left for Green Bay—in those days the "big city" of forty thousand—when he was four. In Green Bay, too, Josephine opened a beauty salon that kept the family alive through the Depression. It apparently did well and even supported employees, including at one time the owner's husband.

Leo was growing up something of a sickly child. Having survived a difficult bout of pneumonia and mastoiditis, he developed complications and for almost ten years suffered from chronic ear infections, went through regular ear-tube placements, a tonsillectomy, repeated adenoidectomies—and, to top it all off, an appendectomy. He was no stranger to hospitals. Between setting up her business and caring for her son, Josephine had her hands already quite full when, on September 6, 1935, just as Leo was starting second grade, she gave birth to her second child, another boy. His name would be Jacob—or Jack.

One impression Len retains from his life in Green Bay is moving a lot. Just the list of the schools he attended fills the listener's mind with a kind of chopped salad of saints' names: Howe Public to St. Willebrod's Parochial, then St. John's, St. Patrick's, and back to St. Willebrod's, before settling in for four years of Central Catholic High. They rented here and there—the Great Depression lifestyle—but one house seems to stand out for Len, and he mentions it frequently: the first one, where it all began for him, at 711 Eliza Street. Astoundingly, the house is still there, on Eliza Street, quite as it was before and unchanged, at least on the outside. It stands like a voluminous likeness of a memory, not frozen and yet not moving on from the past eighty years gone. Same features, same colors. It stands like a provocative question: How near can we come to going home again?

Josephine's salon, Bay Beauty Shop, resided in downtown Green Bay, and her life largely revolved around it, while Leo's life revolved quite a bit around her. There is something about recurring suffering that makes the young very early conscious of their caretakers' love—a satisfied need for consolation, perhaps, or a precarious well-being strengthened by the assured presence of adults. Good parents make us feel safe, a hundred times more so when we are in pain, so sick children often grow up close to their parents—and it happened so for Leo, but there was more between him and Josephine than shared suffering.

Every weekend during the school year and daily in the summers, they went to Mass together. On the way, they talked about things: about work, about business. They were living the Depression, every day a new struggle for income, and the elementary-school-aged Leo was acutely aware of it. He'd ask his mother how much the shop had taken in the day before, and forty dollars was a cause to rejoice. Thirty dollars was good. Twenty was trouble.

He still remembers the angst of the question and the ache of the answer on those twenty-dollar days. "Hard to think that an eight-year-old could be so worldly burdened," he says.

I imagine it was a common enough feeling, a common enough picture in 1937: a woman and a child, bent imperceptibly under the burden that pressed upon their shoulders, walking to church in the morning.

And then Sandra was born, Josephine's third and youngest child, and the burden of the previous years paled in comparison with her new and daily battle for survival.

"I'd always been very close to Mom, but that closeness suddenly grew to a very, very painful closeness,"[10] Len would write about this time. The year was 1940. Leo was eleven years old.

He doesn't know exactly what went wrong at Sandi's birth. Too young to understand quite what it meant, Leo watched a ridge from the forceps delivery slowly dissipate on the baby's forehead and adjusted to a horrifying, upside-down reality: his mother was now sick. For the rest of her life, Josephine would suffer from severe and painful heart palpitations and fatigue, enduring incapacitating days-long episodes. Len's recollections make me think that Josephine might have developed peripartum cardiomyopathy, so it makes sense that she was eventually prescribed Digitalis, but he doesn't remember its bringing her much relief. Nothing brought much relief; her son's heart spasmed helplessly by her bedside.

Many decades later, Professor Leonard Swidler would write, "I remember how I sat alone on the floor next to her feeling totally helpless, with my heart in my throat desperately praying that she would not die. This attack must have been especially intense—they got increasingly severe with the passage of time."[11]

---

10 Swidler, "A Life in Dialogue," section "Pre-Beginnings—Mom," para. 9.

11 Ibid., para. 11.

It was unexpected therefore for Josephine's family, with a surreal sort of feeling of exchanging fire for a frying pan, to see how well her battered heart was handling the stress of colon cancer after twenty years of cardiac disease. Until the last day, it never let her down. She and her heart fought valiantly through three years of treatments and major surgeries, and in 1962 it was cancer that took her life. Samuel lived another twenty-two years and joined the love of his life in 1984.

Len gets terse when he talks about his mother's death, and I can sense more than see something of a hole in him. I'm not sure if it's his heart or the pit of his stomach. Somewhere in the center of his being, where body and soul collide, there's an aching lack in Leonard Swidler: his parents' absence. Then he stretches in his chair, hands behind his head, and a wide, dreamy smile creeps back onto his face. It helps that he believes—I feel palpably just at this moment—that it's only a matter of time. They'll see each other again.

Talking to Len

(On gratitude and a crisis of faith)

RA   Len, you write in your notes that in college you went through a "phase of dire darkness." It was a crisis of faith. Can you talk about that: your doubts about God's existence and how you resolved them?

LS   I think this sort of doubt was there before I joined a discussion group on Reform Catholicism and talked with other people. I can remember spending quite a number of hours over in the church at the college, by myself. It was an agony for me whether God exists— a normal kind of teenage puberty. You begin to ask questions of everything that seemed just there: Is that really true?

RA   Does everyone question this?

LS   Everyone who thinks, it seems. My three-year-old Carmel once asked me about earthworms. She hated earthworms, thought worms were evil. So once we were walking together after a rain—lots of worms everywhere coming up out of the ground— and she asked, "Is God good?" I said, "Yes." "Then who made the earthworms?" She had this perfect reverse logic: if evil worms are here, who is God?

RA   What did you say?

LS   I really don't remember. It was her question, that she asked it, and she was three, that floored me!

RA   Was it evil that prompted *your* questions?

LS   No. I don't recall what did. When one is raised as a Catholic, God is a given. As you get into intellectual life, you just begin to ask questions and you realize: this one's a biggy. I have to say, right now at age eighty-four, I can't say to myself, "God exists." Frankly, I don't think anybody can say that, really. I can't come up with an explanation to myself for how the universe as I know it exists without there being what I call "God." But I can't prove it.

RA   And yet you are at peace now while you weren't then. What was the agony? What was the crisis?

LS   If God doesn't exist, what is the purpose of anything? All becomes meaningless. It really was a crisis. I spent hours there, thinking, *What if God really doesn't exist?*

I don't have a clear recollection of how it ended, just that eventually it didn't bother me anymore. I thought of other things. I got focused on the short-term good, on the meaningfulness of this and that—parts of human life. It drew my attention from this all-or-nothing dilemma. But I still think about it riding my bike and meditating. I spend time being aware of myself now. Am I the only one here, present, or am I within a presence? I think I am within a presence. I don't know, but I trust. It is illogical to say "know"—the whole business of anthropic principle. To say this is a sheer accident is such a massive challenge that I can't say "yes" to that. It flies in the face of everything that's reason, *telos*. No one can prove it because of the nature of our thinking capacity.

RA   A closed system.

LS   Yes! So that's where I am. *Que será, será.* Hegelian, I guess. All I can do is live now, in the now, as best as I know how. Then other things come in—gratitude and so on—when I see so much given to me, and not just physically. I have a much more optimistic outlook than many other people; that's a gift. I got it from my mom: not DNA, but loving affection.

RA   Possibly DNA, too? There are people prone to depression just by virtue of brain chemistry, and you are not.

LS   Right. This is a gift, not something I've earned. What I'm trying to say is that I'm very at ease with myself. And sometimes
my feeling is: "You're missing the bad stuff you shouldn't be at
ease with, you dummy!" But other times I feel I've had a loving
mother and childhood, good health and good friends that support me, and education, and I was born with a brain that can
make use of it. We've been told that faith is a gift—well, it's not
just faith. I've been so gifted! And I really am grateful, yet I sort
of accept it as a matter of fact. So I feel the need to give back
whatever I can—and no angst about that.

CHAPTER 5

"On These Magic Shores": Childhood

They tell you much of your upbringing, but some sort of beautiful, holy memory cherished from childhood—that may be the best upbringing of all. . . . Let only one good memory linger in our heart, and even this might serve one day to save us.

—FYODOR DOSTOEVSKY, *THE BROTHERS KARAMAZOV*

As is usually the case, Len's recollections begin sometime after birth in chaos and confusion—a hazy pin-prick pattern of images and feelings, droppings from the metabolic stream of context, darkened by time and empty of understanding. They are rarely in themselves interesting or informative, our first memories, yet it can be interesting to ask why our brains hold on to a certain memory so early on and not another. Who remembers her parent's hands lifting her out of bed? Who remembers a sudden expanse of the natural world: the first snow, the sun, the splash of a sea? Who, a momentary terror of loss at being left alone in a supermarket?

Len Swidler's first memories carry a painful awakening to the reality of death, and no one, not even Len knows what it meant to him then and how it shaped him. All he has in his mind from his life in Cherokee, Iowa, is two images: his grandmother's deathbed and a body of a kitten, nauseous, crushed into a mess of black blood, bones, and fur stuck to the back wheel of a car.

"Horrible," he says, shudders, and changes the topic. He had to have been no older than two when this happened.

They moved to the town of Cumberland, Wisconsin, in 1930, and Len recalls it much more swiftly and with great liveliness. Little demons start jumping in and out from under his eyebrows.

LS   In the summertime, we kids used to follow ice delivery trucks. Air conditioning and refrigerators were inventions of the future. People had ice boxes in those days, and trucks would come along with ice cakes, so the "ice man who cometh" would take the pick and chip at those slits in a hundred-pound block of clear ice and break off a fifty- or twenty-five-pound piece. We would go in the back of the trucks and follow them because some chips would fall off—crystal-clear, not like ice from refrigerators now, all full of air. They were so cooling on hot summer days!

       Another thing, farm trucks would come through carrying peas on vines, and we'd run behind and pull off the vines and eat the peas.

RA   Little thieves.

LS   And there'd also come through some trucks with rutabagas, and we'd swipe some off the back and eat them. They were farm-sweet!

RA   Are most of your Cumberland stories about stealing stuff from trucks?

LS   [*laughs*] Well, I had not yet learned about confession, so I have no residue of guilt to this day!

Then, in 1933, came the life in Green Bay: Mother's Bay Beauty Shop, learning to have a brother and then a sister, changing addresses, going to school—one after another—and, of course, playing football.

historical interlude

As a new immigrant, two decades ago, I memorized the words "The Green Bay Packers" before I could hope even remotely to understand what they meant. I simply heard them too many times and learned them as an expression. As an idiom. As much as football is an American institution, the Packers seem to be an institution in American football.

I suppose, it is not surprising. America admires a victor, and the Packers have won thirteen championships, including four Super Bowls—more than any other NFL team—since their inception in 1919, which also makes them the third oldest NFL franchise. Yet the legend has something of a humble beginning.

In the summer of 1919, a young and, as it would turn out, quite stout athlete Earl "Curly" Lambeau and his friend George Calhoun kicked around an idea of getting together a football team. It was really quite that simple: a casual conversation on a street corner between former high-school football rivals. By August they had enough guys who were interested, and the Indian Packing Company, where Lambeau was working as a shipping clerk, agreed to sponsor the jerseys and give them access to its football field for practice. Although this was the extent of the company's involvement—and the company itself didn't last through the first season—the team became and forever stayed the Packers.

They played in a field with no bleachers, on donations from the fans, but their very first season brought ten wins and one loss, and people with money began to take notice. It wasn't smooth or easy: Through the early twenties, Lambeau gained, lost, and re-gained backers, put up his own money to buy back the franchise, battled insurance and a litigious fan who managed to send the team into receivership, until the formation in 1923 of the Green Bay Football Corporation. For over ninety years the Packers would stay in Wisconsin and turn their realistically modest town of Green Bay, which even today counts a tad over a hundred-thousand people, into the revered home of the Packers—the team that not only leads the National Football League in championships but is second only to the Chicago Bears in the number of Pro Football Hall of Fame inductees, and those names include giants like Reggie White, Don Hutson, Brett Favre, Ray Nitschke, Bart Starr, Forrest Gregg, Herb Adderley, Willie Davis, and, of course, Curly Lambeau and Vince Lombardi, the great coaches of the twentieth century.

This is what makes me think that the special place the Packers occupy in America's heart is due to something more than their winning record: this team, so much the epitome of American football, is unusual for American football today. Though the third oldest NFL franchise, it has resided in its home town longer than any other team. It is literally the last vestige of the "small town teams" that once populated the NFL and holds a unique distinction of being the only community-owned major league sports team in the United States. The Packers are a publicly owned corporation operated as a nonprofit ever since 1923.

I know America loves a victor, but even more than any sort of victor, America loves a self-made person—a triumph of small over big through excellence, persistence, and eternal optimism. This, after all, is America's biography. Like David—the runt of the litter with ruddy cheeks, a pebble, and a mountain of determination—the Green Bay Packers came out against Goliath-sized giants of football and declared themselves and stood their ground and won. They never lost sight of who they are and where home is, and their home loves them for it with a passion powerful and tender. If you are from Green Bay or a surrounding area as far as Milwaukee, you must be a Packers fan. The story of the Packers, it seems to me, is a consummate one of the American dream.

end interlude

TALKING TO LEN

(On football, brother Jack, and seclusion from the world)

RA   Was football a part of your life early on?

LS   Oh, very much. Green Bay is the Mecca of American football, you know. I went to the Packers games; I saw real heroes like Don Hutson, the "magic" pass receiver. He weighed only 175 pounds, which was my playing weight in college, and this encouraged my football fantasies for decades to come. I thought, *If Don Hutson can play pro football, why can't I? It's not the size but skill that really counts.* All the grade schools had regular football teams, and I played right guard and then center and linebacker.

RA   Were you good?

LS   Let's just say, I had a lot to learn on defense that first year. Over the years, I improved, cultivated an ability to sense how a play was developing and to bring down the ball carrier before a blocker could get to me. I remember a game from my senior year: we were playing a hotshot team from Madison. I blocked a couple of punts, intercepted a pass, and made several tackles, so that I was listed as All-State Honorable Mention among the State high school football players that week. Of course, that turned out to be the acme of my football career.

RA   What about college?

LS   That was bruising. I intended to play, even got a small football scholarship in my freshman year at St. Norbert, but things turned out very differently than I thought they would. I topped out at 175 pounds, and all these returning ex-GIs were comparatively massive and with additional years of experience. I was lucky to make the fourth team. I remember, though, we won our first game 56-0 and were undefeated the whole four years I was an undergrad.

RA   But you never got to play.

LS   Right, which is what disgusted me. At the end of my freshman year I figured it was no fun and stopped playing, though I might have continued if I hadn't gotten so involved in my Catholic discussion group.

RA   But you did then coach some kids in football once you left the team?

LS   It was the grade school my brother Jack was in. I don't remember a great deal, just that Jack played right guard. He was not very tall, maybe 5'6", and weighed close to 200 pounds. He was strong. I remember also that once he broke his leg during a game, and I insisted he continue to play—which he did.

RA   Were you a very tough big brother?

LS   Here's a story: We lived at 913 North Chestnut in Green Bay, and
       at the end of the block lived a football player from the Packers,
       Hank Bruder. They had a child the same age as Jack and a bit of
       a bully. I coached Jack in fisticuffs. One day Jack and Hank Jr.
       went at it, and Jack dropped the fists and bit Hank's arm, which
       ended the battle. I remember hearing from my mom that Mrs.
       Bruder complained to her they had to take Hank to the hospital.
       I thought, *Good for Jack!* Though I didn't coach him in that.

RA   Did you play with Jack a lot?

LS   Oh, yeah, all the time. Frequently I would babysit him. He looked
       up to me as his big brother. Sometimes it was fine with me, some-
       times a terrible drag. I remember one incident quite vividly. On
       Chestnut, there were two piles of lumber with six to eight feet
       of space between them and a plank stretching from one to the
       other. I thought they were ten feet high then. I remember Jack up
       on top and me below. With me egging him on, he began to "walk
       the plank"—and fell off! I don't remember anything after he hit
       the ground. In my memory, he is still falling sideways up above
       me. I presume he came out all right, though years later, when the
       story would surface during party reminiscences, I would allow
       that perhaps some permanent damage was done to his brain.
            We were hanging out together quite a lot, so he became
       much older in his interests than he would normally be. Only in
       high school he got his own friends and got into trouble of his
       own. He'd drink beer a lot, get drunk, that sort of thing.

RA   Did you come back from college to straighten him out?

LS   Not really. I left for seminary from Green Bay when I was twen-
       ty-one and he was fifteen, so he was on his own. That's when he
       got into his difficulties. Once—it was not his fault—he was driv-
       ing a car, and an eighty-year-old man stepped out from between
       two cars, and Jack hit and killed him. He was exonerated as far
       as the law was concerned, but it affected him deeply. I was not
       there at the time.

RA   How did you learn of it?

LS   I don't remember. I was probably down in the novitiate, cut off from the world, and learned of it only much later.

RA   Do you regret that?

LS   I don't have a recollection of feeling bad in that way. I suppose I did feel that way, but I don't have any recollection.

RA   What about now?

LS   Back then, it was perfectly natural. I was going to be a saint, and it meant being cut off from the world. Yes, I was to be nice to people, but the internal communion was to be with God.

RA   Still, people pay a price for cutting themselves off from the world. Your brother went through something terrible and maybe needed you, and you weren't there for him. Now, as the person that you are, do you have any thoughts about that?

LS   Now? It's so wrong-headed I'd have to say it's silly. The whole business of even changing your name the way we did back then, all that . . . Which one sees happening in all of these religious experiences people have, like Mohammed Ali, which is the rage today.

RA   What are your thoughts about cloistered communities in general, then?

LS   I must admit I haven't quite thought about it. My life experience has been moving away from that. My circumstances moved me away. I was thrown out of Norbertines, then seminary and leaving there, and going to university . . . Those were all . . . the first steps I was forced into. So when I went to a diocesan seminary, my first goal of becoming an intellectual was threatened. So I went to a university, which maintained my goal of an intellectual life but put at least my earlier understanding of sanctity in jeopardy.

So asking this question now, about seclusion . . . I guess I'd have to say, there are different people with different psychological make-ups or in different stages of their lives where seclusion makes sense. What I learned from history: there is a kind of rhythm of withdrawal and return that is healthy and appropriate. It may very well be that certain people do best in a more contemplative mode. The numbers will be small percentage-wise. Every lifestyle has its strengths, temptations, exaggerations, and destructive properties.

CHILDHOOD (CONT'D)

As Josephine and Samuel spent long hours, often into the night, culling for income the depleted pool of the Depression-impoverished Green Bay, they left their two—and then three—children in the care of what Len refers to as "a rather long parade of maids" and what we today would probably call "nannies." Of all his nannies, Len most fondly remembers Milly Winicky, who nurtured him and Jack through the war years and took them to her Polish parents' farm near the town of Pulaski. He remembers long, days-at-a-time Polish weddings and learning to polka and to hop-dance.

Milly's boyfriend Larry was inducted into the Wisconsin National Guard, Len thinks, in 1940—a time of such shortage that the new recruits were training with broomsticks for rifles—and in 1942 was deployed to New Guinea to fight the Japanese.

historical interlude

The Papua campaign is not well remembered, not nearly as well as even the nearby battle of Guadalcanal—it did not hold the same strategic importance—yet its horror is hardly comparable, and its casualties are higher in number and three times higher in rate than at Guadalcanal.[12] The offensive on Buna, Sanananda, and Gona—part of the Pacific campaign executed by American and Australian troops—began on November 16, 1942, but the Japanese, concentrating on holding Guadalcanal, had withdrawn to the beachhead around Girua River months before and had plenty of time to entrench where American commanders had believed fortification was not possible. With bad intelligence and a poor understanding of local conditions, the Allies underestimated everything about what they were facing, and the battle that was supposed to be over in two weeks took more than two months and a horrible toll in human lives.

12 Most information about the Papua campaign is drawn from two sources: "Papua" and Hopkins, *The Pacific War,* 142–43.

None of the campaign leaders except General Douglas MacArthur had any familiarity with jungle terrain, and he wasn't there. With their feet in swamp water, dense foliage teeming with insects overhead, and thick, knotted roots all around, soldiers quickly became exhausted from marching and contracted an overwhelming rate of tropical disease. Two out of every three men suffered from something awful: malaria, dengue fever, dysentery, bush typhus, ring worm. Starting out with no tanks or artillery and with inadequate air support and poor supply tactics, they soon found themselves hungry, in tattered uniforms, and fighting with rifles and grenades against a well-bunkered enemy. One can hardly imagine how low morale can fall under the weight of apparently never-ending death, disease, and futility. The Japanese seemed undefeatable.

Only weeks into this disaster did the tide begin to turn with a change in allied tactics—the arrival of tanks and artillery support and new supplies—and the toll that time was taking on the enemy. The Japanese soldiers, too, began to run out of ammunition and rations, and when the Allies finally took the last of the three strongholds, Sanananda, on January 22, 1943, they found evidence of cannibalism among the starving people.

When all was said and done, counting the dead, the missing, and the wounded, the allied casualties numbered 8,546. This official number doesn't seem to include the sick, and how many died later of their conditions' complications or were scarred forever by two months of hell on earth is a question I cannot answer. Of course, this number does not include the Japanese killed, wounded, sick, and starved.

I come from a place that bore the brunt of World War II, so wounded by it that to this day, seventy years later, blood is seeping from the ground and graves span endless fields. Celiac disease is torturing the wartime children of starvation, national treasures are ruined or missing, and no family is complete. Nightmarish history and mottled memories, bitterness, and pride. Almost twenty million Soviet soldiers laid down their lives on the front lines, as did millions of civilians behind the lines. Russia, having fought many wars on its scarred and burned-up land, has grieved and wailed and buried—and learned to remember.

America hasn't fought a foreign enemy within its borders since it began to become itself, since the Revolutionary War, though the scars of the Civil War are of their own, special kind. America sends its children away to fight, and that's a different kind of grief: the quiet and helpless kind. America stays innocent in a sense, beautiful, blossoming, barely touched, and they disappear and leave, some to come back in stars-and-stripes-decorated boxes, others in cages of their own minds. Those who know and those who remember the details of wars that have taken American lives are only a few, because it happens just so far away.

I sometimes wonder which way is better. I get so hurt by the good people who don't remember, so afraid that they don't realize the horror of war—so appalled by the ease of their decisions, their dismissal—and our children who see the troops honored here, don't see them in muck, on the brink of humanity, over there. But, then, Russia remembers, yet that hasn't stopped it from the horror of war, and the damage has been so devastating—economic, psychological, physical—that the wounds never heal.

There is no "better."

end interlude

Leo Swidler was barely a teenager when all this was happening on the opposite side of the globe and did not know the details, but the names of Buna and Gona, little jungle villages, are burned into his memory. "It seemed," he says, "that they fought there endlessly."

Milly's boyfriend Larry did not die in the Papuan swamp. In a fairy-tale-like happy ending, he returned home and at the end of the war married his Milly, and together they lived out the rest of their lives. Len knows this because, around the start of the millennium, the two brothers were visiting together at Jack's home in North Carolina and got to talking about old Milly. Jack, telephone aficionado that he was, found her in a nursing home and got her on the line. She was in somewhat precarious health but still never far from her Larry, also by that time declining.

"*Sic transit gloria—et juventutes—mundi!*" Len declaims in Latin, one of his favorite ways to stump an unsuspecting interlocutor. *So passes the glory—and youth—of the world.* Yes, well—as long as they pass peacefully and in the company of Larry.

Financially, the war may not have been better or worse for the Swidler family than the thirties, but it was different. Len recalls a sharp shortage of certain specific things and their rationing: meat, sugar, fats, oil, gasoline, tires, etc. The last two were a particular problem for his Uncle Mac and Aunt Gertrude, one of Mother's younger sisters. Uncle Mac and Aunt Gertrude made their living "checking stores." Traveling from place to place, from state to state, they made unannounced visits to chain-store locations and evaluated the honesty of their staff. In the summer of 1944, Leo went along with them on a store-checking adventure from Missouri to New Mexico. It would be his summer job.

RA   How did this "checking" work?

LS   In those days, for every sale the clerk would write a bill of sale with a carbon underneath, and I would get the carbon or the original. If it was a clothing store, I would go in and pick out two shirts in my size. While he or she was writing out the slip and ringing up the money in the cash register, I would have "noticed" a tie rack, $1.50 apiece. When she came back, I'd say, "I'll take two ties," and drop them into the bag with shirts and give her exact change—and then I'd go.

       We'd do that for all the clerks. At the end of the day, my uncle presented himself and went over the slips. If there was a slip for two shirts and not a slip for two ties, it meant the clerk stole the three dollars. There was one clothing store in Texas, not very big, but it had seven clerks. In this store, all the clerks stole! It was quite startling. Even the manager's daughter was stealing!

RA   For seven clerks, wouldn't they notice the same person—you— doing this over and over again?

LS   Well, there were three of us doing it, and we were careful. Now, sometimes my uncle and the manager would confront the thieving clerk with the evidence. I think he would get half of what they'd stolen if they confessed and repaid. I imagine it would not be an easy task. My uncle had a strong way of talking—could scare the living daylights out of a clerk—but it would take a toll on him.

RA   Do you know the manager wasn't stealing? If even the manager's daughter was caught?

LS   It was a franchise, so he'd get a percentage at the end of the month. He'd be stealing from himself.

The summer of 1944 turned out to be a remarkable one for Leo just by the number and depth of experiences it brought. He was in Tulsa,

Oklahoma, with Uncle Mac and Aunt Gertrude on June 6, when the mad ringing of church bells, braided into the honking of cars from every direction, woke him up and drove him out of his room, still disoriented, into the multitudes jumping in the street, hollering, and the blasting of the hotel radio. He doesn't remember many more details about D-Day—only the flooding adrenaline of it and an enormous grass field he saw later, at a military base in Carlsbad, New Mexico, covered with brand-new silver B-26's, still unmarked, sitting wingtip to wingtip as far as the eye could see.

Carlsbad marked the end of Leo's journey with Mac and Gertrude and the beginning of a new one: to Los Angeles, where he would stay with another aunt and work for the last month of his summer at a defense plant, building wooden life rafts at a "princely" salary of eighty cents an hour. It seemed to Leo that his every day in L.A. started with an identical weather report, which promised the smog to dissipate by 11 AM, and ended with him collapsing facedown onto the couch.

He rode home in a fifty-car train filled with troops on furlough, through Texas, Chicago, and four endless days and nights, watched America roll backwards, and talked. His world-weary neighbors educated the kid in the ways of life and left tiny cracks in his innocence. He let them—sometimes out of carelessness; sometimes, curiosity.

LS   I remember one soldier pointed to a woman sitting in another soldier's lap, and I didn't know why. He told me they were having sex. It stunned me so much that I still remember to this day. Such a deep shock.

RA   You had four days to get to know these guys.

LS   I rode in the only air-conditioned car, and everywhere else people looked as if they'd melted and run down into their seats. When we went through Amarillo, it was 120 degrees! And all these guys were traveling across the nation to go on furlough. Everybody seemed to be stationed at the opposite end of the country from their homes. I assumed it was because they didn't want them to run AWOL.

RA   Did you think it was sad?

LS   I can understand why they'd make such a move. If you'll be sent off into harm's way, you need to focus on the training, so as better to survive.

Still, in the summer of 1944, by far the deepest impression in Len's memory was made by the Carlsbad Caverns. When he begins that story, his voice slides seven decades into the past and sparkles with a teenager's awe before the miracle of an elevator descending 754 feet down into the Earth.

"It's like a city underground," he says. "A wonderland."

Under the Chihuahuan desert, under sizzling, thorn-covered canyons, more than a hundred caves bubble in the dark and deep where almost three hundred million years ago a fossil reef was framing a filigreed coastline of an inland sea, in the time before dinosaurs. Ages passed, the reef was buried, then sulfuric acid dissolved limestone deposits. Once the water drained, cave formations grew in the humid air—stalactites hung from the ceilings, stalagmites rose to meet them—during the last ice age, as pine forests reigned up above.

People came and installed colored lights, laid down pathways, opened a cafeteria, and named the formations after the twists of their imagination. Over four hundred thousand spectators come down to the Carlsbad Caverns every year, and they stand, dwarfed, before the bony Witch's Finger that rises from the floor like the first protrusion of doom. The bashful Veiled Statue hides her face behind the pall of flowing hair. The Monarch reigns over the invaded underworld, and his crown spans the height of the cave.

Leo took his walk through the Caverns with Gertrude and Mac and with yet another aunt, Mercedes, his mother's younger sister. Barely fifteen years older than he, Mercedes lived in Carlsbad because her husband was stationed there on the base. She had just had her daughter Joanne not long before.

RA   The caves impressed you very much.

LS   Oh, unbelievable! It was amazing. Stalactites, stalagmites . . . Aunt Merce commented on one—it was a mound with a dripping in the middle, so it looked like a woman's breast. She said, "Joanne would like this!"

RA   Did you like Mercedes?

LS   In many ways I liked her best of all. I remember she came to Green Bay to live with us for a while—must have been the next summer, right after the war. She'd divorced her husband, and I heard he was a "ne'er-do-well."

That next summer I was working construction, digging ditches. At Bay Beach at the tip of Green Bay there was a dance hall, and she wanted to go to a dance. She was thirty, I was sixteen—I thought she was antique. "Come on, Leo," she said. "Take me to the dance." "Gee, well, okay." You know how it is when you're young. I'd work all day, heavy physical stuff, come home bone tired, then change and go dance till midnight on Saturday or Sunday. When it came to dancing—wow, full of fun! She just seemed so to me, maybe because we were closer in age. We struck a bond together.

RA   Did you do lots of dancing in high school? Lots of dating?

LS   I went to an all-boys Central Catholic High, staffed by young Norbertine priests, and I never went on a date while in school, except nine formal dances in my senior year, and those girls came from St. Joseph's Academy. I went with eight different girls. That's because one girl asked me back to a Sadie Hawkins dance.

RA   You didn't date at all?

LS   Nope. I was in a play my senior year where I met those girls. It was called *Corduroy Road*, written by Father Guyon. Took place in French Canada. My best friend Gene played one of the lead parts. I don't remember the part I played.

RA   So the girls made more impression than the part?

LS   Yup.

PART II

Downstream

CHAPTER 6

Naval Engagements and Other Teaching Moments: St. Norbert College

Live as if you were to die tomorrow. Learn as if you were to live forever.

—MAHATMA GANDHI

ST. NORBERT COLLEGE IS your typical pretty campus on a bend of the Fox River: a mix of older and newer buildings, parking lots, gardens, and lawns, multi-voiced din pouring in and out of classrooms. A polished wooden pier protrudes out over the water, offering visitors a panoramic view of the other bank—all curly greens through the summer, the white of tidy little houses peeking through the foliage, and a light, soaring sky. The College built this waterfront with a gazebo stage maybe a couple of decades ago, and here its renowned graduate came at the change of the millennia to be honored by his *alma mater* with a Distinguished Achievement Award and an honorary doctorate. He spent an evening thinking of what's passed, taking in the space, leaning over the railing that hadn't existed when Leo Swidler was a St. Norbert student.

Much of the campus didn't exist in 1946. It was sparse then, without a lot of feel to it: two big buildings—Old Main for offices and Boyle

Hall for classrooms—facing each other across a yard; the church with an abbey attached, where priests had their shelter and students studied theology; and an old Quonset hut in the back. Father O'Keefe, a biology teacher, with a handful of his student helpers, nosed tirelessly through the dirt, planting trees. A big field lay open for football practice behind Old Main, dry one day and muddy the next. Len remembers the chaos of registration on a September day of '46. The lines of young men, most of them ex-GIs just back from the war, two or three abreast, were spilling out of the gym and snaking around the field, four hundred yards long— almost all of the freshman class.

The College has changed in seventy years; only Old Main and Boyle Hall still look the same. The red brick trimmed in gray stone of the old St. Joseph Church has a few small additions. A modest white statue of St. Norbert stands to the side. He is holding up a monstrance to remind us of the saint's penchant for adoration of the Holy Eucharist. Inside, space-filled twilight bids one to exhale all hurry. Everything calls to quietude: slender, pointed windows; hoary bricks of dusty red; unpretentious modern chairs that face each other rather than the altar, choir style, from right and left. A wooden ceiling floats over crossbeams and reflects in a wooden floor. This is all recent, the breath of new spirituality. Seven decades ago, this was a traditional chapel with pews and what Len calls "pedestrian décor."

The site had had humble and troubled beginnings, trying to serve a local community, struggling with money, and rebuilt more than once, until Rev. Bernard Pennings arrived in De Pere in 1898. He acquired the building for the Norbertines and quickly turned it from a local church into the worship center of a parish, a grade school, a high school, and a college. It also housed the national shrine of St. Joseph until 1969, when it was moved to St. Norbert Abbey on De Pere's east side.

Leo's meeting with the founder of the De Pere Abbey was brief and chance, one of his first as a college student, and he calls it to mind whenever I ask him what attracted him so about the Norbertines. Passing in front of Old St. Joe's, he saw the elderly abbot shuffle along the sidewalk. Abbot Pennings looked down at a piece of chewing gum stuck to the ground, then smiled at the embarrassed freshman, and said, "At least they didn't spit it out in church!"

Four years at St. Norbert were very full for Leo Swidler. He started with high hopes for football and soon dropped out, but his junior and senior years were taken up by Reserve Officer Training Corps: Leo needed only two years of officer training because he'd had ROTC in high school. Involved by then deeply in his growing desire for the consecrated life, he retained sketchy memories of it—and yet, he never fails to mention ROTC, whenever he talks about college.

RA   Were you proud to graduate from ROTC?

LS   Oh, yeah. Gold bars, the uniform. The ceremony was held in the quad between Old Main and Boyle, and it was June, good weather. Mom and Dad and brother and sister came. I can see the set-up with folding chairs, a stage: green and gold. Our graduation speaker was Msgr. Sheen. He was very famous then, very flashy and dramatic, had a huge radio and TV following.

RA   Was that Fulton Sheen?

LS   That's the one.

historical interlude

Venerable Fulton J. Sheen, the archbishop of Rochester, New York, was indeed at the height of his career in the 1950s and 1960s. From his radio broadcast *The Catholic Hour* to his TV shows *Life Is Worth Living* and later *The Fulton Sheen Program*, almost thirty million people gathered weekly to hear him speak. Thought of by many as an early televangelist, he was very concerned with the propagation of faith and is famous for converting to Catholicism some well-known and creative personalities, including Heywood Broun, Fritz Kreisler, and Louis F. Budenz.

A curious anecdote is often emphasized by the venerators of Archbishop Sheen's prophetic gift. In early 1953, the Archbishop delivered a dramatic reading from Shakespeare's *Julius Caesar*, substituting Caesar's name with Joseph Stalin's and the treasonous cohort with the names from the Soviet political elite. At the end of the broadcast, Sheen stated aloud, "Stalin must one day meet his judgment." Only a few days later, Joseph Stalin died suddenly of a reported stroke, and even to this day not everyone is satisfied with the explanations we have of the circumstances of his death.

Fulton Sheen wrote over seventy books, organized for the poor, and affected millions of minds with his words. He died in 1979 at the age of eighty-four. In 2002, the cause for his canonization for sainthood was officially opened, and ten years later, in 2012, Pope Benedict XVI declared that he had lived "a life of heroic virtues." This brought Archbishop Sheen a big step closer to beatification and granted him the title of "venerable."

end interlude

RA   Len, did you like Msgr. Sheen's speech at your ROTC graduation?

LS   To be honest, I don't remember it. But I remember during the McCarthy hearings I was at seminary, and we all gathered to watch *The Fulton Sheen Hour*. He said something about "gorgonzola cheese" being smelly—a clear reference to McCarthy, who was a Catholic, being a negative. A hidden message in plain view. I liked that.

RA   What about the rest of your ROTC? What else stayed with you?

LS   Really, I mostly remember graduating. Except, we had one summer camp at Fort Riley, Kansas, I recall. By this time I was really into interior life and stuff, aiming to be a monk and what not. I remember one captain, when we were on a march, coming to talk to us about taking salt pills, telling us how best to walk with a "rolling gait" because we had heavy packs and long distances to go. He was regular Army, had been in the war. He was a wiry sort of guy, compassionate—that's what struck me. Advising me with concern. I thought he must have been a damn good officer.

I keep thinking he was a red-head, but it might be because I always think of him together with this one story my Japanese professor told me. It was World War II, some island in the Pacific. All the Japanese officers came together in a room, waiting for Americans to take over, and they were certain they'd be shot. Then an American captain walks in, a red-haired sort, and says, "Hi, gentlemen!" and passes around a pack of cigarettes.

I am not surprised that, of all his ROTC experiences, Len's mind's held on to this captain. It seems a common thing that our deepest impressions and most formative experiences are created less often by events or even ideas—save the most dramatic—and more often by the people we encounter. We crowd each other's lives and bump into each other, knocking each other off our paths and leaving dents in the virginal shapes of our childhood souls. Those who hurt us and those who care for us, those who terrify and those who provoke to action and thought: It is the people in our lives who leave enduring traces and direct our journeys most of all. They bring about events; they call attention to ideas. When I ask Len about his college years, he tends to start and end with his teachers.

Father Vincent DeLeers was more than a professor but also a spiritual guide. He had taught Leo chemistry at the Central Catholic High still as a Frater, after his discharge from the Army in 1943. He had served in the war as a tank commander and from the first day set a tone unlike anything the kids had come to expect from their previous teacher, a much older priest.

"Where are you in your textbook?" Frater DeLeers asked and pressed from that point on. At the end of the class, he assigned homework pages and warned, "Be prepared for a quiz."

Len rolls his eyes and lets out a sharp laugh, telling the story. "Ha! Father Dionne, the previous teacher, never gave quizzes! But the next day: lo and behold, Vince gives a quiz! Of course, we were shocked and did miserably! From then on we had a quiz every day—and it really worked."

Vince DeLeers was a professor of philosophy at St. Norbert. Len cannot name the courses, but he remembers the questions, those early connections exposed for him by a brilliant mind.

"Can there be action at a distance?" Prof. DeLeers kept asking. "Is it possible for me to think something here and affect something there, without a physical link?" What was he getting at: compassion? prayer? the "butterfly effect"?

When Leo joined a discussion group on Catholic Reform, he discovered Father DeLeers there, and then again, and again, in all the places where Leo's heart felt at home—they weren't that much different in age, both young and full of ideals, kindred spirits. It was Vince DeLeers who introduced his loyal student to classical music, the lifelong thread of salvation that would keep Leo tethered to the Eternal through any darkness, pull him out of silence, fatigue, and doubt, and become for him the epitome of Beauty Divine.

They were novices, Leo and a couple of his fellows, when one day Father DeLeers walked by the music room at the Abbey where they lounged, listening to a record.

"What are you listening to?" Vince demanded.

"Mozart."

"Well, okay." His face softened. "That's real music."

Vincent DeLeers has had a hilly life of climbs, tumbles, and vistas since Leo Swidler left his tutelage. After serving a while as Dean of the College, he left the Norbertine order to get married, had and raised children, got divorced, saw his children marry, and petitioned to return to consecrated life, which was granted with a caveat: to come back to the community, but without priestly privileges. In the fall of 2013, Len visited the Priory at St. Norbert and found some familiar faces, among them Vince's. No longer of an impressive build, no longer sporting his once dark and wavy hair, distracted by Alzheimer's, he greeted his former student from a wheel chair, but his face radiated utterly irrepressible joy under a white, flighty mane, and together they sat and talked—not like sixty years ago, not as a teacher and student, but forever kindred spirits.

There were others. "Father Steinmetz," Len says, "was pure idea." Soft-spoken and unobtrusive to eye and ear—pale, gray-haired, a bit thicker around the waist. He taught metaphysics, and it seemed somehow appropriate that, delivering Aristotle's concepts of reality, he was the very embodiment of moderation. In one semester he created the mold into which all of Len Swidler's thought poured for decades: his paradigm. With a genuine reverence for a master of trade and with a little lingering surprise, Len ends his recollections of Father Steinmetz with this: "I was always astonished that fifty minutes were over when I thought it was only starting." I think, maybe, this is the highest compliment for a teacher.

Father Ruess gets a different treatment.

"Smart alec," Len says, squinting pleasurably like a cat in the sun. Father Ruess was a history professor and, from what I hear, quite ahead of his time. He held conversations in class, which was unusual in those years and earned him a reputation of a "weird" prof. He asked them questions and mocked the vernacular English that reigned in the streets.

"How can you say something in one word that's really three words?" he'd put to the class and, after a bit of commotion and guessing, reveal that "D'yeat" stood for "Did you eat" in his riddle. The students loved it.

Len speaks very briefly of Father Ruess, and yet those sarcasm-infused sessions must have had an impact on him because, in his graduate work, Len followed in this professor's footsteps. He wrote his doctoral dissertation in the field of intellectual cultural history.

"Any more funny stuff?" I ask Len about his college experience.

Oh, yes. How silly of me to ask. A sharp and benevolent sense of humor pervaded the life of the Norbertine Order and its college, guided young priests toward self-awareness, helped endure inevitable trials, developed in students healthy intellectual skepticism and a balanced relationship with authority. Darkness overtakes humanity without regular injections of funny stuff.

"Well, listen. We had an 'Errr Derby' for teachers who said 'errr' a lot. One could say it seven or eight times before completing a sentence. He taught religion—awful. Our Education Department was a butt of jokes: you know, 'If you can't do, teach.'" Len makes an apologetic gesture with both hands. "Imagine the shocker when I took this one course with Father Claridge, and we had to read a book a week!"

Father Claridge appears to have been a fascinating character: not only a professor in the Education Department but also a librarian and a nuclear physicist. Rumors circulated around the College that he had worked in Chicago on the Manhattan Project. He also weighed about three hundred pounds and was by popular consent dubbed one of the two "blimps" on the faculty.

Len does not recall the name of the other "blimp"—also a priest, not as tall as Father Claridge, yet thoroughly rotund—but recalls clearly one of his favorite moments in the library. The two men met in the narrow space, maneuvered to let each other pass, and, as they began to move apart on their ways, Father Claridge remarked to his like-figured peer, "We should have a naval engagement." The lone student watching this muffled his giggle with a fist. He thought it typical of Claridge and exceedingly clever.

"Blimp" #2 taught Latin, and Leo took a course from him on early Christian writers: Augustine, Cyprian, and so on. Latin was a challenge for Leo. It just didn't have any rules of word order, not like English.

"Where is the verb?" demanded the exasperated student.

And the answer came from his presence-filled teacher always equally calm and unhelpful: "The verb is understood."

As Len tells me of his struggle with Latin, remnants of long-ago frustration flashing on his face, I cannot help but start cracking up. Prof. Swidler is famous—or, in some circles, infamous—for injecting Latin phrases, words, and sentences not only into his writing but his everyday speech.

I am laughing because I am a Russian-English bilingual who learned English as an adult, and I can relate to young Leo's explosive rage. A foreign language—it is more than a task, more than a mystery. It can seem like an injustice, a conspiracy against you personally. Because . . . it makes no sense. It cannot possibly work! When my family and I came to the United States—frightened, mentally battered, and clueless refugees—and turned on American television, we were convinced that, in some sort of sick game, Americans just pretended to understand each other. What was this language that didn't sound anything like what was written? A language with more irregular verbs than regular, more exceptions than rules, affirmatives and negatives in the same sentence?

A language is a little like a mountain valley: You either grow up there or discover it after traversing the mountains, weather-beaten and exhausted, appreciating every blade of grass, and then you rest, having brought the outside world with you, never to be the same. Or you collapse on the way.

Len Swidler is fluent in Latin; he is fluent in German. He thinks in those languages alongside English, adding dimensions to be deciphered in his conceptual constructions—and I mentally tip my hat to our "Blimp" #2. He did his job well. So, I am thinking, did Leo's other teachers.

RA   Len, it's beginning to sound like all you did in college was study and train. Did you have any fun?

LS   Ha! I used to play cards with ex-GIs for money. I'd learned to play with my grandpa, who was a horrible card shark; he liked to win because he cheated. I played smart. I didn't cheat. It was part of my "semi-sinful" life. See, you have to remember that tuition was a hundred dollars a semester. If you could pick up three or four dollars a game, consistently three times a week, you could pay for college. Now, I didn't get this much. I'd win once in a while and had all kinds of fear and trembling about losing, though really it wasn't about morality. It's just that I could lose a couple bucks or win a couple bucks.

        I had a friend, Ray Sauvey—local, from Green Bay. He was this small, wiry guy, and we got along very well. I remember we'd go sit on a turret in Old Main and eat our lunch. We got involved in the discussion group together, so it bonded us.

What Len most often calls his "discussion group"—or simply "the Group"—was by all accounts much more than that. Organized by a local couple, Agnes and George Hohlmiller, the Group brought together maybe three dozen people from all walks of life—students, blue collar workers, and intellectuals—to talk about new writings and hot topics in contemporary Catholicism, and to follow discussion with decidedly targeted action.

"Observe, judge, and act!" Len recites the Group's unofficial motto to three claps of his hands.

The Hohlmillers were a middle-aged, middle-class family. Len remembers George as an upper-echelon bureaucrat for the Green Bay electric company and Agnes as a homemaker—both college-educated, having let their children out into the world, and ready to focus on a bigger picture. They had a spacious house near the Fox River, and every Tuesday night an assorted crowd packed itself into their living room for the weekly meeting. Students sat mostly on the floor; soft seats were reserved for the older and honored guests, who included at times the Registrar of St. Norbert College, Father DuPont, and Leo's beloved Father Vincent DeLeers. Everyone was supposed to have read some materials beforehand, meant to initiate the conversation, but students tended to show up "cold" and plunge straight into it, lacking, according to Len, in timidity.

Len retains a particular memory of the evening when Dorothy Day made an appearance at the Tuesday discussion. She had been a well-known and already controversial figure for years then but didn't make a big splash at the meeting. Unobtrusive, she tucked herself into the corner of the couch, knitted, and said, as Len put it, "rather little." He kept glancing at her and thinking that she reminded him of the knitting Madame DeFarge from *A Tale of Two Cities*. Thankfully, given that her unwavering pacifism accounted for one of the major controversies surrounding Dorothy, any similarity between her and Dickens's "vengeance incarnate" remained confined to knitting.

Len cannot recall how he got involved with the Group or who invited him. By the time he joined toward the end of his freshman year, not only were their discussions well established, but their activism had also begun to yield visible results. St. Catherine's Library and Book Shop was founded by the older members just before Leo's appearance on the scene, and he got there just in time to help them make the place remarkable. Named after its patron saint, St. Catherine of Alexandria, the library and shop sold and loaned books of spiritual and social significance, offered meeting space, and soon ventured into food preparation and organic farming. This was a thoroughly green undertaking decades before "green" meant anything but a color to anyone.

"We were into good food," Len tells me. "You could pick up ground whole wheat and cereal and bread there. I was really proud of baking whole wheat bread, though, to be honest, my culinary arts did not progress much beyond that."

The library has closed since, and whole wheat bread is on the shelves of every grocery store, but after sixty-seven years, the book shop survives. In 2009 it moved, nestled now next to the St. Francis Xavier Cathedral in Green Bay, called Cathedral Book and Gift. They no longer lend books, no longer serve as a meeting place for students, and the only organic food they sell is the Mystic Monk coffee. Still, changing names, changing places, and changing with the times, the legacy of Agnes and George, and of everyone swept up by their activism in the 1940s, endures to our day.

I dare say that it endures in the person of Leonard Swidler, too—in everything he's done, in what he's become. Leo had started his college career as a chemical engineering major and finished it as a double major in history and philosophy. There is no mystery in what pushed him to discover his true calling: His fascination with the subjects themselves notwithstanding, it was the Lay Apostolate Movement that seeded in Leo's heart reflective spirituality where formal piety had lain, nurtured out of it concern for social justice, and blossomed into true activism and genuine devotion to the Christian cause. The Group made Professor Swidler the man he is—as he says again and again.

"Thinking back to it, there was a great deal of integrity and intensity on the part of these people." Len's voice deepens in an audible homage. "They obviously thought a lot about mentoring the youth. And they mentored me right into the monastery."

As time passed, the Group's activities branched out more and more. They sponsored everything from folk dancing to serious conferences, some several days long, that aimed to reconcile spiritual and liturgical involvement with everyday living. Leo organized several of them as an upperclassman. At a nearby convent, they celebrated the Eucharist and practiced Gregorian chant, becoming eventually a respectable *schola cantorum*.

"We took up plain song, Gregorian chant, and became enamored with it," Len says. "There was some convent in Green Bay, the Good Shepherd Sisters, which had 'wayward girls' there. They ran a laundry, and they had a chapel, so we got some sympathetic priests to say Mass on Saturday mornings, and we went to practice and sang."

historical interlude

The Monastery of Our Lady of Charity of the Refuge in Green Bay is one of many such houses—about forty worldwide. They are related to the Good Shepherd Sisters, but they are not the same. When the man now known as St. Jean Eudes founded the order of Our Lady of Charity in France in the mid-seventeenth century, he could no longer watch, passively, the plight of the single, widowed, and abandoned women spiraling through destitution and shame into a life of prostitution in the streets of Caen. In the heart of a saint and in any sane mind, the sin of each is the burden of all, and Eudes turned to the nuns who would form a vowed community dedicated solely to saving the "fallen" women. By the time of the French Revolution there existed seven houses of Our Lady of Charity, and it is from this stem that an offshoot institution, the Order of the Good Shepherd, eventually sprang.

The convents of Our Lady of Charity of the Refuge became widely recognized reformatory places and, over the centuries, expanded their care beyond women who had led, in the eyes of their communities, unsavory lives to those in danger of stepping off the "righteous path" and to younger girls—say, the children from "immoral families." Their mission has been to convert and preserve through prayer, hard work, and discipline. Some "inmates" came voluntarily. Others were sent by their families, yet others by the State in places like Ireland, and the practice has not remained without controversy.

Much like the monastery in Green Bay, Our Lady of Charity houses have commonly run laundries operated by the "inmates"—the penitents, often called "magdalens" thanks to the now-debunked Christian myth that Mary Magdalene, the most influential woman in Jesus' movement and his "apostle to the apostles," was a reformed prostitute. In Ireland, the Magdalene Laundries employed unwilling workers as young as nine years old from 1922 to 1996, and the inquiry surrounding them reached its apogee just recently in 2013 in a large monetary settlement from the State to several hundred "survivors" of laundry life, after multiple testimonies and a finding that over a quarter of the women had been sent to the nuns' care by the Irish State, often with no idea why.

The court case and the ensuing "McAleese report" brought to light the conditions endured by the magdalens on the tail end of the clerical sexual-abuse scandal that all but destroyed the reputation of the Catholic Church. In this case, no allegations of sexual or physical abuse were made against the Lady of Charity Sisters. On the contrary, former inmates overwhelmingly agreed that they were well taken care of. Instead, they spoke of crushing unpaid labor, endless scoldings, and humiliation. It wasn't the question so much of abuse as it was of whether or not these reformatories should have existed in the first place, in the way that they did.

It is a poignant, unceasing question for human communities: how to enforce our moral code, knowing that time will pass and our understanding will deepen, and the code will change. How to look in the mirror—how to face each other, one body of humanity fractured into victim and perpetrator—when morality has changed, when we just begin to comprehend that our "right" has been wrong. Yet we cannot abandon the moral code, fluid as it is, and stop enforcing it. We are communities. Some values endure forever. We don't know what maturity will come to us tomorrow, but today we believe in some inalienable rights; if we did not, we would have nothing left but wrongs.

It is a poignant question, a poignant time for the Sisters, for any state that used convents as reformatories, a poignant moment for us all. Good intentions and the roads they pave . . . What frightens me is that we can be wrong without doing anything wrong. Throughout the laundries' existence in Ireland, by sending women there the State believed it was curing social ills, and by balancing care with harsh treatment the nuns believed they were saving souls. Ireland is not alone in this.

I've been able to find rather little about the Green Bay laundry, but the principle, naturally, seems to have been similar. The monastery took in women and girls for everything from unwed pregnancy to truancy, most of whom (but not all) came of their own volition and some of whom stayed to take vows and become Sisters themselves. There was hard work there, and there was prayer, and there was care. I have heard, anecdotally, stories that have little to do with moral reform and everything to do with simple, undiluted compassion. One inmate was referred to as "slow"; the nuns thought she wouldn't do well in the outside world, and so they offered, and she stayed at the monastery for the rest of her life and worked in the laundry under their care. A grave in the Order's cemetery bears her name. A widow came to live with five children, and of her four daughters, three chose the life of a Lady of Charity nun.

end interlude

Leo's fascination with plain song took root from the Group's trip to Ohio. In the wake of Pope Pius XII's encyclical *Mediator Dei* in 1947, the world was abuzz with such phrases as "lay apostolate" and "liturgical renewal." The encyclical, by some still considered the most important of his papacy, emphasizes the spirit and sacrament of the liturgy, warns against formal piety, argues for liturgical expressions that develop with the times, and calls for active participation of the laity. Where the Mass is concerned, this was probably the loudest herald of Vatican II, and the Council would draw from Pius's writing fifteen years later.

All over the globe—for sure in America—throngs of Catholics rejoiced and took up the cause of liturgical reform, organized talks and lectures, analyzed, exchanged ideas, and participated, participated, participated. The Hohlmillers grabbed their group and drove to Loveland, Ohio, where an expert on the topic was to give a presentation.

Now, more precisely, they weren't going to Loveland but to a nearby property called Grailville. Yes, it is what it sounds like: the Town of the Grail. Back in 1921, a Dutch Jesuit priest named Jacques van Ginneken had founded an organization of lay Catholic women who would bond in community, grow in spirit, and act in the world unbound by the walls of convent cloisters. In 1940, two members of the Grail movement crossed the ocean to the United States, and in 1944, Lydwine van Kersbergen and Joan Overboss, together with fourteen other sisters, moved to a farm near Loveland and called it Grailville.

Today, Grailville is a spiritual and educational retreat center for women and the center of the Grail in the U.S., but others exist throughout the country, and other Grail communities speckle the Earth. The Grail in the U.S. is on the forefronts of feminist theology, and it is no longer just a Catholic movement. In 1969, its women opened the doors to members of other Christian denominations, and in 1975, to Jewish women.

When Leo Swidler came with the Group to Ohio in 1948, Grailville was very new, but it was entirely in keeping with the Group's spirit and mission. He was taken by the organic farm and by the talk on lay apostolate, and he was fired up from that day, I dare say, till death—because it's been sixty-seven years, and the fire is still burning.

The Group would return to Ohio several times. They were kin, these people: a lay order of women banded together for the conversion of the world and a mish-mash from Wisconsin, boys and girls and grandparents. In every way that mattered, they were kin.

Talking to Len

(On eroticism, mutuality, and the consequences of words)

RA   You were quite a diverse group.

LS   In a way. My friend Ray and I were the more intellectual ones and obviously the "fair-haired boys." There were two Frigo brothers, older, who came from Italy and founded a creamery in Wisconsin that became very famous. The Frigo cheese is well known, might still be around. They were "good Italians," you know? Had lots of children. One child became a Norbertine; we'd be in the novitiate together. One of their children married one of the gals in the Group who had the most glorious laugh! An Irish woman, and married this clunker. [*He smirks.*] I always thought she could have done better, like me.

RA   Did you have a crush on her?

LS   I didn't quite, but she had this glorious smile, and this laugh, like magic! Lit up the room. Very musical. In the summertime we were working on some kind of long-term project, where there was the Coyle family (I'm obviously partial to the Irish), and there were the Coyle son and the Coyle daughter. Her, I had a crush on. Absolutely gorgeous: not just to look on but the whole magic of a person, just sucked you in. When she moved into the room, you knew it. All these decades later . . . Youth is interesting. Even at eighty-four, that stuff never totally goes away.

RA   What stuff?

LS   The draw of the erotic.

RA   What is the erotic to you?

LS   I could go back to my earlier readings and say, "Woman, thy name is erotic."

RA   So the erotic is the feminine?

LS   *Pour moi.*

RA   Do you find the erotic in nonhuman?

LS   Some music. Some ideas, maybe. Maybe the beautiful. They kind of fuse in my mind.

RA   So, what is eroticism?

LS   I don't know. I'd say joy, pleasure, beauty. It's what comes to mind. Then my mind just moves to the good and the true. That's just the way I operate—maybe, cliché, but it's the way it moves. So when I did medieval metaphysics, I always felt, *Wow! The good, the true, and the beautiful!* I find that very erotic.

RA   But eroticism? The relationship between the human being and the erotic?

LS   I guess, wanting to be one with beauty, goodness, and joy. So, I guess I tend to feel in totally positive terms—I mean, *vis-à-vis* myself and other persons and God. Positive. That's why I dislike my earlier negative Catholic upbringing about sin, and one of the things about Islam that I dislike is the very term, that Islam means "surrender." It's a betrayal of God's creation. We're not supposed to surrender. I understand what it means, but I dislike it. For me and people like me, it's the wrong way to go. I frankly think it's the wrong way for people in general; it doesn't allow people to be fully human, but truncates us. Two people—say, a couple in love—are supposed to expand each other, not shrink one into the other. If I were in a position to have sex today, it would never be enjoyable unless it were mutually enjoyable, equal.

RA   You believe that "surrender" in Islam is lack of mutuality?

LS   Yes. Words have consequences. In English, whenever we use the word "man," we immediately, even if unconsciously, put women in a subordinate position: "Women are failed men." Just using the word screws with our heads. The word "surrender" defiles the creator, not just the creature. I understand how it got there— God is infinitely greater than we are and so on—but that's hyperbolic language; it's abstract. It's all right to use hyperbolic language if you know what you're doing, but it still has effect, even if you know you're doing it. So whenever I have a choice, I don't use that kind of language.

RA   You say that eroticism is being one with what you named as erotic: beauty, goodness, joy. It evokes in me a mystical pursuit. Would you say that eroticism is worldly mysticism?

LS   Yes, though I'd rather say "earthly," stuff of the earth. In *Practical Mysticism* by Evelyn Underhill, the opening chapter says that mysticism is "knowing of the real." It goes on to describe what I would call "natural mysticism": being open to sense-perception, interior perception, things around you. Mysticism is expansion of consciousness; there's depth to it far beyond what we normally think about or speak of, but in a certain sense it's fundamentally the same thing.

The image I use for myself is a sphere. You expand the perimeter one teeny-weeny bit, one nanometer, but the resulting volume expansion is huge and the same for the surface. So is the result in human consciousness. Or here's another metaphor: A snowball starts down a mountainside. When it's tiny, it's no big deal. When it's huge, it needs only travel an inch to expand a lot.

So at a certain stage, any advance seems something qualitative. When you read somebody like John of the Cross or Teresa of Avila, you wonder: How could I ever approach such an experience? In an earlier time I wanted to be an intellectual and a saint, spent all this time on my knees. But now . . .

RA   Do you feel at peace with your quest?

LS   Well, look. I am aware it's possible for me to deceive myself. Still, I've been doing this long enough. Like a fiddler on the roof, I'm on the edge, and I have to be careful that I not become overly comfortable living on the edge. But I am balanced here on the edge. I am relaxed.

CHAPTER 7

From Prayer to Contemplation: the Norbertines

We are hard pressed on every side, but not crushed; perplexed, but not in despair; persecuted, but not abandoned; struck down, but not destroyed.

—SECOND CORINTHIANS 4:8–9

BY THE TIME YOUNG Leo approached his college graduation, he had well become a member of the Norbertine family: His St. Willebrod's primary school was mostly staffed by the Norbertine priests; his high school was completely so; and St. Norbert College seemed to have sealed the choice. Leo was attracted to the world of mind and spirit in which the fraters lived, he was by then deeply involved in Catholic Action, and he had resolved to become an intellectual and a saint—and in 1950 it was a well-known truth that to be a first-class Catholic one had to be a priest. Or, in the case of the unfortunate sex, a nun.

Thus the decision was made, and toward the end of his last semester Leonard Swidler applied to join what was officially called the Order of Premonstratentians, since St. Norbert had founded his legacy in the twelfth century in the French town of Prémontré. The youngsters called it the Order of Monstrous Pretentions. Lovingly.

The novices were inducted on June 6, 1950, and stayed at the De Pere Abbey, next to the College, for the first few weeks, before moving on to the novitiate. Leo was still there when, on June 25, the North Korean forces crossed the border into South Korea, and recent allies—the U.S. and the U.S.S.R.— began their first proxy war. Leo's letter from the Green Bay Draft Board arrived on Monday—his deferment had ended the day he stopped being a student—so he was to report to the Greyhound Bus depot the next Monday, at 6 AM, as a new private in the U.S. Army.

Distressed, Leo knocked on the abbot's door. Abbot Sylvester Killeen wasn't a new person in Leo's life. He had served as the principal of the Central Catholic High School; he was the priest who had instructed and baptized Leo's father. They had two options: The Order could obtain another deferment for their new novice available to seminarians, and if it didn't work, Leo would activate his commission and ship out as a Second Lieutenant. They had a week. The next three days passed on what Len describes as "pins and needles," but on Thursday Abbot Killeen called with the good news that the deferment had arrived.

Len thinks on occasion about the timing of his life and his birth. He missed narrowly two wars that could have cut short or changed his life forever: World War II had ended nine months before he graduated from high school; the Korean War started just as he graduated from college. He had classmates who were drafted into the military and sent to Korea, at least one killed in action. Absorbed in his deepening interior exploration, he didn't reflect on it then, not much. But, now, having stood witness to America uprooted by Vietnam, Afghanistan, Iraq, Kosovo, Cuba, Grenada, and the never-ending violence—America soaked in blood and post-traumatic stress—he wonders what sort of Leonard Swidler would have emerged, should he have survived as a "shave-tail" infantry Second Lieutenant, from the black gamut of deployment.

In the meantime, twenty-one novices—the largest novitiate class in St. Norbert Abbey's history—moved to a large three-story mansion on Lake Mendota, across from the University of Wisconsin at Madison. They would spend a year there getting instruction on every aspect of religious life from the novice master nicknamed "Buck," studying, learning to chant the Office—of course, in Latin—and to sing Gregorian Chant at daily Mass. This last one Leo already knew. They would work at their chores (Leo was helping Brother Pasquel in the kitchen) and build a stone retaining wall against shore erosion.

Actually, Leo didn't go by "Leo" nor by "Len" while in the novitiate. This was still the time when every incoming brother or sister in the church received a new, "religious" name, and Mr. Leonard Swidler, at his induction, became Frater Cyprian.

"It wasn't a bad name," Len says and smiles. "Nothing like the one our Frater Youngest got!"

The youngest member of the class was the last to be doled out a name. Tom DeWayne, with Frater Cyprian's condolences, had to contend with being Frater Evermode for an unknown to me number of years but has since, Len recalls, become an abbot, dropped the religious "Evermode," and gone back to his baptismal name, Thomas.

As for Frater Cyprian, he studied and prayed. When I ask him what he did for recreation, he cannot remember. He remembers studying. He'd always been interested in the Latin Fathers: Jerome, Augustine, Lactantius, Tertulian, Cyprian—Cyprian especially, considering he was a "Cyprian" himself. He remembers reading about interior life: Dom Marmion, St. John of the Cross, *The Imitation of Christ* by Thomas á Kempis, everything by Réginald Garrigou-Lagrange.

Frater Cyprian did not have time for recreation. He was busy becoming an intellectual and very busy becoming a saint. Every minute he was not required to be somewhere else he spent in the chapel, on his knees, in an intense and persistent effort to move from what he calls "discursive prayer" to what he calls "contemplation," from talking to "being with."

Nothing was easy, and not everything went smoothly that year. It was a cold winter, down to -29°F, and the novices slept in bunk beds on the unheated third floor, piling several blankets on top of themselves through the frigid nights, getting up in the mornings exhausted from the blankets' weight. Lake Mendota froze solidly, deeply, in the way of arctic waters that become truck roads during the winter months, and it was a clear Sunday afternoon when the young men decided to skate over the lake to the University campus.

If you have been to the North in the winter, you know the brilliance of its sunny day. Winter days are short in the North, so into the precious hours between the late sunrise and the early twilight they spill the most powerful light that human eyes endure. Each surface is snow, and, bouncing sunlight back into the air, all rounded lines, the world shines and sparkles in unthinkable purity. A sunny, snowy day lifts the spirit, dispels depression, fills the soul with hope and a glimpse of heavenly clarity.

But, it's a short day, and the calm doesn't often endure. By the time the novices started on their way back across the ice, a stinging wind had risen into their faces, and the road home turned from a fun ice-skating outing, only a couple of miles long, into a grueling battle with the powers of winter. The voyage across the lake took them several hours, and, once it was done, Frater Cyprian discovered that he was sick. Something was wrong with his eyes.

Len doesn't know what he contracted or developed and doesn't remember the diagnosis. He knows it was awful and painful, and his perfect twenty/twenty vision would never again be the same. For three days he lay alone in a darkened room and emerged from it nearsighted, but at least he could see light.

For the second year of novitiate, the cohort returned to the DePere Abbey, where most fraters began work on their Bachelor's degrees in philosophy, and Cyprian, having already accomplished that, moved on to studying theology with twenty or so others. Theology was taught on a four-year cycle, and new students simply entered it at whatever year it happened to be when they joined. At the start of their fourth year, the students could be ordained "simplex."

Always early in the morning (probably from 7 to 9 AM), theology courses were scheduled so the older fraters and professors could be free for their jobs at the college. As Frater Youngest in the group, Cyprian sat in the front row and could not see two fourth-year "theologians" sleeping in the back of the class: Frater Rowland De Peaux (nicknamed "Cookie" for his work as a cook during novitiate) and Frater James. But everyone would partake in heartfelt entertainment when the professor occasionally called out, "James! Wake up Rowland!" And then a bit later, "Rowland! Wake up James!" The class giggled.

RA   Were they advanced through the years and ordained anyway, even though they slept through theology?

LS   I suspect so. [*laughs*] We all thought it was hilarious. But the morality of it never rose to the level of consciousness for me then.

RA   And now?

LS   What do I think now? Given the state of theology in those days, it wasn't a terrible loss.

In a way, life was the same for Frater Cyprian as in the year before; study and prayer still filled his time and his soul to the brim, yet life was different. For one thing, he had his own cell: a simple room but full of light, with a bed, a desk, a chair, a bookshelf, and a crucifix. Speaking of it today, Len calls up no feelings one way or the other. "I have feelings about my study here, at the house," he says. "I feel at home with my easy chair and books all around and music and what not." There was none of it, it seems, at the abbey. He remembers no pictures on the walls and no personal things of meaning, but he did have books. *"Ad usum Leo Swidler,"* he'd written on the inside covers.

Second, Len remembers recreation—at least, of a sort. On Thursday afternoons, Frater Cyprian with several fellows walked to a nearby tuberculosis sanatorium to visit patients. Far from a lighthearted diversion, these trips provided an exercise in compassion and food for thought, the effects of which Len Swidler is feeling to this day.

historical interlude

Tuberculosis is a scary diagnosis, even in the twenty-first century. It takes months of powerful antibiotic cocktails to treat, and not every case responds to the drugs. In the early 1950s, we did not have powerful antibiotic cocktails. Streptomycin had been discovered only a few years earlier and was still a long way from commonplace; Isoniazid—the first oral mycobactericidal—was just about to come out in 1952. Since the nineteenth century, sanatoria had spread throughout Europe and the United States for thousands of sufferers who had no hope of a cure. All they had were hopes that the disease would naturally subside, a few experimental and surgical techniques—such as deliberately collapsing a lung to let the lesions heal—and a belief that total rest could help the body fight.

Patients at TB sanatoria in the 1940s and early 1950s lived according to their wealth and class, but they had one thing in common: the regimens of rest that ranged from "absolute rest," which demanded a patient lie flat and not move or even read, to allowances of walks and light work for those who were on their way to recovery. The afflicted could be there for years.

A professional thirty-two-year-old woman, who, in the 1940s in England, was diagnosed with TB, recorded her doctors' instructions in her diary thus: "Absolute and utter rest of mind and body—no bath, no movement except to toilet once a day, no sitting up except propped by pillows and semi-reclining, no deep breath. Lead the life of a log, in fact. Don't try, therefore, to sew, knit, or write, except as occasional relief from reading and sleeping."[13]

end interlude

This woman survived her TB and, eventually, through strength of body and character and through what some people call "luck," returned to active life and died at the age of eighty-six, but not everyone was either this lucky or this strong. Far from everyone had education enough to keep engaged while idle. As the young men from the abbey went from bed to bed at the sanatorium, trying to bring comfort and diversion to its monotonous routine, Frater Cyprian saw people on those beds whose minds and spirits had all but atrophied, and he wondered: If he had to lie still for a year, for two years, what would happen to his burning enthusiasm for an inner life? Would spirituality survive a trial by boredom?

Thankfully, not everything in life, even for a devout new novice, is somber and reflection-filled. Recreation at the abbey in the spring of 1952 involved a week's stay at a cottage in northern Wisconsin. The fraters long anticipated their vacation—a time away, by a large creek, and a change of routine—and Frater Cyprian's group, once its turn came, went up under the supervision of the newly minted Father Rowland De Peaux (remember Cookie, who slept through his fourth year of theology?). It seems, however, that outings for Cyprian's novice class didn't tend to go well.

They had heard from the group that had occupied the cottage the previous week about the most fun activity: rafting down the stream of the creek. It was done in two-person rubber rafts, and Cyprian and fellows were all geared up for a day of beauty and adventure on the water. What they did not consider were the heavy rains that had fallen between the previous group's trip and the day our reckless friends pulled out the rafts onto what was no longer a placid stream but a raging, roaring river. This was advanced white-water rafting—an adventure they had not signed up for.

Four young men traveled, let's say, swiftly downstream in two rubber rafts: Father Cookie in the first with Frater Ray Schmandt, Cyprian with another frater (incidentally, one of the Frigo children from his "discussion group") in the second. When the lead raft disappeared around the

13 Hurt, "Tuberculosis sanatorium regimen," para. 9.

bend from Cyprian's sight, no trouble registered in his mind, and "team two" gleefully chased after it—but, clearing the turn, they couldn't see their friends. A moment—and they realized they were hurtling toward a dam that the speed of the creek had turned into a four-foot waterfall.

Four feet is not much of a waterfall. Unless you are flying at it, out of control, in a tiny rubber raft.

Careening over the top, Cyprian managed a horror-colored snapshot of two heads in the water below, four hands grasping frantically for the cord attached to the raft, and the raft tossed around by the cascading torrent, dancing and slamming down onto the gasping, disappearing heads. And then his raft tilted and went down.

Some might say that the four men were outstandingly lucky that day; others, that "someone upstairs" was looking out for them. What we know is that it was time for none of them to die. Cyprian's raft, against many odds, came down flat and right side up, still holding on to both of its occupants, who could then grab the other two and pull them out onto the edge of the little concrete dam. Len can still see in his mind's eye the soaked, stunned, and shaking Rowland taking his first steps on *terra firma* and collapsing on his knees, hands folded in a prayer of thanksgiving.

The name of Rowland De Peaux came up more than once in my conversations with Len, and every time Len's eyes sparkled, and he reminded me that Father Cookie owed Frater Cyprian his life. I think, in retrospect, Len kind of likes this story.

At the end of the 1951–52 academic year, Frater Cyprian's novitiate was over, and the time came for his class to take their first (temporary) vows. Young frater was looking forward to becoming truly a Norbertine; this was, however, not to be.

He was called into the office by Abbot Killeen—quite out of the blue, he felt, and he didn't know what was happening. He stood before the abbot's desk in his white habit gathered in by the white leather belt of a novice. The abbot sat behind the desk. What Len remembers of the conversation was short and brutal.

"The council has decided that the Norbertine Order is not really the right one for you," the abbot said. "Perhaps you should think about the Trappists."

Unlike the canons regular Norbertines, who follow the rule of St. Augustine, the Trappists (Cistercians of Strict Observance) are monks, follow the rule of St. Benedict, and keep near-perpetual silence. The studious and excessively serious Frater Cyprian, whose habit had worn holes in the kneelers of the abbey's chapel, must have impressed the elders of the Norbertine Order as a more fruitful candidate for a life of prayer and silent contemplation than for a life of preaching, teaching, and parish service.

Looking down at this decision from the height of many decades, Professor Leonard Swidler is happy with it. He likes the way his life has turned out. But on that spring day in 1952, the two sentences just uttered by Abbot Killeen struck him like a bolt of lightning. It was a disaster. He stood stunned and mute, "like a dumb beast," he recalls. "Like somebody hit me in the forehead with a two-by-four."

It took several long seconds for him to find something to say: "May I keep my Norbertine breviaries?"

"Yes," the short answer came, and all was over. Walking back to his cell to pack, through an awful feeling of freefall in his stomach, he was trying to comprehend the immediacy of a simple yet still bizarre fact: he was no longer Frater Cyprian.

One thought beat against the inside of his skull: *Oh my God! Going home and telling my mother!*

Father Vincent DeLeers stood in the hallway. He already knew. Cyprian's unofficial spiritual director, he knew the young man better than most, and his obvious disagreement with the council's decision was the only relief and the only consolation on that tumultuous day. Len doesn't remember what Father DeLeers said, but he remembers sorrow on his face and pain in his voice as they said good-bye.

In the scheme of Leonard Swidler's life, his dismissal from the Norbertines ran more deeply than his own disappointed plans for consecrated life in one particular order: being ordained had been more than his dream; it was his family mission. "Every Irish mother had a vocation to the priesthood," Len would write later in his reflections, "through her first-born son!"[14]

This isn't true any longer, but, carried by the currents of the early-twentieth-century culture, Leo, who adored his mother with the tenderness he reserved for none other, fully expected her to have a heart attack should he betray her expectations. How could he tell her his road

14 Swidler, "A Life in Dialogue," section "Authentic religion . . ." para. 8.

to sanctity had been cut short? How could he come home a reject from the spiritual elite?

Worry, grief, and shame converged on Leo's soul, weighed it down, pushed it into a dark place, and in a dark place he stayed for many months. Still, a decision had to be made on what to do with his life now that he was no longer a Norbertine.

The Trappists, suggested by Abbot Killeen, did not appear to Leo a viable alternative. After all, he still had his two goals: to become an intellectual and to become a saint. The existence of a silent monk may have allowed him the latter but not, he thought, the former. Of course, Thomas Merton was a Trappist monk and by that time had published several books, including *The Seven Storey Mountain* and the initial *Seeds of Contemplation,* but the 1952 Leo Swidler did not have the luxury of many years of hindsight, may not have felt himself equally exceptional, and was still attached to the Norbertines. Whatever the reasons, after a few weeks of anxiety and depression, he, as he puts it, "psychologically staggered" toward his next chapter: contacted the bishop of Madison and asked to be taken on as a seminarian.

This is how, come fall of 1952, Leo found himself continuing his studies in theology at St. Paul Seminary in St. Paul, Minnesota.

When I asked Len why he had thought that the life of a parish priest would offer him a better chance to become an intellectual than that of a silent monk, he said briefly, simply, with a kind of self-deprecating smirk and with a swiftness that made it clear he had considered it before: "I wasn't thinking very clearly."

Talking to Len

(On prayer, the immanence of God, and why we are both Christian)

RA   Len, do you pray? What is your prayer life like now?

LS   I don't pray in an older, customary sense of using words, nor even in the, let's say, Ignatian sense of meditating and imagining I stand at the foot of the cross. I simply try to put myself in the Presence. And that's it.

    Of course, it's not very satisfying. I don't get any answers back in a normal sense. Nor do I, on the other hand, have any deep angst. You know, I can read about and understand where Luther was, for example: that deep angst, "Am I saved or not?" But I don't have it. I guess maybe the main three virtues of love, hope, and faith—or trust—operate for me.

    In one sense, hope is preeminent. Trust is paramount, but it's built on hope. Love . . . Love is all-encompassing, even if it turns out that my "trust" was untrustworthy and hope was in vain. Love is its own reward. It asks for nothing more. So I buy that.

RA   When did this change from your conventional prayer life happen? You used to love word-filled prayer.

LS   A long time ago. Already in the monastery. In the novitiate.

RA   You stopped praying?

LS   Well, no. I was required, of course, to come together and chant the office and all that. And it's not that I found it meaningless, but it's not where my anchor was any longer. It was a bit like Asian meditation—emptying oneself out—but not exactly. I just have to use the word "presence," and I am totally aware that this is part of human psychology, probably has all kinds of neural bases, about which we are learning more and more, all very fascinating. Yet I am quite convinced that human consciousness cannot be reduced solely to the firing of neurons, and precisely what it is is really a mystery. I think about it: Where was Andie those seventeen years of Alzheimer's, when she was shrinking into nothingness?

RA   Why do you think this happened, this shift so completely away from verbal prayer? After all, you wanted to be a priest, and if you'd become one, this would have been part of your daily life.

LS   It was part of my daily life in the monastery, too, but those are just stepping stones. Why the shift? The stuff that I was reading: Marmion, some of the mystics, John of the Cross, Teresa of Avila, so many others—it's just you are presented with either a huge magnet or a dark hole, and it's both, depending on where you are. And we won't *know*—and that word is really loaded—until beyond the grave. In fact, we don't even know if we'll know beyond the grave.

So, see, Luther and others, they worried about what was going to happen beyond the grave, as if it depended on our knowledge of it—or lack or distortion of knowledge. It doesn't. I pick up from St. Paul: "Now is the time of salvation." This is the way we ought to live: now! And when "now" is the way down into the tomb, then we go.

RA   Is prayer all about life beyond the grave?

LS   Not at all.

RA   For many Christians prayer is connection, focus, formulation of praise, thanks, ecstasy of presence. What about those? Why did you shift away from those, too?

LS   I do get something of the ecstasy in music, and I share it. I don't listen to music alone. I listen to music—especially instrumental—with "God," if you want to use that term.

RA   Why not?

LS   I am reluctant because it has all kinds of baggage. For me, it's pure image, but I often use it: "He's got the whole world in his hands." And the music, it's not just "God," it's everybody I love.

RA   This is the second time you put the word "God" in air quotes.

LS   The term narrows it down so blooming much!

RA   Okay. I think I know what you mean when you say you are reluctant to use the term "God" because it's narrow or carries baggage, but you are Christian and a mystic. What is really wrong with the word "God"?

LS   It immediately, unavoidably does things in one's mind. Analogously, when speaking English, if we use the word "man" or "mankind," it distorts the image in your head, by connotation more than denotation. "God" sounds so pedestrian.

      Mind you, I am intellectually totally persuaded by the principle of sufficient reason that the cause/goal of all that is surely cannot be less than Leonard Swidler and more bright people in the world, so Ultimate Reality is a personal being. To not have Person flies in the face of all reason. If I can think all these beautiful things, obviously, more so can the cause of me, even if by way of emergent Being. If it's there potentially, it's there. Of course, as you learn more and more about how things operate in the world, you can't avoid being a million-person Socrates: "Man, do I know that I don't know!" Reading the weekly science section of *The New York Times*—just a slight inkling of "Ahhh!"—the incredible intelligibility that operates in reality!

      So if you want to say, "Praise!"—yeah. But I don't even do that. It doesn't seem appropriate to me. Even the word "surrender" seems to me to belittle God. We humans are radically free, and to submit degrades God and us. We are free and should stand free. Not to do that is to betray the Creator of freedom. So I should and do love you for you, not for God.

RA   This presumes a sharp separation between me and God, though, a very sharp line of transcendence. Otherwise, there is no offense: Loving me for me and for God would flow naturally into each other.

LS   My understanding is that I love you for God by loving you for you, period.

RA   Then, you don't need the opposition.

LS   I wrestled with this in the novitiate, and no; this instrumentalizes you.

RA   Don't you have to become an atheist if you keep going in that direction?

LS   Well, there is much that is secular. Charles Taylor's *A Secular Age* talks about "immanent transcendence." It hinges on how you understand these terms, but if you mean by that that there is something greater than *moi* but it's within the realm of "created reality"—if you project humanity as the ultimate—it's hard to make that skin impermeable.

RA   That's Humanism, of course: ideals greater than myself focused on the spirit and future and value of humanity. The beauty of Christianity is that it doesn't stop at the level of human reality and doesn't cut divinity off. It doesn't make us choose between the immanent and the transcendent but blurs the line of that binary just enough for the mystery to make itself known. The transcendent Divine become immanent in the world and fully so in a human.

LS   Right. With Jesus and Christ and all that, you can have all kinds of literally wonderful levels of depth of understanding. You can't have immanence without transcendence.

RA   You might say that's why I am a Christian.

LS   Me too.

CHAPTER 8

The Road Not Taken:
St. Paul Seminary

I'll tell you what it is—it's the synagogin'—the tabernaclin'—the psalmin' that goes on in this hoose, that's enough to break the spirits o' ony young creature.

—SUSAN FERRIER, *THE INHERITANCE*

WHEN LEN RECALLS HIS time at St. Paul Seminary, the emotion that seems to dominate his narrative is amusement—which is not to say that he learned nothing or found the entire experience utterly without intellectual stimulation. In fact, in his reflections he writes with positive fondness about his two years of dogmatic theology. The professor, a then-young scholar Father David Dillon, was, in Len's words, "filled with serious scholarship and great enthusiasm for Thomistic theology."[15] To the delight of his deep-digging student, he did not use the formulaic, "pre-digested" nineteenth-century scholastic handbooks by Tanquery but the *Summa Theologiae* itself, with the help of commentators such as John of Thomas and Cajetan. Mr. Swidler basked in the rays of Aquinas's mind and needed little else to find his life exhilarating.

On the other hand, to the rest of his academic schedule—all the classes outside of the four-times-weekly sections with Father Dillon—Len

15 Swidler, "A Life in Dialogue," section "Life in St. Paul's seminary," para. 1.

refers pithily as "intellectual jokes." The two Fundamental Theology classes reportedly consisted of an ongoing translation from the Latin textbooks into English proclaimed by the professors from the podium.

"Snoozeville!" Len rolls his eyes with the disapproval of more than a disgruntled former student but of a teacher who's had to stimulate his own students' interest in esoteric subjects. "Boring. I soon decided I could read the Latin a lot faster by myself."

And he did. Having finished the textbooks in a couple of months, he sat in the back of the classrooms and read the Russian classics: Dostoyevsky's *Crime and Punishment* and *Brothers Karamazov*, Tolstoy's *War and Peace* and *Anna Karenina*. Who knows how much general education Mr. Swidler managed to catch up on in Snoozeville 101!

The Scripture course, apparently, was even worse than Fundamental Theology.

RA   You write in your reflections that your Scripture class was "so criminally bad" that you "did not even learn enough to begin to realize what a disaster it was." Although you are not primarily a biblical scholar, you've published scholarly books dealing with the Bible. So, how was it a disaster? Did this prevent you from becoming a good biblical scholar?

LS   The teacher was an adjunct named Saxey, and at the time it just was clear to me and everybody that he was a zero. Nothing. He wasn't even pious! It was just ripples in the wind and no content. It was like reading the St. Paul telephone book. I don't know what he was doing. After the first few minutes no one paid any attention, and he was babbling up front. Only afterwards, when I began to read the scripture scholarship on my own, did I realize, *There is an awful lot here!*

RA   You don't remember what he filled the time with?

LS   No. After the first few minutes he could have been saying the most riveting things, but our switches were off. So vacuous . . . It's the vacuity that must have been impressed so strongly on me.

And yet, this is not Len's most bizarre memory from a seminary classroom.

"The wildest of all," he says, "was the Church History class!" He leans forward, grins, and there they are again: little demons dancing in his eyes. He is about to tell a story of mischief and noble chaos.

LS   For this class, all four years of theology students—about 250—were jammed into the *Aula Maxima* (the "big room"), the whole top floor of the classroom building. I don't know how it got started, but the tradition was in full bloom by the time I got there. When Father Billy Busch entered the hall, all hell broke loose! All the senior students began shouting at the top of their lungs and grabbed their chairs and pounded them on the floor, ceaselessly, for six to eight minutes! Chaos, unbelievable chaos—and we the newcomers in the front, gaping uncomprehendingly, turned to salt like Lot's wife. I cannot describe the pandemonium.

    In the meantime, Billy walked up onto the stage, sat behind his desk, and serenely observed this roaring chaos in front of him—and when the bedlam diminished to a mild roar out of sheer exhaustion, he started with a loud, "Errr," and paused, which triggered a repeat performance for another three minutes, only to die down again, eventually, followed once more by Billy's throat-clearing and two more minutes of screaming. At least twenty or thirty minutes would go by like that. Unbelievable: grown men, mostly ex-GIs, studying to be priests, would carry on like this.

RA   And why did they? What was all the rioting about?

LS   It was just the presence of Billy. Why, I don't know. Inner earth eruptions. The students were the eruption, and he was the opening gap.

It was quickly becoming clear to Leo Swidler that his first goal in life—to become an intellectual—was not greatly aided by being a seminarian. What took him by greater surprise was realizing that his second goal—to become a saint—would have to be an uphill battle against authorities no less powerful than the Rector of the Seminary himself. Of course, definitions of sanctity vary, and Leo would come to reevaluate his own concept of it time and time again, but basic human decency has always seemed to him an absolute prerequisite.

The *Aula Maxima*—the only auditorium large enough to gather the whole student body other than the church—was used by the seminary, besides the infamous Church History class, for delivering spiritual meditations, most often by Father Ryan, a brother of the better known Msgr. John A. Ryan, a moral theologian and social rights activist, famed among other things for his advocacy of the minimum wage and a light-hearted but respectful title "Mr. New Deal." Father Ryan had the distinction of having gone completely bald, which, naturally, earned him the nickname "Curley" and which, unfortunately, was his most pleasant feature. Curley's meditations Len characterizes as "dour enough."

Still, the dour Curley he could handle. It was the occasional meditation delivered by the Rector, Msgr. Rudolf Bandas, that made Leo increasingly uncomfortable and sent him searching for a word to describe the Rector's message. The word he eventually found was "aberrant."

Msgr. Bandas—or, as Len refers to him, Rudi—sported, in opposition to Father Ryan, a full head of dark, wavy hair and what Len calls "arch-conservative" ideas.

"He was obviously hung up on sex." Len shakes his head in helpless disbelief. "Not unusual given the nature of mandatory celibacy. He'd say that his mother had to sit in the back of the car, and we mocked, 'Never sit next to a woman of the opposite sex!'"

Whenever he led the spiritual meditations, the Rector would spend his time of influence on the hearts of future priests by expounding on the dark forces working to corrupt the soul of Christian American youth. He didn't name the forces, and the rhetorically masterful gloom and mystery of his innuendo made the threat of corruption seem ever more ominous. It took Leo a few of Rudi's speeches to understand that the Monsignor was talking about the Jews.

historical interlude

Father Denis Fahey (1883–1954) was a priest of the Holy Ghost Fathers, of Irish origin, and a theologian often quoted by Father Charles Coughlin, the "radio priest." Denis Fahey believed deeply and uncompromisingly that the world must accept Christ the King on Christ's terms as Denis Fahey understood them, that modernity must not encroach on tradition, and all those who corrupted the Christian spirit with "naturalism" must be made to yield by any means necessary. The "corruptors" on Father

Fahey's list included Satan, communists, demons, freemasons, and Jews. In his 1953 book *The Kingship of Christ and the Conversion of the Jewish Nation*, he wrote, " . . . as we must stand valiantly for the rights of Christ the King, the true Supernatural Messias, and strive to reimpregnate society with the supernatural spirit of the Mystical Body, we must combat Jewish efforts to permeate the world with naturalism. In that sense, as there is only one divine plan for order in the world, every sane thinker must be an antisemite."[16]

Denis Fahey considered himself one of the sanest thinkers of his time.

end interlude

I come from Russia, where one acquires the skill of distinguishing the shape of a Semitic nose at first glance, along with a root of a Semitic family name, in early childhood, almost instinctively, as one distinguishes a man from a woman and a friendly face from a menacing one. That's why, as soon as I was introduced to the Founding Editor of the *Journal of Ecumenical Studies*, Professor Leonard Swidler, in November 2006—from the moment I heard his name and saw his features—I carried a tentative assumption of his Jewishness. That he was Christian eventually required an explanation. That he was Irish added to the explanation's flavor.

Growing up Catholic did not save little Leo from experiencing Antisemitism, though, on the scale of one to ten, he judges it "at most a two." In Russia we say, "They hit your face, not your passport."

He remembers especially one encounter with the neighborhood children, who could not, of course, have determined his heritage from any facial features but must have found out that his father was Jewish, and there they were, taunting and calling him a "dirty Jew" and throwing stones. Leo was nine then, or maybe ten. He doesn't remember being badly hurt, only badly scared—and feeling guilty of something he knew not what. Such is the fate of all victims: to wonder if they'd brought the abuse upon themselves.

He remembers also that his best friend was among the taunters, the only attacker who got what was coming to him the next day. This isn't uncommon, but I wonder if it was Leo Swidler's first betrayal.

In his autobiographical reflections, Len would write, many decades after this episode and after he left St. Paul Seminary behind:

16 Fahey, *The Kingship of Christ*, ch. VI, para. 3.

Antisemitism in a Catholic seminary after World War II? How was this possible? Well, I learned that it was quite widespread, and it took the revolution of Vatican Council II (1962–65) to begin to exorcize it. Of course, at the time I felt rather strange when I realized that the Rector was talking about Dad and me! Later in life I had different terms to describe what I then felt about the poison that Rector Rudi was purveying—to me and my older ex-GI confreres who had not long before fought a bloody war to stop the world's most heinous antisemites.[17]

17 Swidler, "A Life in Dialogue," section "Life in St. Paul's seminary," para. 5.

Talking to Len

(On Christian Antisemitism
and the historical Jesus)

RA   How did you eventually realize that Msgr. Bandas was referring to the Jews in his meditations?

LS   For one, he kept referring to Father Denis Fahey, although that connection is something I only discerned later, out of seminary. I can't remember how, but somewhere along the line I learned about Fahey, who ironically is a Holy Ghost father, and later I taught at Duquesne, founded by Holy Ghost Fathers. Bandas never used the name of Fahey, though. He was indirect and dark, but there was a lot of that. It was obviously pressing on his psyche. I connected him with Fahey because of the wording "corrupting of youth."

RA   Why were you so surprised by the presence of Antisemitism in a Catholic seminary after WWII?

LS   I found it astonishing because it was so filled with hatred. Antisemitism is that way. Of course, much of Christianity had a streak of vitriol and Antisemitism.

RA   For most of its history.

LS   It always struck me as out of place and not just ethically reprehensible but intellectually stupid, cutting yourself off at the knees. Jesus and Mary are a couple of kikes? They are adored!

How could these Christians put two and two together and get seventeen? Intellectually bamboozling. When Jews were driven out of Spain, they were given a place to come in the Papal States. Popes often protected the Jews in the Middle Ages.

RA   And yet, didn't they get driven out by a papally sanctioned Inquisition?

LS   Spanish, not Roman. It was complicated and depended on who was pope. Anything becomes thinkable when you begin to realize most Christians have no idea of any of that stuff: the Borgias, the blood and intrigue . . . What strikes me is the intellectual gap on the part of Christian, especially Catholic, Antisemites. It proves Goebbels's point: If you tell a big enough lie, people are more likely to believe it.

RA   Why especially Catholic?

LS   I guess Catholic theology and piety are much more focused on Jesus than Christ—not exclusively, of course. So, it's Jesus and Mary. They are two very obviously Jewish human beings. The Protestant focus on *Christos* can take you out of this world; there is no "earthiness," so you can think of the Jews as "earthy" people and despicable as a consequence. But here you are, supposedly madly in love with these two Jews, and you hate Jews.

RA   Catholic theology, perhaps wrongly but historically, did focus for a long time on high Christology more than on low—on the Divine Christ, so to speak, more than on Jesus of Nazareth.

LS   But in a lot of the piety you imagine yourself at the foot of the cross—the suffering Jesus. It's all very palpable. To make this case, you have to focus on the earthy Jesus. That's the intellectual disconnect. They make a mental summersault and think of Jesus as a Christian, but nobody asks the question. If you could back up fifty to seventy years and have a group of Catholics in front of you who were potentially Antisemites and ask them, "What religion was Jesus?" They would have to think about it and say, "Jewish, *but* . . . " Or something like that, but they didn't ask.

RA   Today, it is common to teach Christianity—and about Christianity—from a historical perspective of its Jewish roots. Do you think, then, it's important?

LS   Absolutely, since the early 1980s, the third Quest for Historical Jesus. I wrote an article in 1971 called "Jesus was a Feminist." All you had to do was ask the question. Once you've asked it, the scales fall from your eyes, and you say, "Of course!" It's hidden in plain view. The same with Christian Antisemitism; it's a nonstarter intellectually. In philosophy people correctly say that it's the questions that are important, not the answers. Once you ask the correct question, the genie is out of the bottle.

Forward to Marquette

Leo would spend two years at St. Paul Seminary, struggling and thinking, finding his way. In 1954, he decided not to take ordination to the subdeaconate but to leave for Marquette University to get a Master's degree in history before moving on to the University of Wisconsin for doctoral work. He can still hear his mother's voice, obviously perturbed, tender, questioning. Her oldest son was turning his back on consecrated life, for good.

"Do the girls excite you?" she asked.

RA   Did she think this was the reason?

LS   She must have figured the celibacy thing was *the* reason or a major reason, or she wouldn't have asked the question.

RA   What was the real reason?

LS   When it got closer to the end of the second year of theology, ordinations would be taking place. I had had one year of theology before, so it would be my third year. We'd be ordained to the sub-deaconate—they've eliminated it since then—which was a major holy order, so it meant permanent vows: celibacy, breviary. My twin goals were to become a saint and an intellectual, which struck me at the point: I would have plenty of challenges that would force a saintly response, but being a parish priest was not an intellectual life. At the abbey, commitment to celibacy and to religious life was all one thing; it was not a question for me. In the secular priesthood, they are parallel but not one thing.

RA   What do you mean?

LS   When you choose religious life, you are choosing a group of men as your family (men in my case) instead of marriage and family, but as a diocesan priest you are not choosing any family, just a thing called "priesthood." You commit yourself to no family, and it seems like a big gaping hole. So, I'm quite sure if I had not been forced out of the order, I would have come to permanent vows and ordination with no hesitation at all. But I went to seminary on the rebound, so to speak. I guess, there was no other order that attracted me that summer of 1952, just the idea of the priesthood—in those days, to be a man and a "real" Catholic, you had to be a priest.

RA   Why start from scratch?

LS   I don't think Marquette would recognize seminary credits. In those days you didn't get a secular degree in Catholic theology; you'd only do it to get ordained.

RA   Why Marquette?

LS   Why? It was closest, it was Catholic, it had a graduate program. What did I know? You certainly did not want to go to that atheistic University of Wisconsin. You could not go to a secular school. People were told they'd be excommunicated. I remember in 1966, '67, '68, we had some priests who wanted to come study at Temple and requested transcripts to be sent over from St. Charles Seminary here in Philly, and they refused. The priests arranged to have the credits sent to LaSalle (our local Catholic university) and picked them up and brought them to our office.

   So at Marquette I did an MA in history with philosophy and English lit. as minors.

RA   You had majors and minors in a graduate program?

LS   Then you did.

In the next three years, by 1957, at the godless University of Wisconsin, Leonard Swidler would meet and marry the new love of his life, Arlene Anderson, and would be transformed by her from Leo into Len. It is Arlene, a Catholic scholar in her own right, whom he credits with making him think of himself as a feminist.

PART III

Upstream

CHAPTER 9

If Feminism Was Good Enough for Jesus . . .

No future life could heal the degradation of having been a woman.
—DOROTHY RICHARDSON, *PILGRIMAGE*, VOLUME 2

WHEN I ASKED LEN to list what he thought were his most important pursuits, he named dialogue first and feminism second. This corresponded nicely to his own list of most important accomplishments: *After the Absolute,* his most renowned book on dialogue, which features the Dialogue Decalogue, reigns there in first place; and "Jesus Was a Feminist"—a 1971 article in the January issue of *Catholic World* turned into an eponymous book in 2007—he proudly puts second.

Jesus Was a Feminist is an attempt to show that the historical Jesus—Yeshua from Nazareth—radically departed from the cultural norms of his time and place in treating women as equals, that women's roles in Christianity have been drastically undervalued through history, and that our discipleship to Yeshua demands of the universal church an attitude of immediate gender equality. The 2007 book opens with a summary of Len's "most dramatic conclusions" reached "after many decades of research and reflection":

> The first one is . . . that Jesus was a feminist—and that presumably his followers should imitate him in that. . . . I published that

claim over a third of a century ago. Still, it remains news to many Christians, including the leaders of the Catholic and Orthodox churches.

The second dramatic conclusion that I draw is that Jesus—contrary to a two-thousand-year mistranslation of a key Gospel passage—did *not* reject divorce and remarriage!

The third is that proto versions of two of the canonical Gospels, namely, Luke's and the Fourth Gospel, were written by women. . . . [T]he time has come for us to recognize publicly that the penultimate version of the Fourth Gospel was written by . . . Mary Magdelene. . . .

The fourth, and most sweeping, conclusion is that we would not have Christianity today if all the materials on Jesus' teaching and life that were gathered and handed on by women were missing.[18]

TALKING TO LEN

(On Jesus and feminism)

RA   You often call yourself a feminist. This seems significantly to define your self-image. How did you come to it?

LS   Of course, I was always an unconscious feminist because I grew up with my mother, who supported a family in the Great Depression—not because my father was a delinquent but because it was impossible to get jobs for millions and millions. And the way my wife Andie was treated made me conscious of the disabilities women had to undergo in the intellectual world.

RA   For example?

LS   For one, she said she would have gone into math if she could as a child, but women couldn't then. She had one experience when she went to the library—a public library—to get a library card, and no, she couldn't have a card under the name of Arlene Anderson, and she couldn't be Mrs. Arlene Swidler. She had to be "Mrs. Leonard Swidler." It was infuriating and consciousness-raising. This was the early 1960s. We were teaching at Duquesne,

18 Swidler, *Jesus Was a Feminist*, ix.

and her experiences at the English Department were of the same sort: She'd come home from meetings irritated at times and tell me about it. I described it to myself like this: They discussed a topic X, and Andie would say, "What about this?" And no one would say anything. Next, twenty minutes later, some professor Joe Schmuck would articulate what she'd said, and everybody would be, like, "That's fantastic!" That happened not infrequently.

Andie became a full-blown, active feminist, and I went along with sympathetic vibrations, so to speak. When we moved to Philadelphia, it was not too long before I began to feel that we needed in the Religion Department at Temple a course that dealt with gender and women in religion, and we had no women on the faculty. I brought it up and had a negative response. I decided with Andie's help to offer the course—no one was going to do it. So that's how I got started.

In the process, when it came to dealing with Christianity and women, in the library I found quite a few books about women and Paul, but none on women and Jesus. At most, books had a short chapter, but more likely a paragraph or a page, saying that he was nice to women. Period. So I did what any undergrad in those days would do: got a bunch of 3x5 cards and re-read the Gospels. The evidence was obvious: Jesus never did or said anything negative about women; on the contrary, he did and said much positive and counter-cultural. At that point I delved into the context: the role of women in Judaism at the time of Jesus, which came out, of course, as very subordinate. That's how I wrote this first article that came out in 1971: "Jesus Was a Feminist."

It was published in *Catholic World*, and I distilled that down to eight hundred words and sent it to *The New York Times*, and, lo and behold, they published it. That provoked two or three letters to the editor that got published. What I remember is two letters from rabbis saying that I mis-described the role of women in Judaism at that time, that there were many outstanding women thinkers in the Mishnaic period, such as Bruriah, the wife of Rabbi Meir. As a result, when I went on sabbatical in Tübingen in 1972, I think, I dug into the material there at Institutum Judaicum and produced the book *Women in Judaism*. To summarize: Of course, the status of women, like Josephus said, was seen, according to the Torah, as inferior to men. There were over two hundred pages of evidence of their inferiority, along with other religions, including later Christianity.

RA   Of course, that's later Rabbinic Judaism, after the first-century Palestine, after the fall of the Temple. The same is true for Christianity. What about Jesus?

LS   Jesus treated women as equals, contrary to his culture, which is what I call a feminist. His stance on women, along with pacifism, are the two that cannot be found in the culture and are later rejected *de facto* by Christianity.

In the mid-seventies, Andie and I edited a book on the ordination of women. But the Vatican issued a decree saying women can't be ordained, and by that time situation had changed from '66. Now there were a number of women with degrees in theology, Mary Daly one of the first, so Andie and I edited this volume, a response to the Vatican's decree, taking their arguments and dismantling them. That also led to the launch of the movements for the ordination of women—the one that this launched is WOC (Women's Ordination Conference). I was always a male auxiliary support to Andie's efforts.

From that work I produced, through a lot of research and study, a book called *Biblical Affirmations of Women*, and that was the last thing on the topic that I published for a long time; there were now lots of highly trained and motivated women in the field, and I was needed like a fifth wheel. Only when Andie was very ill already with Alzheimer's, I published the book *Jesus Was a Feminist*, yet I have a feeling that New Testament scholars don't take seriously this line of argument, not even to reject it.

RA   Why do you think that is?

LS   My thought is two-fold: I am not a member of the club. I don't go to the Society of Biblical Literature meetings, so I can't do anything worthwhile. For others, were my name Leona instead of Leonard, I'd be taken more seriously. In the book, I look at Jesus through this set of lenses as if I were a member of this all-boys club.

RA   Is it possible the volume is not good? Or conversely, maybe the world has changed enough that your book is simply not important or controversial enough to make a splash? Maybe, it's a good thing?

LS   Maybe that's the answer. That would be a benign understanding. But, about five years ago, at the World Council of Churches—possibly 2008—in Geneva, around lunchtime we went to the cafeteria, and I got in line, and some white fellow in his middle fifties was in front of me. I put my hand out and said, "Hi. Leonard Swidler."

And he says, "*The* Leonard Swider?"

I'm like, "Yeah."

"*Jesus Was a Feminist*?!" He says, "In seminary in Chicago we had to read your essay 'Jesus Was a Feminist.'"

That's what I remember now. The essay must have made a searing impression on him.

RA   That's indeed impressive.

LS   Something similar happened just recently, in September 2013, at the annual meeting of the North American Academy of Religion in Chicago. During a coffee break I was chatting with Elizabeth Sung, a professor of systematic theology at the Trinity Evangelical Divinity School about a course she offered on ecumenism, and I gave her my name card. She looked at it for a couple of moments and said, "Oh my God! 'Jesus Was a Feminist'!" I asked where that came from, and she said she'd read my article about ten years before, and that it had helped her decide to go to seminary and eventually to become a systematic theology professor. So, you know, whatever some say about the claim of this article—and the subsequent book—it seems to be a gift that keeps on giving.

RA   I suppose what I'm saying is that between the time your essay came out and the publication of the book, both the scholarship and gender relations have changed quite a bit. The difference in reaction to your article and to the book could be discouraging or encouraging.

LS   And connected?

RA   Right. The book might be a flop in academic circles because it is outdated or because the essay has helped create a world in which your book is no longer an outrage, a surprise, or even interesting.

LS   Could be. People would tell me how my essay opened their eyes and all, and I was thinking how the reality of Jesus was sitting there for two thousand years, and nobody saw it! And I'm like a kid saying, "The Emperor has no clothes!"

RA   Well, the idea had ripened to where the society was ready to see it, no?

LS   And I was the first to see it. I would say that in terms of impact, of reproductions, "Jesus Was a Feminist" and "The Dialogue Decalogue" were the two most important things I've done. Each was translated into thirty or forty different languages.

IF FEMINISM WAS GOOD ENOUGH FOR JESUS (CONT'D)

September 3, 2013

Dear Dr. Swidler,

I hope you get this. I need to say "thank you." I am one of those people who carried your article around for years.

In 1982, as a sophomore in college, I dug up your 1971 article "Jesus Was a Feminist" in the dusty bound magazine archives in the library at Kent State University. I copied your article and placed it in the front of my Bible, where it has stayed for more than 30 years. The old, slick photocopy paper faded, but before it got too hard to read, I copied it for many religious sisters and friends of mine.

I could not deny back then that God was calling me to be active in the world, use my gifts for others, be a leader, look for ways to create more economic justice, serve others in addition to a family I might have. That was not the message I heard from my

Catholic church at the time. . . . Your article reassured me that
I should listen to the Holy Spirit working in me and accept that
others may not get it, but I got it.
     . . . Thanks for putting the words on paper. Today I found
the book you wrote in '07. Glad I can share it with my daughters.

Cathy Ivancic,

Business Owner, Consultant, Mother, Wife,
Believer, Christian, and Feminist

Naturally, not all responses to Len's feminist Jesus have been so positive. In fact, one "member of the club," contrary to Len's assumption, cared to read the book, and what bothered her had little to do with the author's gender or societal memberships. In her 2008 review published by the Society of Biblical Literature, Kathleen Corley from the University of Wisconsin-Oshkosh writes, " . . . Swidler reconstructs an overwhelmingly negative view of Judaism in Palestine of the first century but uses late rabbinic sources for his reconstruction." If he were to use only first-century Palestinian sources, she believes, a picture of a more progressive society would emerge: "Women were in the Zealot movement and the movement of John the Baptist, may have written writs of divorce, owned their own property, and kept their own finances. Even the Gospels themselves show that women moved freely out in public and were in no way separated from men socially." She accuses Len of ignoring all the feminist scholarship that, since 1971, has worked to correct our anti-Judaic impressions of ancient Israel: Ross Kraemer, Amy-Jill Levine, Elisabeth Schüssler Fiorenza, Bernadette Brooten, Judith Plaskow . . . [19]

Nonspecialists also had a mixed reaction. A Canadian writer and social activist Scott Neigh found the book of some value and interest, but his online review raised a series of concerns, including one that echoes an aspect of Kathleen Corley's last point:

Also of concern is the danger of theological antisemitism contained in this approach. . . . one way that it has historically manifested is by Christians emphasizing the great things that Christ brought by denigrating how Jewish culture/religious practice did things before that point. . . . Though Swidler explicitly says

---

19 Corley, Review of *Jesus Was a Feminist.*

... that he is not intending to do this sort of thing, I think it is at least possible that he ends up doing it anyway.[20]

Len, of course, disagrees. He does indeed use later sources in the book, but as a buttress to his method he points to an existing school of thought, to scholars who rely on Rabbinic literature as a continuation of the spirit of Pharisaic Judaism from the time of Jesus and before. The portrait of Yeshua himself Len draws mostly from his own reading of the Gospels. He feels in all respects justified and concludes that "*Yeshua was a feminist, and a very radical one.*"[21]

I suppose the good news is that his book did not go quite as unnoticed as he had thought, and, in the end, I feel he did not write it for the scholarly reviewer. He wrote it for the interested yet popular reader like Cathy Ivancic, and on her it made every bit the impact any author could only hope for. As a matter of fact, this might well be a good example of why Len often feels like an ugly duckling of academia: he doesn't tend to write for precision of analysis, depth of research, and minutiae of attribution. He writes in broad strokes and overarching ideas, in provocative statements and memorable alliterations. He writes for an appeal of the heart and reverberation of the soul. He writes for the message—a goal more often of journalism and literature than of purely scholarly work.

What does this mean? What does it change? If Len cared for the academic standing of his position, he could have responded when Kathleen Corley's review was published.

Of course, he still can. That's the saving grace of academia: the debate is always on.

---

20 Neigh, Review of *Jesus was a Feminist*, para. 11.

21 Swidler, *Jesus Was a Feminist,* 33 (*emphasis* in the original).

CHAPTER 10

Hostels, Hostiles, and a Big World: backpacking through Europe

A good traveler leaves nothing behind and requires no destination.
. . . Know this secret, or you will be lost.
—*Tao Te Ching*

THE MID-1950S TURNED OUT to be big for Leo Swidler. In 1954 he would leave St. Paul Seminary and start his Master's program at Marquette University. A year later he'd take a step into the unknown of public education and quite fully find himself in the intellectual boiling pot of academia, its arguing and questioning, its ever-shifting centers of moral gravity. Then and there, he would meet Arlene Anderson, fall in love, and discover just how much he was willing to do for one woman. He'd leave behind his familiar nickname and become Len—because Andie preferred it. But before any of it began to happen, there was the summer of '53, and it was one of those summers.

Not since the impression-packed work trip with aunts and uncles nine years before had Leo gone on a true outward adventure. He'd stayed mostly close to home, and his exploration had been of an inner, spiritual sort, but things were changing. On some level ready to tear his plans for a priestly vocation, he was turning in a radically new direction this time, and, frightening or exciting, the giant secular world was waiting in all directions—a multi-colored, multi-lingual, wonder-loaded map.

It was, I think, a perfect moment for Leo to leave his cradle-land and look the world in the eye, and he chose a perfect companion for his first journey abroad: He took Jack, and for ten weeks, together, the brothers went backpacking through Europe.

From their summer-job earnings of the previous year, the boys had saved $640 each, of which $400 went toward a roundtrip ticket to London. The airplane they boarded was the ultimate in luxury, the definition of awesome in the early fifties: a Boeing 377 Stratocruiser, a double-decker with four massive propellers and a recently invented pressurized cabin.

Mechanically, it appears, the plane was less awesome, thanks to faults in its radial engines. For the duration of their existence, the fifty-five Stratocruisers used by the airlines made the news with thirteen accidents that killed 140 people, and by 1960 they were largely supplanted by jets like the Boeing 707.

Of course, the boys didn't worry about—most likely, didn't know—any of this. All they knew was that they were two of nearly one hundred passengers who could relax in soft seats or sleeping berths or come down to the lower deck's lounge and bar. This, incidentally, is where the young Swidlers happened to be seated among eight fortunate others. Airline personnel did not seem to include a bartender, so after a while, the passengers began freely pouring the liquor themselves. Leo especially liked one character in a seersucker suit who dispensed a pearl of wisdom with every drink, and the one advice now-Professor Swidler, for some reason, has retained for sixty years, was this: "The best way to travel is to wear one suit and carry a suitcase full of money."

Len moves his overgrown eyebrows up and down in a gesture of comical significance, raises his index finger, then plants it in his knee. He may remember the seersucker suit's advice, but he doesn't follow it, at least not in the spirit it was offered. In the metaphor of Len Swidler's life, his suit indeed is one, his car's got rust holes in the floor, and whatever money he carries is destined for those whom Len has spotted along the way: those with not enough. But Len is laughing, and I with him: it's an amusing image, he with a suitcase of money.

The image of a twenty-four-year-old Len with a suitcase of money is especially amusing. He and Jack disembarked in London armed only with backpacks, $480 for the pair of them, thumbs for hitch-hiking, and some addresses for places to spend the night—student hostels and German

Catholics involved in Catholic Action and Nazi resistance, whose names Leo had gotten from a German economics professor teaching at a college across the way from his seminary. Germany, however, was still a while away. The adventure began in England.

England

They walked about London and took in a Shakespeare play at the Old Vic Theater, then another—those were good, but Len does not remember exactly. It is only the third stage that he remembers in shuddering detail, the one in Stratford-upon-Avon, at the Shakespeare Memorial Theater.

Stratford is a small town in South Warwickshire, about one hundred miles northwest of London, past Oxford and halfway to Manchester, on the river Avon—you might say, in the middle of nowhere. Few people would have known where it is or why it is, except this is where Shakespeare was born, and so this is where we go to touch the sacred ground that sprouted theater, to breathe the air of English poetry. Here—of course, nowhere but here—is the home of what used to be the Shakespeare Memorial Theater and is now the Royal Shakespeare Theater. Here, the most spectacular of the best artists come before us onto the stage, transformed into the personae we've known since birth as friends—and as enemies. And they ring out of their lips and pulses, from the trembling of eyelashes, all, to the last drop, eternal longings of the human plight: rage, sorrow, madness, and ecstasy, the abandon of desperation, the quicksand of suspicion, the beauty of shed inhibition. And they pour those precious drops offstage at our feet—salvation and contemplation flowing and ebbing, crashing into the self-erected walls of regret, soaking the delicate fabrics of our hearts. And they nourish, and they drown: Shakespeare.

In the summer of 1953, Shakespeare Memorial Theater was doing *Lear*. Michael Redgrave in the role of the king. Who could walk away from it and forget?

Philip Hope-Wallace from *The Guardian* went to see the production on July 15th of that year. The next day, his review itself was poetry:

> . . . *a really fond and foolish old man, pathetic because absurd in his quite unfrightening parade of power.*
> . . . *the study of a man seeking in wandering wits a refuge from intolerable reality . . .* [22]

---

22 Hope-Wallace, "Michael Redgrave as Lear," paras. 4, 6.

Len presses his fingertips together when I ask him to describe that evening. He leans forward and lingers, and I realize he is looking for words. "It was . . . *cri de coeur.* A cry of the heart!" A stage almost bare under a minimalist, nearly abstract set, and Lear's massive, robed figure—wretched, blind, mad with grief—clutching to his chest Cordelia's tiny body. And nothing else, and nothing to change, ever again. "He seared the air with his lament," Len finally says. "It was heart-wrenching."

Paris

Paris was next. To my great chagrin, Len's stories of it do not live up to Shakespearean passion by a very, very long shot. He talks mostly about chaos in the Parisian streets. The metro was in what seems to Americans its habitual *modus operandi*: on strike. The ground transportation stunned Jack and Leo with reason-shattering din.

"It was enough to drive you nuts!" Len screws up his face at a hint of recollection of that sound. "Especially if you were trying to sleep."

Like bizarre, noisy leukocytes through stone capillaries, cars were squeezing through the narrow streets Paris had inherited from the Middle Ages, blowing their horns whenever they approached an intersection. They seemed to compete at how mighty a bawl each little Fiat or Citroen could bellow out.

Len's face suddenly lights up: "When I got there, I realized why Gershwin's *American in Paris* sounds the way it does! The rhythmical *bleep-honk-honk* in his piece. It must have been some sort of custom to honk at an intersection, you know. It was awful. Doubtless, that's why they subsequently passed a law forbidding the honking of horns at intersections."

Yet, the single strongest impression upon Leo's fragile psyche was left by a place even more prosaic than a street corner: a toilet stall. The bathroom at the youth hostel where the Swidlers stayed was apparently co-ed, though Leo had not realized it until, seated comfortably in a stall, he heard two American girls come into the spaces on both sides of him and proceed to talk loudly over his head. Poor young man, as shy as they came, froze, mortified, praying only that he make no sound—God forbid the girls say something to him—until long after they left. Probably long after the whole building went to sleep. Nothing else memorable seems to have happened in Paris. Mercifully, the brothers were free birds, and Germany beckoned.

Cologne

The Gothic Cathedral is the eternal watchman of Cologne. They began to build it in 1248 and, after two-and-a-half centuries, left it unfinished until 1880, to become one of the largest churches in the world, but since the thirteenth century it has reigned over the city through famine, war, and winds, and nothing has ever brought it down. Leo and Jack climbed one of the Cathedral's twin 515-foot spires and gasped at the destruction underneath. All of the old city, the whole center was ruins and rubble, traversed here and there by cleared streets, for miles in every direction.

The Cologne Cathedral was hit several times—fourteen by some reports—but stood tall through World War II, shedding only occasional stones, like tears, over its decaying charge. That in the midst of near-total destruction of Cologne from Allied air raids the Cathedral never collapsed has been a subject of speculation and anecdotes in Germany and beyond. Some say that the Allied pilots navigated by its soaring spires toward the end of the war and so left it, purposely, standing. Leo was told by a local citizen a different version of events: that the residents deliberately shined enormous search lights onto the building during night air raids, thinking the British bombers would aim at it and miss, and were proved correct.

Without any evidence to support it, this latter story sounds to me both true and suspect, in different ways. Knowing what it was like in Soviet cities brought to the brink of annihilation in the war, I have a hard time imagining that Cologne would have enough power for enormous search lights in the city center that was bombed literally into nonexistence. Nevertheless, people are capable of miraculous things when they try to save their children and their cultural treasures. During almost nine hundred days of the Leningrad Blockade, the citizens of the city, frozen and starving, climbed up the spire of the Peter-and-Paul Fortress, up to the golden domes of our cathedrals, to pull camouflage cloth over them, and those, too, stood through the war. The citizens of Cologne could have found a way.

Still, when I imagine the Cologne Cathedral towering out of the endless field of debris, lit up to be spotted from miles away, I doubt it would still be there if the bombers wanted it gone. I wonder instead if they didn't indeed avoid it. For navigation? Perhaps. Or, maybe, for its utter and breathtaking beauty. Or, maybe, because, a bit like a big red cross, the search lights intersected upon the last thing of peace still whole in that dark and broken world, and it was a church.

One of the names Jack and Leo carried with them belonged to Maria Schlüter-Hermkes, the widow of an honored jurist Johannes Schlüter, who had worked for the Prussian Ministry of Culture, developed several treaties, and worked closely with the then-nuncio Eugenio Pacelli, the future Pope Pius XII. Frau Schlüter-Hermkes had connections at the university, where Len seems to recall she had built a student center, so, besides warm beds and warm hugs, she soon offered her American guests twenty marks and a student escort to the opera.

The student greeted the foreigners in a manner still customary in post-war Germany: He shook their hands, clicked his heels together, and bowed. *I could get used to this,* thought Leo to himself, but the magic of the Rhineland had barely begun. The boys' escort apologized for speaking poor English and, in Len's words, "proceeded the next couple of days to sound like Shakespeare." He took them to their first live opera, Richard Strauss's *Der Rosenkavalier.* Mesmerized, Leo drank in every note, keeping his eyes closed—though, I must confess, it was not from sheer pleasure; he just didn't want to look at the stage, where the young "knight of the rose" Octavian, sung by a graceful contralto, was romancing "his" voluminous beloved, Sophie, about twenty-four sizes larger than her suitor.

Der Rosenkavelier is a comedy about love, gender roles, and age gaps. It's a comedy of inconstancies and inconsistencies, and I find it a little bit fitting that Len's first encounter with operatic comedy about mismatches that match should involve a comedic element of mismatch. As he gesticulates, trying to show me just how huge Sophie was looking onstage, I watch and listen and say nothing. It's pretty clear, the size of Cologne's *prima donna* didn't do him any damage because this first time began Len's lifelong love affair with opera.

He loves all music—above all, classical, orchestral, sacred polyphony. And opera, opera . . . Len and Arlene always held season's tickets to Philadelphia's Academy of Vocal Arts, and once she could no longer go— and after she passed away—he held on to the tickets and now invites his friends. I am one of those lucky few. With Len I go to the Kimmel Center, to the Cathedral, and to the AVA. He listens with all of his body, drinking it in, and it doesn't even have to be good. I am a much more severe critic. Len listens to music; his eyes are closed. And then, he needs nothing else.

RA   Len, you have a tradition you keep on Good Friday. Talk about that.

LS   It started some years ago. We come together—these are all people who know German—we come together at Patrick Burke's house. He has a CD production performance of *St. Matthew's Passion*. Bach's best. Dietrich Fischer-Dieskau sings one of the parts; it's a stunning ensemble, recorded in the early 1960s in Munich, when we both were there. We sit, and we have the text in front of us, and we listen. It's all very quiet except for the music. We take a break in the middle. Altogether it's about three hours.

When it starts out, it's just music, you're following the text, but as it goes on, it begins to develop a whole feeling like you're in a different space. Especially the solos. I noticed reading the texts that they are old pious German songs, the theology of which I totally can't accept, but when they're sung, they're utterly transformed. They become somehow translucent, and they mean something profound and moving. Somehow Bach and the singers transmute pious trash into transcendent theology. So, you know, the experience of these three hours is incredibly aesthetic and also deeply spiritual, and it doesn't become less so with repetition, year after year. It never fails to move me that way. I gather it's very similar with the others.

Then we share food together, which we would never do on Good Friday in the old days. But we take the term "good" seriously in this case. I cannot imagine a more appropriate, deeper, spiritual and religious kind of way of keeping Good Friday than what we do there.

Rheingau

In 1953, Leo and Jack left Cologne and traveled down the Rhine, to the winemaking country and bucolic landscapes of the Rheingau. In Rüdesheim am Rhein, they wandered along the shores of the river so famous for its dreamy spots that, in Germany, the town is second only to Cologne Cathedral in the yearly number of tourists. They stopped at all the wine cellars they could find, locked arms with wine-mellowed strangers, and swayed to the rhythm of local drinking songs—and a little bit to the fog of alcohol—and they sang:

Wer soll das bezahlen	*Who should pay for this?*
Wer hat das bestellt,	*Who ordered this?*
Wer hat so viel pinke-pinke,	*Who has so much dough?*
Wer hat so viel Geld?	*Who has so much money?*

In Bingen, they regarded with awe a white-and-red stone tower on a little island in the Rhine. The Mouse Tower, rebuilt many times since the Romans had first erected a structure on this spot, is the subject of an enduring and terrifying folk tale that makes one want to cut the Brothers Grimm a little slack. It revolves around a historical personage, Hatto II, the archbishop of Mainz from 968 to 970 CE. He was apparently known as an oppressive ruler, and it is his death that the Mouse Tower legend describes, though no evidence seems to exist that the story is factual.

Hatto, the legend goes, was cruel and avaricious. He stored up food and sold it to the peasants at back-breaking prices, and no plea had ever reached his frozen heart. His treasures grew; his people starved. One spring, the lowlands were flooded by the overflowing rivers, and famine overtook the province. Though villagers begged Hatto for pity on behalf of their children, he only laughed. Again and again, he said, "My wheat is too precious to give it to hungry rats!"

Yet the peasants would not let up, unable to watch their children die of hunger, and finally the bishop bade them go to an empty granary and wait for him, saying he would bring them food. At last there was joy, and the people gathered into the granary, blessing Hatto's name. Children stopped crying, knowing that night they would have bread.

When the time came, the bishop arrived, but, instead of entering the building, he ordered his servants to lock all the doors and set the granary on fire. "You have pestered me like rats," he said, "and now you shall die like rats." Unmoved, he listened to shrieks of horror and pain from inside until nothing was left but ashes and then returned to his palace for dinner.

That night, Hatto was awakened by a scampering sound and tiny squeals and in the morning discovered, shocked, that a magnificent portrait of him had been gnawed to shreds by rats, face first. A servant ran in and could barely tell him through trembling lips that a mass of mice and rats was approaching from the granary.

At full gallop the terrified bishop fled from the rats, but they pursued. He jumped into a boat and rowed across the river with all his might, but they pursued—many drowned and many more swam to the shore after him. He ran into a tower on a small, rocky island, barred all the windows and doors and crouched in a dusty corner, but they pursued. Rats and mice climbed on the walls, gnawed through the wood barring the doors, and the dread of his victims was nothing compared to what he felt then.

When the mice got inside, they covered the bishop. He fought them and stomped on them, beat them off and clawed at them, but they surged like the tide breaking on a cliff. Little was left of the body when servants dared enter the morbid space some days later.

Such is the story of the Mouse Tower near Bingen-on-the-Rhine. They still point it out to strangers as the place where Bishop Hatto had met his death.[23]

Germany enthralled Leo, carved a space within his heart, and nestled there for good. Germany suffused him with itself and seeded a bit of its essence in his every fiber: the sound of its speech and song, the beauty of the land, the taste of the wine. He would return to Germany again and many times, to study and to live, and then again to travel. His older daughter, Carmel, would be born there. He'd become so fluent in German that even now he has a hard time on occasion finding words in English for some feelings or concepts that, for him, are just so in German. Carmel didn't speak English for the first three years of her life.

Every summer Len takes his granddaughter Willie and goes to Germany for a long vacation on bicycles, and every week he goes to her house—really, of course, the house of his younger daughter, Eva—to teach the girl the language. I would say Germany was the love of Len Swidler's life had he not had dialogue, had he not had the church, had he not had Arlene and his students. Human beings are capable of loving so much, so deeply, that even we marvel at ourselves.

Germany embraced Leo the first time they met, in 1953, and never let him go—but Jack and Leo's trip was not yet over, and so on they moved, to Holland.

---

23 For a full story, see, e.g., *Folk Tales*, 186–92.

Holland

They had a few addresses of Norbertine abbeys in the Netherlands where they could ask for free lodging, but hitch-hiking, by definition, does not allow for precise planning, and one day the brothers found themselves alone at a rural intersection, with no Norbertines in sight and an evening looming. Mostly, they'd overestimated the liveliness of Europe's post-war traffic—after all, the economy on the Continent was still in shambles, people barely ever traveled for pleasure, and when they did, they didn't usually drive. Even the British rarely left the country for breaks and holidays. As far as Len recalls, they were allowed to take out only £50 at a time. So when the truck carrying the Swidlers, who were trying to get to Amsterdam, turned in the "wrong" direction and the boys decided to get off and wait for another ride at a crossroads in the midst of spanning countryside, it turned out to be decidedly a mistake.

They spent a long Saturday afternoon by the roadside, waiting for anything on wheels, but encountered no one save two young women on bicycles who were coming, as it later turned out, exactly from the opposite direction: from Amsterdam. Finally, with darkness thickening in the sky, the brothers resolved it was time to look for shelter where fate had dropped them.

Their choice wasn't large: at the northwest corner there stood a tavern, at the northeast corner, a Catholic church with a rectory. To the south, they could see a few houses, and all around, endless fields. This was farmland. Jack and Leo exchanged a glance and took a chance on the church, where a few minutes later they could see the priest's back disappearing into the sacristy. Leo shouted in English, to no effect. *Maybe, he doesn't understand!* They rushed after the man, into the sacristy, just as the door opened to let him out—he was leaving, their hope for a comfortable night! Leo called out again, gathering up his crumbs of German into a sentence. *Will he stop?*

He did.

He turned around and closed the door. He faced two young men squarely and poured onto their heads a long, wrathful tirade, only part of which Leo could parse. What he got was the gist of this waterfall of insults: "Lousy Germans!"

"But . . . we're not German!" Leo whimpered. "We're American!"

"*Soll ich das glauben!?*" *Should I believe that?*

The pastor turned on his heel and slammed the door.

Dismayed and with nothing to lose, the boys trudged across the road, swearing quiet oaths never again to mention Germany to the Dutch. To their pleasant surprise, the tavern was hopping with merry peasants, song, and drink, and they soon found out that a yearly week-long celebration called *Kermis* had just begun. Leo had heard of *Kermis* from Dutch towns around Green Bay. Related to the roots for "church Mass," it is a celebration of the founding of the local church, a town's traditional "church birthday." On this Saturday evening, the party went full swing, and American travelers—who spoke exclusively English—soon became honored guests inundated with free beer and toasts to the United States.

Jack was eighteen and loved beer; passage of time slowed down for him considerably once he stepped through the tavern doors. Leo preferred wine, so after a bit of merry-making he began to ask the locals what strangers could do for beds in this corner of the world, and—luck or blessing—they directed him to a hostel within walking distance. Holding up Jack, who by then was in what Len characterized as "a very happy mood," Leo made his way east and down a small wooded road to a hostel by a little lake. The two bicyclists who'd passed the brothers on the crossroads earlier that day were already there. The girls were pretty, the night was starry, the vapors of their last drinks still carried the boys' thoughts high and light, and the young people spent the rest of the evening in beach chairs, talking of pleasant things.

It is funny now, this story with a frantic beginning and a nice ending, yet it wouldn't be complete without one final chord. It seems, in the course of their meandering conversation on Saturday night, the Swidlers told the vacationing Amsterdamians about their hostile encounter with the village priest, and it seems the girls were Catholic. They went to an early Mass the next day, Sunday, and it seems, they spoke to the pastor. Long story short, when Leo and Jack timidly walked into the modest red-brick sanctuary, flooded with light, for the late-morning Mass, there was the priest this time: unapologetic but welcoming and friendly.

Venice

As well as all their adventures ended in Holland, the boys left it with easy hearts—back south across Europe, for Italy.

Italy—a land almost mythical to an American mind. An epitome of romanticism, a fountain-burst of the Renaissance, the home of St. Peter's

Church. Italy, the land of siestas, spaghetti, and serenades. The land of Chianti, where the sun goes down only to throw soft shadows of mood lighting over Cupid-touched couples. The land of love.

Of course, it is also the land of Mussolini, the birthplace of fascism—and in 1953, the memory of it was fresh in everybody's mind.

Leo and Jack were looking for Italy's miracle, and they got to know its irony, too.

Venice greeted young Americans with the sparkle of canals and swan-like gondolas. Though short on money, they were willing to splurge on a motorboat tour of the city, especially since two gentlemen in raincoats and slouch hats made them an offer at a reasonable price for the next morning. All the gentlemen needed was a deposit so they could, they said, buy some fuel for the boat. The brothers obliged, and the next morning at 8 AM, as agreed, they stood ready to be picked up. Needless to say, the morning came and went without a motorboat tour.

This would probably have cemented the boys' stereotype of the ubiquitous Italian crook had they not run into a different kind of Italian on their train ride along the Po River Valley. In the excitement of all the happenings, Leo left his camera hanging on a little hook by the seat and realized it just as the train was rolling away. A camera was a big deal: not only was it expensive and contained memories of their adventures but it was, in fact, not his. He'd borrowed the thing from his cousin Mary. Not counting on much success but desperate enough to try, the boys boarded the next train in the same direction, rode to its final destination, and filed into the Lost & Found.

"Has anyone by chance turned in a camera from the last train?"

"Please describe it in detail."

Holding his precious find in his hands, Leo mused. There were honest people in the world, and some of them, apparently, lived in Italy.

Rome

Rome was . . . big. Rome had everything: crowds, palaces, and ancient ruins. But to Leo, Rome was the Vatican, and for the seminarian he still was, all roads indeed—still—had to lead there, to the holy ground. The brothers wanted to see the pope.

historical interlude

Pius XII is one of the more complex figures in the history of the modern Catholic Church, one of the more controversial—certainly, worthy of note and a marked influence on the life of one Leonard Swidler. Born Eugenio Maria Giuseppe Giovanni Pacelli, he hailed, quite obviously, from Italian nobility, yet he was the pope who, in 1946, shifted the national balance of the College of Cardinals away from the traditional Italian majority by elevating a number of mostly German bishops connected with the German Resistance.

World War II took over Pius's pontificate from its beginning, just after he was installed March 2, 1939—incidentally, on his sixty-third birthday—and for the next six years, nothing else mattered. His choices during the war are more than debatable, more than notorious. Seventy years later, they are still divisive to the world that lives in the shadow of history's bloodiest century.

It is an uneasy question to ask: whether the pope is the most powerful leader on Earth, one who guides over a billion followers, or the least significant head of state, whose sovereignty extends not even over one whole city. This question became even more poignant when powerful fascist regimes surrounded his tiny Vatican on all sides, when the same regimes that exterminated civilians were threatening to destroy his very church, when those same regimes wielded massive armies and moved walls of fire, like tsunami, around the world.

Pius XII was a peace-maker and a natural go-between. In the way he knew how, he did not remain passive in the face of atrocities. He facilitated communication between the Allies and the German Resistance, issued permission to American Catholics to aid the Soviet Union in its fight against Nazism despite the church's—and his own—almost rabid phobia of anything remotely communist, and went on the radio and spoke, again and again. Some say his repeated denunciations of violence against innocents "sometimes on account of race alone," his protests against deportations of Jews, his cooperation in saving nearly nine hundred thousand Jewish lives worldwide—by Catholic convents and churches and within the walls of the Vatican—are the actions of a saint. After the war, more than one Jewish rabbi publicly thanked the pope for help.

Then, there are others. As the world reeled from the unthinkable loss of lives (not only Jewish) that was the Holocaust and tried to wrap its collective consciousness around its own ability to allow this to happen, the pope's efforts began to seem insufficient. Criminally insufficient. He was called "Hitler's Pope," a Nazi collaborator, and an Antisemite. He was called unfeeling and indifferent.

These accusations are still around, but I am here to assure you, they are unfair. Pius XII was never indifferent toward the suffering of victims, whatever their race or creed. More thought-provoking are those who say his denunciations of mass murder were vague, and his immovable stance of "impartiality" was the moral failure of a diplomat who found himself in the position of a wartime leader. There are times, perhaps, when impartiality doesn't exist. When the Light is battling Darkness, there is no in-between, and, trying to stand outside, one is crushed into nothing or cut in half—or worse yet, swallowed whole. One is guilty of not being the Light.

Who is right? I don't know. Few of us are truly the Light. Most of us do what seems best, minute by minute, and later find we've failed in some way or another. Everyone asks these questions. The U.S. and the U.S.S.R. didn't rise up against Nazism until we were attacked, and, standing amid our ruins, counting our losses, we ask how much suffering could have been avoided had we had the courage to act earlier, before evil stormed through our gates. What if we'd taken a stand, along with the U.K., Australia, New Zealand, Canada, South Africa, India, and Newfoundland, in 1939? What if we'd had wisdom, foresight, and moral fortitude enough, even when trouble was maybe still in someone else's house?

It was complicated. Many forces shaped history and many currents. It was complicated for Pius XII, too, but for good, at least more than for ill, he emerged from the gamut of World War II with declining health but unbroken spirit.[24]

He has a fairly diverse post-war legacy, this pope. Another might have let his flock sweep up the ashes and spit off blood, rebuild and re-center a little, but not Pius: He kept up the controversy and refused to be pigeon-holed. Doling out "liberal/conservative" labels, we don't know what to do with him.

In 1948, he interfered in Italian elections by threatening with excommunication anyone who would vote for a Communist candidate. Two years later, he solemnly declared the Assumption of Mary to be part of Catholic faith, becoming the only pope to invoke *ex cathedra* papal

---

24 For a summary of Vatican archives from the period, see Blet, *Pius XII and the Second World War.*

For a perspective on Pius XII's actions, see, e.g., Phayer, *Pius XII, the Holocaust, and the Cold War.*

infallibility since it had been defined in 1870 by the First Vatican Council. His 1947 encyclical *Mediator Dei* on liturgy reform and the lay apostolate revitalized progressive Catholics everywhere, and yet, in 1950 he put out his now-infamous *Humani generis*, a staunchly conservative push-back against modern approaches to theology.

In this entirely undiplomatic denunciation, Pius XII declared the Teaching Authority the only source of "authentic interpretation" and ordered theologians to agree with the Magisterium on faith and morals even in matters that had been previously left open to discussion. He prescribed that all Catholics doubt the theory of evolution and labeled it a communist plot, swept aside the idea that humanity had more than exactly one human originator (Adam), condemned attempts at ecumenical dialogue as "eirenism," and mandated a literal reading of the Old Testament as interpreted by the tradition of the church only, so God forbid anyone engage in exegesis or, worse yet, consider any biblical narrative "on a par with myths or other such things." To seal this house-cleaning deal, the pope inserted into the encyclical a reminder that everything he said "demands consent"—even ordinary teachings—since, if he chose to say it, it was no longer subject to discussion, for he did, after all, speak for Christ.

Pius XII became very ill in 1954 and, though he did some work in the next four years, never fully recovered. He died of heart failure in 1958 in his summer palace, Castel Gandolfo, and the funeral procession for this beloved son of Rome reportedly gathered greater masses than any event in the city's prior recorded history. He was succeeded by Pope John XXIII, who would throw open a window and convene the revolutionary Second Vatican Council—the Council that, between 1962 and 1965, would change the face and the heart of the church and, in the process, would draw from the spirit of Pius's *Mediator Dei* while drawing all over his *Humani generis*. Toward the close of Vatican II, Pope Paul VI opened the cause for canonization of Pius XII, and it is still proceeding today amid controversy, so characteristically his.

end interlude

It is this pope that Jack and Leo Swidler came to Rome to see in the summer of 1953 and, after asking around, were told that Holy Father was at his summer palace in Castel Gandolfo, about fifteen miles outside the city. Cooler breezes, the azure Lake Albano, seventeenth-century architecture . . . The boys couldn't wait.

They planned to catch a bus to Castel Gandolfo in front of Rome's notorious Altare della Patria ("Altar of the Fatherland"), a gigantic heavy monument of glaringly white marble with Corinthian columns, ostentatious staircases, and fountains, that commemorates Italian unification. An equestrian sculpture of Vittorio Emanuele II—the first king of the unified Italy—reigns before it. Italians generally dislike the structure because of its pompous disharmony with the surrounding architecture and because, to make space for it, the state destroyed a considerable portion of the medieval Capitoline Hill, and in its nine decades of existence the monument has earned several unflattering nicknames like "The Wedding Cake," "The Typewriter," and "The English Soup," the latter a local term for a highly ornate dessert.

Jack and Leo got to the bus stop so early that they were first and cemented their place in line—or so they thought. Slowly a few others arrived, and just when they thought they'd be quite comfortable, a chirping and fluttering black-and-white gaggle of what looked to Leo like "tiny Italian nuns" descended and surrounded them. Apparently unfamiliar with the custom of waiting in a queue, the tiny nuns bunched all around, and when the bus rolled up, they burst through its doors like a water stream through a broken dam, knocking aside both Leo's and Jack's considerable American frames.

"Oh my God!" Len rolls up his eyes and shakes along the length of his body. "Jack was 220 pounds of solid muscle! I was no shrimp either: 5'11" and 180 pounds. In a flash, they totally filled the bus, including standing room. I forced myself into the doorway, and Jack, who had finally picked his stunned self up, got his two feet just inside the door, backwards, grabbed the two bars on either side of the door, and simply pushed and crushed backward with all of his strength. The driver closed the door, and Jack and I, along with some thirty versions of Sister Mary Euthanasia, were happily off to see the pope!"

After a long, hot ride and a long, hot climb up the hill from the bus stop to their destination, Jack, Leo, and the gaggle of nuns dissolved in the hordes pouring into the village square before the papal residence. It is called *Piazza della Libertá*—Liberty Square—a name left over since 1870, when all kinds of old things were given new names in the first throes of ecstasy of the Italian Unification.

The Apostolic Palace itself, even by the Vatican standards, is of noteworthy size and of epic, ancient history. There has been a palace on this spot for nearly two millennia, ever since Emperor Domitian erected one for himself in the first century CE. After a series of other estates, the Genoan family Gandolfi constructed a villa here in the early thirteenth century, and in 1596 the Vatican came to own the place, which finally completed its long conversion from the center of Christian persecution to the residence of Christian leadership. Clement VIII immediately declared it among the possessions that were never to be sold, and by the late 1660s the palace we now know and love was completed, with Bernini's design. Urban VIII had already begun the tradition of the popes' spending vacations here on Lake Albano, fourteen hundred feet above the sea, where the skies are thinner, the winds are fresher, and the foliage is shadier in the sweltering months of Italian summer.

Since then, Castel Gandolfo has felt the feet of Goethe and seen the faces of many a poet, philosopher, artist, and scientist, and every manner of saint. Hans Küng has gone there to meet with Benedict XVI, and George W. Bush with John Paul II. The popes stayed away from there after 1870, once the Papal States had been taken over, but in 1929, the Lateran Treaty guaranteed the Vatican uninterrupted custody of the villas, and soon they returned. Pius XI was the one to dust off the old walls, and he brought with him an elevator, the Vatican observatory, a world-famous collection of space rocks, and a whole agricultural complex of cattle and greenhouses. Thanks to his sagacity, during World War II Castel Gandolfo was able to provide, among other help, a daily allowance of milk to the local population, maternity and birthing care to pregnant refugees, and shelter and food to hundreds of Jews.

After the war, the building, which used to be rough masonry of uncertain color—a sort of gray, it seems from the period photographs, with a reddish hue—was renovated in smooth plaster, and today its five-story façade blends with the rest of the Liberty Square a warm shade of yellow that takes after a well-rummed eggnog, interrupted by foamy white window borders and crowned with a round clock high above a grandiose main entrance of dark wood decked out in gray stone panels. The square itself lies before it smallish in comparison and kind of unobtrusive: three-story buildings of the same palette, shutters of brown or green, the dome of the Pontifical College of St. Thomas of Villanova rising over the roofs at the opposite end. The whole look of it is just so clean and delicious, it is far less ornate than "The Wedding Cake" but certainly more appetizing.

The population of the town Castel Gandolfo does not reach even nine thousand souls, but tourism, of course, swells the number of people on any given day and brings most of the business. Artists like to display their pieces along the walls of the Liberty Square and around the fountain in its center, but that's on the days when a pope is not in residence—or at least not expected to show himself. On the summer day in 1953 when Jack and Leo threaded themselves closer and closer to the palace through the grinder of soaking bodies as if into a barrel of sauerkraut, there was no space for the artists' tripods. No space for anything.

"There were mobs and mobs of people," Len says, "and then a jam-packed square of however many thousands could squeeze into it, plus an extra thousand!"

They squeezed their way in with the churning masses, smudging sweat off strangers and mixing smells, losing sense in the mind-bending clamor, and they waited. They thought it was loud in the long, hot wait for the pope, but when Pius XII stepped out onto the balcony that reigned over the square at the fourth-story level of the palace, the racket that had been drowning their consciousness whipped itself into a world-consuming roar. The throngs howled, thundered, and shrieked, and their shrieks and howls bounced off the walls and reverberated, rendering anything the pontiff said impossible to discern.

Leo could see him up there in his white cassock. He could hear the pope speak first in Italian, then another language, and another. He could hear English but couldn't make it out. The pope raised his hands and spoke a blessing, and the frenzy that had felt to Leo at the level of tension impossible to top, swelled higher and swallowed the universe.

And then it was over. Pius XII turned and disappeared inside the palace, and insanity subsided, and little by little Leo's hearing returned, and so did his bearings. But he could still see in his mind's eye for a long time a fragile figure all in white, hands upraised in a blessing, carried up in the air on the wave of human passion.

And then, the adventure was over, too. The brothers hitched their way back to northern Italy and through Switzerland to France, to go back home. They were lucky and caught good rides: in the company of merry young people and many big bags, in the company of a kind and tired man who slept while Leo drove. They flew home over the Atlantic, and it looked different this time: no longer the world's expanding boundary, just an ocean in a big world.

Leo and Jack had always been good brothers, but, aged almost six years apart, they had not always been friends. Friends they became in 1953 and remained until Jack died in early 2007. Len misses his brother palpably. I can see it in the slight trembling of his eyelashes, the upward curling of the corners of his lips.

"I wish you could have met Jack," he says to me often. "You would have really liked him."

CHAPTER 11

"Their Exits and Their Entrances": graduate studies, here and abroad

He felt that his whole life was some kind of dream and he sometimes wondered whose it was and whether they were enjoying it.

—DOUGLAS ADAMS, *THE HITCHHIKER'S GUIDE TO THE GALAXY*

MARQUETTE UNIVERSITY IN MILWAUKEE is a Jesuit school that has the honor of having become the first co-ed Catholic institution of higher learning in the world in 1909. When Leo began his Master's program there in 1954, it was his first co-ed experience as well.

Leo studied English literature, especially T. S. Eliot and the New Critics. He studied Modern European History and wrote his thesis on the Nuremberg Trials and the Holocaust. He took seminars in philosophy. This was the time when Existentialism was exciting and new, and Professor Donald Gallagher had just returned from a year in France on a Fulbright Exchange. The classroom walls reverberated with the names of Camus, Sartre, and Marcel. Soaked for years in medieval scholasticism, Leo inhaled contemporary thought like inebriating fumes. Phenomenology of Merleau-Ponty, Maurice Blondel's "philosophy of action," Henri Bergson's multiplicity . . . The Cold War drew attention to the questions of individual freedom and responsibility: Nikolai Berdyaev, Emmanuel Mounier . . .

Marquette would not destroy Leo's foundation of Thomistic thought, but it would open his eyes to a choice of quirky architectures from which to build his castle. This would be an ever-growing castle, never again the same.

And then, there was theater.

Len doesn't remember the title of the play, only that it was written by a young professor from the University of Wisconsin at Madison—the only U Wisconsin in those days. The action took place in Lidice during WWII. The Nazis razed this tiny village near Prague as a reprisal for the assassination of Reinhard Heydrich, one of the highest-ranking Nazi officials and architects of the Holocaust, SS-Obergruppenführer, the founder of SD— Nazi intelligence and Gestapo's sister agency. Hitler called him "the man with the iron heart." Two soldiers, a Slovak and a Czech, blew up Heydrich in his car not far from Lidice, and its residents were thought to have aided the attackers—as it turned out, mistakenly. On June 10, 1942, the village was blockaded, its men lined up against the wall and shot, women sent to concentration camps, most never to return. Some children were given to SS families to be "germanized"; the majority, gassed.

Himmler meant for Lidice to vanish from history, but it lives. Around the globe, towns, streets, and parks have been named after it, and the village was rebuilt to welcome home after the war those few who survived. A memorial to its murdered children is connected to the new village site by an avenue of linden trees.

In the play written by an American professor in the 1950s, a local German officer knocks on the door of a Lidice family on the eve of the massacre, comes into their living room, and tells them what's about to happen. Leo played the father.

RA   Len, you acted once in high school, didn't you? And now at Marquette. Did you like it? Did you do it again?

LS   A little bit. The following year, when I went to Madison to the University of Wisconsin, there was a poster there. The same young professor was going to put up the play on TV, and I tried out and got the part of the Nazi officer. That was my TV debut and finale. It was very early in television: TV came to Green Bay in 1953, and this was '55 or '56, pretty new. Black and white, of course. It was all live, I think—so get it right, and that was it. They'd pan in and out with two cameras.

The night of the performance I was supposed to look straight into the camera, and I forgot my lines, so I fudged them somehow. Andie was watching at home, and she knew I forgot them because she had helped me prepare, but she said no one else would know I'd forgotten. True love.

RA   And that's it, never again?

LS   After Wisconsin, circumstances just didn't present themselves. I'm a bit of a ham, you know, so I enjoyed it. I do all these imitations of accents, but . . . Well, "all the world's a stage," right? But not on stage. I've always wanted to be an actor like I wanted to be a tenor.

RA   What happened?

LS   All you have to do is listen to my voice.

RA   I mean, to acting.

LS   I transferred it to my teaching.

RA   How much theater is in your teaching?

LS   Considerably more now than before. I'm much more at ease. I don't do it very often, but I play roles for a few words. And I do like to play with words when I teach—and even when I'm not teaching, as you know. But I am often saddened by the impossibility of utilizing the huge repertoire of Latin jokes and puns that I have. No one understands them anymore, and explaining jokes . . . you know. You might say, I am a pathological punster. Strangely, you know, Andie was excellent at it in the early stages of her Alzheimer's. She hadn't been a punster originally, but, of course, she lived with one, and then, at one point in her disease, she began to come up with these new, cross-lingual puns.

Arlene "Andie" Anderson entered Leonard Swidler's life at U Wisconsin, where they both, always-starving graduate students, were members of an eating co-op at the school's Newman Center. She swept him off his feet, re-fashioned him from Leo into Len, and it didn't take her nearly the two years they spent in Madison.

The Newman Center, the locus of all things Catholic on any large enough and self-respecting campus, naturally offered more than food but a bubbling, chaotic student life, and Len's memories of UW mostly revolve around that social club of a place: the nuclear physics student who played a mean boogie-woogie in the rec room, the lectures by Bishop John J. Wright and Father Bruchberger, a French cleric whose book on the life of Christ was all the rage. Together with Andie they started a *schola cantorum* for Sunday Masses at the Newman Chapel and chanting the vespers with a few grad students before dinner.

Incidentally, it was at this chapel after Mass one winter Sunday morning that Len crystallized in his mind the meaning of the word "irony." The worshipers were asked to leave their things in the vestibule and dutifully did so. Having returned to his backpack after the service, however, Len discovered that an ethics textbook, from which he was teaching at a nearby junior college, was missing from his bag. Three days later, he saw his stolen volume on morality for sale in a used-books store.

Len recalls it now with a smile. To be sure, many things of Madison make him smile. But nothing compares with the famous Catholic Arts Festival—a national, juried exhibition held at the Newman Center. His first year in Madison, Len browsed the pieces on display and basked in their splendor. He thought he couldn't love it more. It seemed only natural that, come next year, an idea somehow materialized that he should run the Festival—except, anything Len Swidler touches tends to grow in his hands into a grandiose undertaking, and the 1957 event became the Christian Arts Festival that included artists from any Christian denomination and broadened the media beyond visual arts to drama, music, and readings.

Len directed a production of the morality play *Everyman*, where he, unsurprisingly, cast himself as the Voice of God. Andie organized and performed in an evening of dramatic readings, and one of her friends put together a concert of sacred music. His face turns happy and wrinkly when he piles up details one upon another for me—memories of the best of times. "It was all just . . . a great success," he says.

They left Madison, not knowing if anyone would take up the reins, if their short tradition would continue, but yes or no, they left with easy hearts; their greatest yet and most thrilling challenges awaited. They were just married, and Len had received a grant from the German Academic Exchange to study Modern European Intellectual History at Tübingen

University—a part of his doctoral work. They were going to Germany. Everything was changing.

After a May wedding, the newly minted Mr. and Mrs. Swidler began to make plans for their move across the ocean. Unfortunately, like an overgrown garden, reality can look pretty from afar, but we become messily entangled in logistics the minute we step into it.

Len's grant gave him enough money to move and begin his dissertation research, not enough for two people to live on. Arlene, on the other hand, still had a teaching position at Valparaiso University that she'd held before the wedding, so it was decided that he would go ahead to Europe and she would join him at Christmas, after saving some money over the fall semester. What the newlyweds didn't know was that by September, when Len boarded his boat, Andie was already pregnant with their first child. Four months' worth of days poured like cooling molasses, but in snowy and garland-filled Tübingen she finally arrived in December, already in maternity clothes.

In the meantime, Len Swidler came to Tübingen knowing exactly what—and whom—he was after. Professor Heinrich Fries was the best-known spokesperson for the then-revolutionary *Una Sancta* movement: a dialogue in Germany between Catholics and Protestants, and Len's dissertation topic. Ironically, the Protestant faculty of theology at U Tübingen had an ecumenical institute attached to it, but the Catholic faculty had nothing, only Heinrich Fries's lone voice for dialogue. He was a professor of Fundamental Theology, a philosophical attempt to show that, even though theology is based in belief, it can be engaged intellectually, through reason. Both of these pursuits excited Len to no end, and Prof. Fries became both his subject of study and his mentor, so when the University of Munich offered Fries to establish an institute just for him in addition to a chair in theology, without hesitation Len followed his advisor.

RA   Len, would you call Heinrich Fries a friend?

LS   I guess I'd say I became friends with him. It was not in the same way as I did later with Bernard Häring, but that's partly because we were always speaking German, and I was still learning. With Häring we spoke English—his choice.

Fries was a very open person. He had this gorgeous red-head housekeeper, who had a young daughter. She was a war widow herself. I thought it was a breath of fresh air to see the very human, friendly relationship the three of them had. I have no idea if there was anything below the surface.

RA Does it matter to you?

LS In a certain sense. Not in the sense your question implies, like I would be judgmental.

RA Yet you brought it up. Why?

LS It would be an interesting insight into male-female relationships and how this was or was not reflected in theology.

RA What do you mean?

LS At the time I thought nothing of it, but you think back, and the whole question of mandatory celibacy for priests comes to mind.

RA It is fairly clear you are not in favor of priestly celibacy rules as they are now.

LS To begin with, there is firm New Testament evidence that several, if not all, of the named followers of Jesus were married. We have no positive evidence about Jesus himself one way or the other, but since all rabbis married and Jesus was reported to have read from the scriptures, some scholars argue his marriage is presumed.

They were Jewish, you realize, and in Judaism marriage and sex were considered a true good. Holy. However, as soon as Jesus' teaching spread outside of Judaism into the Greco-Roman world, it encountered an extreme dualistic mentality: the body is bad, the spirit is good. That's what has led—and still leads—to our widespread efforts to limit bodily pleasure. This is abstinence, fasting, asceticism of all sorts—and celibacy.

Now in Eastern Christianity they stopped at limiting the role of bishops to celibates from the third century onward, and in Western Christianity there've been greater or lesser attempts from the fourth century on to make priestly celibacy mandatory, and they succeeded in the twelfth century, though not infrequently honored more in the breach.

RA   I hear what you're saying: priestly celibacy is not rooted in the Bible or in the life of Jesus himself. But the third pillar of Catholic doctrine is tradition, acknowledged and overt, fluid and accumulating. Isn't there something to be said for customs, laws, maybe interpretation of laws that develop with time? We do a whole lot of things that aren't in the Bible, refuse to obey some commandments that are. Times change.

LS   Yes. Look. Various pious reasons are given for mandatory priestly celibacy. A big one is that a priest must be free to devote his life entirely to serving God, which of course implies that noncelibates are *ipso facto* also-rans. Obviously, such claims are lies. Just think of other, noncelibate professionals: Orthodox married priests, Protestant ministers, medical personnel, social workers, police . . .

The true reason for mandatory celibacy is two-fold. The first is the continued prevalence of the "bad body, good spirit" mentality. The second is that celibacy gives the hierarchy almost total control over the clergy and, through them, over the laity.

RA   You believe the rules should be changed, I assume.

LS   I hope that Francis will call a representative council, which will make priestly celibacy optional. As I was saying about my Doktorvater Fries, I had an impression of family from his living, and it was good. I never knew the nature of it, but in my recollection, it was a very wholesome relationship.

RA   Did your friendship continue with Prof. Fries?

LS   Oh, yes. I translated some of his books. One was *Resignation in the Church*, where he argued that we should not resign ourselves to the wrong but keep at it always for reform. He was my kind of guy. You know, he had an outstanding sense of humor and was very persuasive. They invited him to go to Vatican II, but he didn't, and I never had a chance to ask him why.

It was Heinrich Fries whom Len approached, shortly after his arrival in Tübingen, with what was then a unique request: to work toward a degree in theology. Professor's eyebrows climbed: these were the 1950s, and the animal called "lay theologian" had yet to evolve. Both men, of course, knew this, but Len insisted: he had done work in Latin, Greek, philosophy, and theology, and nowhere did he see a good reason, either rational or legal, to shut him out.

Fries shook his head: if anything stood between Leonard Swidler and his goal, it would not be reason but tradition. No modern pontifical Catholic theological faculty had granted a theology degree to a layperson—but all right, he would take up the topic with the faculty. Believe it or not, soon the decision was made to start a new tradition.

This is how Leonard Swidler became, as far as he knows, the first layperson in modern times to earn a degree in Catholic theology. He was granted a Licentiate in Sacred Theology from the University of Tübingen in 1959 and returned to America with much to brag about: a new achievement, a new family, a new home culture, and a whole new perspective.

Talking to Len

(On student rebellion and the popes)

RA   Len, you made some remarkable connections while you studied in Germany in the late fifties, didn't you? This is when you first took a class from and corresponded with Hans Küng, now one of the most famous—and controversial—theologians of our time, who became your close and lifelong friend. But, let's start with Joseph Ratzinger, better known as Pope Benedict XVI. What's the story? How well do you know him?

LS   I met him then, and met him again when he was Cardinal Archbishop of Munich in 1979–80. I was becoming involved in the Oberammergau Passion Play then, working with them to bring historicity into it and clean up its traditional Antisemitism—but more on that later. He wrote me a letter thanking me for my work with the Passion committee, and that's our only personal contact after Tübingen. At Tübingen University, he was on the faculty while I was there and for a while after I left. In our first issue of the *Journal of Ecumenial Studies*, in 1964, we published an article of his. In a way, you know, he was no big deal yet. He was a deal, but not a big one.

RA   You once said Professor Ratzinger "ran away" from Tübingen in 1971. What do you mean by that?

LS   Yes, "running away" is exactly the right verb to use. In '71 he left Tübingen and went to the University of Regensburg in Bavaria, one of the ten new universities that West Germany created because the medieval universities they had were overflowing with students. Doing that is like leaving Harvard to go to a community college in Oklahoma. It's not even going sideways but downward!

RA   Let's leave aside the question of what's wrong with an Oklahoma community college. Why did he leave?

LS   Pretty obviously because of the terrible experience he had with the students' rebellion at TU. He was incapable of handling it— unlike Hans Küng, who handled it so well that the students held a "torch light parade" when the Vatican attacked him, about the same time, in the late sixties. So there is this interesting sort of context: the different ways they responded.

RA   We all have heard of the 1968 student riots in Europe, especially France, and especially Paris. "The revolution that never was." But this is Germany. What were the rebellions really about?

LS   Well . . . I would say, pseudo-Marxist. That mentality was rife around the world, and Marxism was still avant-garde for a lot of people. It was going to be put into force, by force, from below, that kind of thing. It really swept across the world—a manifestation of revolution from below—and several dimensions came together to "push" this mentality: Vatican II, the Civil Rights movement, the war on poverty. I'd say, it was one of the creations of the baby boomer generation. The "greatest generation" came out of the Great Depression and fought in WWII, then went on to have the baby boom and tried to create the world of suburbia. Of course, the sixties and seventies rebelled against that.

RA   And, if I'm not mistaken, he started out on that liberal path himself, didn't he?

LS   Joe Ratzinger? Oh, he was and worked as a moderate reformer during the Second Vatican Council. In fact, he was a *peritus* for Cardinal Frings of Cologne—an expert advisor—and one of the leaders of the reform effort. Ratzinger started out a good scholar—a young scholar at the time—doing the research and writing work for Frings. Hans Küng was a *peritus* not for any particular bishop but for the Council as a whole.

During the Council Küng and Ratzinger were on the same side, on the side of liberal reformers, which was Ratzinger's mentality at the time—but the student rebellion obviously so scarred his psyche that he basically turned hyper-conservative. Come to think of it, this is very similar to what happened to Pope Pius IX. He was elected in 1846 as a liberal, and all of Europe was expecting him to clean up the open sore that was the Papal States—and he started, but then, too bad for him, there flared up the year of revolutions all around, including Garibaldi, who killed his Secretary of State. He had to flee for his life and was eventually brought back to Rome behind French bayonets, which experience so traumatized him that he became the reactionary that history now remembers. I think something like that happened to Ratzinger. Students taking over his classes . . . frightening.

I remember once I was in Munich visiting Prof. Fries when Joe was the Archbishop. Prof. Fries and I were talking at dinner, and he mentioned how priests of the archdiocese resented Ratzinger because of his arbitrary, authoritarian manner. Then he was quickly catapulted to head of the Holy Office under John Paul II, where, naturally, this manner of his continued.

RA   Then, what would you say of his almost unprecedented retirement from the papacy?

LS   It's an extraordinarily positive move, this I must say. Might be a little ironic, but it is exactly what he'd advocated earlier, while he was at Tübingen. I think that this action on his part is going to have ramifications for the future of the church not only at the level of the papacy but all the way down. I envision people saying, "If the pope can resign, why shouldn't bishops resign? Why shouldn't Monsignor Hooligan resign? Why let them get old and sick? Why wait until they are seventy-five? There is a more rational way of doing it."

RA   Have you ever tried to contact the pope, discuss policy, bring issues to his attention? After all, you knew each other when you were young and liberal.

LS   I wrote him two public letters. The first one was something I just tossed off, and I thought that was going to be the end of that, but in fact it went sort of viral. I was surprised. I recall writing it because, as head of the Holy Office, he took some actions and issued some documents concerning women—and didn't consult with any women. So my letter in effect was, "Dear Joseph, what you say may or may not be true, but you should really consult with women before going off on your own."

And then, when he was pope, he attacked a group of priests in Austria, and again I thought, *Why didn't he consult them?* So again, I wrote, "Dear Joe." This went even more viral. There is a French translation and, I think, a Spanish translation. I was astonished.

RA   Any reaction from the pope?

LS   No. I think there was some guy, an international lawyer, who knew the public relations person for Benedict, who made sure a copy was sent to him. So I think there is a reasonable likelihood that he may have seen it, though response was null.

I wasn't surprised, of course. Let me tell you about one episode. Then-Cardinal Ratzinger wrote an essay, in which he attacked relativism as something to be staunched, and named two terrible protagonists of it: Paul Knitter and John Hick, both my good friends. It was terrible. For openers, he referred to the Presbyterian Hick as Episcopalian, which is bad enough. But a real intellectual blunder was that he had a series of quotations from Knitter he disagreed with, and he took them from a book by some other author written in Italian. You understand? He was quoting Italian translations of Knitter while writing in German. You don't do that as a scholar.

We'd had a similar situation before with a different author, and it sparked some excellent dialogue, so I approached Ratzinger with the same question: Would he allow us to use his essay and gather responses, and so on—and never heard back. I found a fax number of the Holy Office and sent the invitation again by fax, and I got a phone call one day from a young priest in the Washington nunciature. He said that Cardinal Ratzinger asked him to call me and thank me very much, but the Cardinal was too busy to accept this invitation.

I said, "Well, there is no time limit. If he can't do it by November 1, then how about December 1?"

There was a pause, and he said, "He doesn't make commitments this far in advance."

I said, "I get the message. He doesn't want to respond at all, right?"

The priest just sort of chuckled over there. That was one of our most direct contacts since his cardinalate.

RA   What do you think about Pope Francis?

LS   Francis is clearly committed to a Christianity that is active in the world, one that tries to bring holiness to all—that is, "holiness" which is "wholeness," you know. He points especially to those who one way or another are not "whole," usually made so by society's attitude and treatment, like the poor, sexually non-mainstream, victims of violence . . .

RA   I assume you are encouraged by his gestures of simplicity and humility, crossing boundaries with religions, hinting at reconciliation with women, his whole lifestyle we are so unaccustomed to seeing in the Vatican.

LS   He is definitely a "big tent" type of leader—a church rather than a sect. I don't think he is aiming to reform any major doctrines or practices directly, though celibacy for priests might be an exception. Rather, he is at work changing the Catholic consciousness—and *catholic*, universal consciousness, too. From the moment he chose the name of Francis he was doing it. He asked the people to bless him first, before he blessed them, then rode back to the hotel on the bus with the cardinals, and paid for his hotel bill—all those small things become world-changing. He is refocussing Catholic and world attention on reaching out and helping persons, all persons, but especially the marginalized, rather than on following rules and doctrines.

RA   Speaking of reaching out to the marginalized, what do you think of the newly minted adoration of Pope Francis from the LGBT community? He was just declared the person of the year by an LGBT magazine, *The Advocate*. This is absolutely unheard of.

LS   And yet, not surprising, I think. His remark *inter alia* about homosexuals was, "Who am I to judge?" And it's like nuclear fusion—can power a star to give enough light to produce a whole new life! The Vatican had been judging and condemning them for centuries, but he is changing Christianity to be a thing of joy and love rather than finger-wagging and scowls.

RA   So, you are hopeful?

LS   It is not naïve hope, but let me say this: If he can live and persist for another eight or ten years, Catholics will then suddenly say to each other, "We used to think such-and-such, but we don't any more. How did that happen?" And the answer will be: Francis.

CHAPTER 12

Do We Not Bleed? Healing the Oberammergau Passion Play

Jesus said, "Father, forgive them, for they do not know what they are doing."

—LUKE 23:34

OBERAMMERGAU IS A COZILY sized Bavarian village of just over two thousand people, and it's regionally known for a couple of things—woodcarving and a NATO school—but it's world-famous for one: the 370-year-old tradition of the Passion Play. In the year 1633, the denizens of the village, embattled by the bubonic plague, made a vow to the Lord to perform the Passion in perpetuity if they were to be spared. The death rate did go down dramatically, and in 1634 performances began. For almost four centuries, with only a couple of exceptions for cataclysms like the Second World War, decennially Oberammergau has been putting on an enactment of Jesus' Passion that now takes several hours, runs from May to October, involves every resident of the village, and draws hundreds of thousands of spectators from every corner of the world.

For a long time, the effort was difficult to sustain economically, but our globalizing planet does have its pluses: The overwhelming tourist crowds that converge on this tiny nook in the Alps have redefined its economy completely. New business, new communal amenities . . . When the town needs something, the locals have a saying: "The Play will pay."

It all takes place outdoors, in a theater that, as of recent construction, seats 4,700 people. In 2010, the theater was packed for 102 days. Living tableaus and acted scenes, music, costumes, and sets—the scale and artistry of the Play are astonishing, especially considering that almost none of the participants are professionals. For the natives of Oberammergau, the Play is a birthright.

It has become inexorably a great—maybe, the greatest—part of Oberammergau's identity. Snuggled into a quaint mountain valley, the village buildings are frescoed with biblical scenes, its streets bear the names of Judas and Mary Magdalene. As if it were jealously watching the people that had become its own, the spirit of the Holy Week is sweeping through Oberammergau in the wind. The village became the Passion Play. Its life became the Vow. In a twist of thought-provoking irony, the natives like to call their hometown the "Alpine Jerusalem."

The irony I find in this self-chosen nickname doesn't come from Oberammergau's fame but from its infamy. Google "Oberammergau Passion Play," and you will see such words as "troubling," "infamous," "controversial," and "offensive" popping up next to "antisemitic" and "anti-Jewish." Since the beginning of any such conversation in the Western world, the Play has been as much lauded for its spectacular creativity as condemned for its rabid, overt, medieval Judeophobia. One distasteful measure of just how bad it was is the public approval that Adolf Hitler issued to the Play for its handling of the Jewish question. This was in 1934, for the tri-centennial celebration.

After the Second Vatican Council put forth its document on ecumenical and interreligious relations, *Nostra aetate*, the church directed Oberammergau to revise the script of its Passion. *Nostra aetate* devoted its largest section to Judaism, where the Council insisted that Jews as a nation were not to blame for Christ's death, that Judaism and Christianity were a theological family, and that Christian Antisemitism was unacceptable. They were going to a whole new height in interreligious relations. The Oberammergau Passion, meanwhile, still sported horned Jewish priests and a chorus proclaiming the "blood oath," which called the responsibility for the murder of Christ upon the heads of the Jews and their descendants. Judaism in it was villainous, Romans barely present, and Jesus decidedly Christian. In the rarified air of *Nostra aetate*, the Play smelled noxious.

The year was 1965. When the 1970 performance did not feature changes, the Vatican withheld its canonical approval. Oberammergau had ten years to find itself in step with the rest of the world, so the village began to fill with advisors, evaluators, and representatives. The Archbishop of Munich, Joseph Ratzinger, appointed a theological advisor. The Anti-Defamation League sent a team, and so did the American Jewish Committee. Some came to help adjust the script, others to critique and give suggestions for the future. Professor Swidler and his people came to build a bridge.

By 1979, when Rabbi Leon Klenicki of the ADL first talked to Len about leading the team, Len was no longer just a half-Jewish Christian but a half-Jewish Christian who'd devoted his life to dialogue. Whatever arguments one might have with his theory, it is hard to argue with one of Dialogue Decalogue's cardinal rules: We cannot define each other's identities. We certainly cannot step in from outside and redefine them. If I define myself—my whole identity as a Christian—in opposition to you, a Jew, you cannot show up and tell me I am wrong. What good will it do? You are the enemy. Not even my church can simply command me to change. I cannot be ordered to stop being me, I can only be ordered to obey.

This, I think, was the danger in Oberammergau when authority after authority, hierarchical and advisory, converged on a beleaguered, traditional little village to set it straight: Yes, the Play could be changed, it could be made more accurate historically and scripturally, certainly more politically correct, but if not careful, it would not become less antisemitic, just less honest.

Len Swidler knew this and more. He was a half-Jewish Christian devoting his life to dialogue, and he was a teacher. So when Oberammergau's Mayor Fink opened the village gates to them, he came, not to tell and not to correct, as much correcting as he might have wanted to do. He came, together with the creators of the Play, to explore: why and how they were doing it, why and how they might want to change something. How they might find a way better to follow in Jesus' footsteps. After all, that's what they wanted. After all, Jesus was a Jew. After all, a bishops' council had realized this, why not the citizens of Oberammergau? Len came to dialogue.

For thirty-plus years since then, he's been going back with his team to keep improving the script and the costumes, to talk about theology and symbolism. He involved friends and colleagues: Gerard Sloyan, a prominent Catholic theologian, came with Len on the very first trip; Ingrid Shafer, long a professor and practitioner of Jewish-Christian dialogue, translated the reformed text of the Play into English. He brought graduate students to help, among them Racelle Weiman, who became a flag-bearer for this cause and his others, who has been Len Swidler's faithful comrade since the first days of her graduate work until this day. She is now the Global Education Director of the Dialogue Institute.

Len didn't change the Play alone, nor were his team the only people trying to change it, but it has come a long way since 1980. When he describes the 2010 production, his face radiates the unbounded pride of a new graduate's grandfather: This now "blatantly Jewish" Jesus is his baby, and the Hebrew he prays from the stage is Len's triumph as surely as if he had taught it to the actor himself.

"I was in the audience in 2010," Len tells me, "and one of the people turned to me and said, 'This is a Jesus who is believable to modern persons!'"

He never forgets to mention this story. That's because he is bragging.[25]

---

25 See "Report" for a fairly balanced summary of progress and further recommendations from the Council of Centers on Jewish-Christian Relations.

Talking to Racelle Weiman

(On the Play, an endangered legacy, and traveling with Len)

RA   Racelle, how did you get involved in the Play?

RW   I came to Temple from Israel looking to do a theological reflection on Christian-Jewish relations and the Holocaust for a dissertation. I hadn't heard of Vatican II yet. And then I met the two Catholics: Swidler and Sloyan. In 1980, they were working on the Oberammergau Passion Play, and Swidler was the guy on the ground to take theology from its ivory tower and bring it to the people doing it, the simple people there. Helping the directors of the Play. I was the youngest in the group and the newest student.

RA   Did you find the work a success?

RW   The trips to Oberammergau were amazing, and the difference between 2000 and 2010 is staggering. I witnessed drastic changes: in the understanding of Jesus, his Jewishness, and more.

    It was Ingrid Shafer, Len, and I who went, and you know, the real workings of it is to see Len's labor with it. He was there from early to late summer, and they were still at the end fixing the sloppy theology. Every time. They learn from time to the next time, but very little: what they feel people will tolerate. It's about how Jewish to make Jesus and Mary, how to make Jesus say *Sh'ma Israel* in Hebrew, etc.

    The big thing, of course, is the drama. They had Judas who was really the only Jew in the group, and the rest looked very pale and Christian. Priests, like Pilate, looked very satanic, and in the script it was clear that Judas was forced by them to betray his teacher. Things like that. These passion plays all tended to be that way.

RA   What was Len like?

RW   Len was very patient and gentle, he would not shake his finger at them but would sit with them—a perfect bridge to his own community. Exactly what you need when there is misconception: a person they have reverence for and who wants them to get it right.

Once he asked me what I found problematic, and I said there were way too few Romans. Historically, Jews were puppets under Rome at that time, so any who looked like they were causing a riot were condemned, but where are the Romans in the Play? So Len told them about it, and they said, "We can't add any more; all the Romans run the concession stand outside."

Funny, right? The play is run by the village people. During breaks you need people to clean up and sell drinks, and that's done by people in bit parts, which is the Romans. So it had nothing to do with theology, but it misinformed the situation. Then we discussed how to create a more visible Roman influence: flags, more frequent passing of the existing Romans through the theater, and so on. It's one of those fun moments that illustrate how nothing is what it seems.

RA   What other issues did you work on with the villagers?

RW   Well, this is pre-Mel Gibson's *The Passion of the Christ*, but we had some of the same situations: Mary looked like a nun and priests were wearing horned helmets. What I mean is, costuming became a big issue. But the costumer was a fancy one, and you can't insult a fashion designer. See? Again, this was not theological. The question became, who can tell her how to modify the costumes?

RA   I know they got rid of the horns.

RW   Yes, and in 2010 they wrote up in their exhibition an "evolution" of the costumes away from Judeophobia. Then, of course, only the villagers are playing it—which means some racial homo-geneity—but this time, in 2010, they made the most German-looking, absolutely blondest guy to be Judas.

And Len would sit after the play with them. I, as a Jew, didn't do it. He did the internal conversation about what would be more honest, what would be more true and less stereotypical.

RA   This sounds like Len, but I've also heard him criticized for im-posing his style of dialogue. How open do you usually find him?

RW   What Len always brings into the room is a loose demarcation between students and faculty. He is never condescending to most ideas, and that engenders loyalty from students. There's no arrogance of academia with him.

He created a Christian-Jewish dialogue at German uni-versities, and there was incredible excitement there to see real, living dialogue, not just to read about it in books. Real struggle confronting the pain of the experience. And I said to Len, "We are not even stopping at a concentration camp." It was never even in his mind. I brought it up, and we decided we would all go to, I think, Dachau. Everybody wanted to go, all the Germans, too. Germans were killed there too, you know. Anyway, this was Len's program, but he was able to hear me. I realized this guy was different from a lot of others. We have different points of view often, but he gives audience.

RA   You've developed a long and close friendship, haven't you?

RW   I went through very difficult times during my program, and Len was the only one who cared that I finish my thesis. He wrote to me, stayed with us when he came through Israel, invited me to events in Europe—where I'd be the only Jewish woman, by the way. He kept me informed of his Trialogue conferences, Jewish-Christian-Muslim. I was one of his *Hasidim*, his disciple. And I ended up doing an incredible dissertation: the Vatican still didn't have diplomatic relations with Israel, and that's well after Vatican II. I asked questions about this long road to recognizing Israel, about repentance. I used the Dialogue Decalogue ideas and con-flict resolution, ethnic and religious. The year I came to defend, the Vatican recognized Israel, and I watched all the key players, all the problems: the canonization of Edith Stein, the convent at Auschwitz . . .

RA   What did Len think?

RW   That's a problem with Len. He was always saying he doesn't believe in these things so he doesn't think they are important. But
just because it's not important to him, it doesn't mean it's not
important to people on the top. He'll talk to anyone but not to
the conservatives in his own church. He'll talk *at* them but not *to*
them. He says you can't talk to extremists, but most of them are
not. He just . . . doesn't do that "intra" dialogue.

RA   Do you disagree on any other issues?

RW   Well, in Macedonia, when I told him that the Bektashi voices
were being destroyed by the Sunni community, he said it was
too bad but did nothing. I said, "You should talk to the Sunni or
to the Macedonian Orthodox about protecting this minority."
But he doesn't get involved with that. He is a networker but not
a human-rights activist. He is not there for the cause. The same
thing happens when I say, "You are not just there to dialogue
with the majority." But he's so open to everybody, he doesn't
question people's motivations.

Here's another example. We were both invited to Bangla-
desh to speak, but suddenly Len gets a visa and I don't, because
their ministry of interior doesn't want a Jew talking about Jews.
So the question is for Len: Do you leave your Jewish partner
and go anyway? He went, and said he would mention this in his
presentation, and his mention was, "It's too bad all of us cannot
be here." So this is about human rights and the fight for them.
The principles of the Decalogue.

RA   Do you think Len is naïve? Too focused on a goal? Has a priorities problem?

RW   Len assumes others use the same terminology he does, but it's
not always so. For example, some Saudis decide they would be
"dialogical," but it really means they want others to be sympathetic to their position. And China is "opening up" to anybody,
so Len is willing to go to this still-Communist country, which is

brutal to the Dalai Lama, where religions are not safe. Same with the Saudis. You can't even bring a Bible there. All those many Filipinos can't have a Mass. It's totally repressive, but Len goes there and doesn't mention religious liberties. It's not enough to mention women's veils.

We've spent a lot of time with Azeri people. One of our associates was from Azerbaijan, stayed and worked here. She says that as a Muslim she is weeping because Wahhabism came into the country, and this former Soviet republic that had had 100 percent women's graduation rate now only has 80 percent, and it keeps going down. How do you go backwards? And Len has no comment and no involvement. Talking about legacy and the next generation.

RA   Do you think that he is making inroads into oppressive societies and tackling one thing at a time, creating ties? Maybe, he thinks that, if you attack all issues at once, you alienate people and then lose the proverbial war for the sake of one battle?

RW   That's not his explanation. What appears to me . . . I think, Len doesn't realize how really evil and devious people are. He is very much a naïve and sweet guy, especially now that he's older. He comes from such kindness that he doesn't believe the other can see differently than he does.

Thursday we were at Ground Zero with the Temple program for students from Iraq, Lebanon, and Turkey—and an Iraqi girl asked a survivor of 9/11 whose father was killed, "Isn't it true that Al Qaeda was just an operative of the American government?" She meant that we did it to ourselves. I'd told Len that they believe these conspiracy theories that we'd created an excuse to go to war with them. I mentioned to Len that it would happen, four years in a row: these lovely young people believe these awful things. But Len doesn't get it. He believes so much in critical thinking . . . When he heard this, he said, "Oh my God, I have to fix my hearing aid! You didn't just say that!" And so on.

I think he just doesn't get people who aren't critical thinkers. He acted like he was floored by this idea. This is a criticism now, it's not a good thing, you understand.

RA   You can't dialogue with a phantom; you have to see the person in front of you.

RW   That's it. Reality.

RA   This is a serious criticism, and hard to reconcile with the kind of work you've described Len doing in places like Oberammergau. But you still enjoy working with him?

RW   Len is one of the best people I know, and he does a tremendous amount of good. We did several Trialogues of scholars together. I went to Macedonia with him in 2003 and to Indonesia in 2000. In Indonesia it was right after the dictatorship, and one of Len's students became a foreign minister, Alwi Shihab. They discussed having a dialogue using the idea that religion is the cornerstone of their constitution, even though Judaism is not recognized among the five religions they officially have.

        Jews are invisible in Indonesia. There used to be a community there, and there are still islands that have a presence, but in reality . . . Len created a relationship with them and asked for a dialogue of Abrahamic faiths, found five Jews: four rabbis and me. We went to Indonesia, and I saw Len in action. It's a beautiful sight!

        There were the head of Indonesia and Prince Hassan of Jordan, and Len represented the Christians, really. Len was wonderful: he made sure that in no way he'd go overboard but that Jewish representatives were treated like everybody else—as honored guests. But the most wonderful thing there was to see that Len was the most important figure in the room, on the level of the President of Indonesia and Prince Hassan. You could sense international reverence for him.

        You know, abroad, Len is treated as the "wise man." He is at the level of princes and presidents—overseas, in the non-Western world. We love him here, but there . . . Not because he does anything different, either. The way he works, he does immediate follow-up with people he meets, he doesn't let the ball drop. Of course, he puts people on his listservs right away.

RA   Oh, those listservs of Len's! Sometimes I wonder if he doesn't publicly broadcast every email he writes.

RW   Yes, it's good and bad, but he brings people into the fold. He sees people without bias—anyone who comes up to him. He is the great connector. He was doing networking before anyone had used that word. In Indonesia, we were able to create a great amount of cachet with the ministry of education and foreign affairs.

RA   You admire him.

RW   There is a way in which Len and I are quite alike. Right before I began directing the Dialogue Institute, in 2006, the last project I did in my previous job Len got involved in, and it's really illustrative.

The Chancellor of Hebrew Union College, Rabbi Alfred Gottschalk, was born in Germany, and when *Kristallnacht* happened, his town was destroyed, and this little boy and his mother got out but left behind a grandfather, who didn't want to go. The grandfather died right before Treblinka of natural causes, and no one knew where he was buried.

Now Rabbi Gottschalk was this incredible person, the leader of Reform Judaism, and couldn't find his grandfather's grave, but in 2006, a German couple found the grave in a Jewish cemetery, and he wanted to put a tombstone on it and to engrave the names of the family killed in the Holocaust. I said it should be an occasion, not just for family. There should be Jews and Christians going and making this village realize the occasion.

This was all happening in Oberwesel on the Rhine. The place has a terrible history of blood libel in the Middle Ages, sixteenth century. They'd found a Christian body upstream, and blood libel ensued, and this Werner became a saint. And when sainthood was taken away from blood libel "victims," it upset people.

Anyway, forty-seven people got bussed into the village, Protestant and Catholic and Jewish, and all dialogued. Len helped me set it up. But the best story is the story of our incredible network. The Germans on the ground wanted to put up a monument in the old synagogue and to do an outreach event after we got to the grave site to put up the tomb. It would cost about 40,000 Deutschmark. In the town, some were for and some against it. The supporters said there'd be a vote in two days in the council. Len and I decided to write an open letter to the town: how wonderful it is that they are welcoming the Jews in the person of this famous rabbi, that they have the open mind to go through repentance, the kind of Christianity we adore . . . In other words, positive not negative. The newspapers promised to print it, and we sent it to all the big Christians in English here in the network and had them sign it within twenty-four hours, over a hundred major signatures. I don't know if we embarrassed the town into doing it or not, but they did it. That's one of the things, I think, that turned around into Len's offering me the director-ship: turning anti-dialogic people into dialogic.

It's an amazing feeling, you know: Wherever I go, people say, "I know that man. I know his work." That's a legacy for him.

RA   Len is turning eighty-five. I imagine, legacy is becoming im-portant to him not only in the work he's done but in who will continue it and how. People like you.

RW   Of course. But he should be more honored. Temple's Religion Department today doesn't know well enough who Leonard Swidler is. For his eightieth birthday, people from around the world came to celebrate him, people of the highest caliber. And the accolades! And not a single member of the department showed up. There is no prophet in his own land.

RA   Do you think of Len as a prophet?

RW   Well . . . He certainly doesn't think of himself that way. You know the way he dresses?

RA   You mean whatever's slightly clean with no more than five holes in it?

RW   Right. We were in Scotland when he was to speak before the Scottish parliament, and he travels with a bag like your back-pack. He was about to go before the parliament, and he had no suit! I had to hijack him and take him to a department store. But when he put on the suit, he looked so good! You know, it is still the suit he wears.

Talking to Len
(On loving persons, rationality, and being liked)

RA   Len, you just showed me a card from Racelle Weiman, a col-
      league of over thirty years and a friend. Why are you surprised
      by the admiration and sincerity in its tone?

LS   I always find it surprising when people like me.

RA   Whenever somebody likes you, you're surprised?

LS   It really is true.

RA   Don't a lot of people like you?

LS   True.

RA   So have you not made the conclusion that it's not a surprising
      development?

LS   Psychologically, it's still surprising.

RA   You are a peace-maker with a sense of humor.

LS   I haven't thought of myself that way, really.

RA   "Blessed are the peace-makers."

LS   [*laughs*] I guess I'm like the vast majority. Ninety-plus percent of
      people are benevolent.

RA   Well . . . I would agree that most people are basically benevolent. To a degree. The majority of that majority thinks small in its benevolence. We are benevolent toward family and friends, sometimes toward neighbors and our immediate encounters. That's why we have wars and prejudice and intercultural, inter-religious, interracial violence. In order to get this majority of us to be benevolent toward "the other," you have to introduce "the other" right into our faces. Get us Muslim neighbors, and we can say, "Oh, these are people just like me." *You* are able to be benevolent on a large scale, which is a very precious quality.

LS   I'm a reasonably good guy, okay.

RA   You've accused Christian Antisemites of being irrational. You find Antisemitism immoral, but what boggles your mind is that they are irrational. And yet you find a pattern in your own life that's founded on good reason, and you are surprised every time you encounter it!

LS   Well, okay, but there is an inner voice that says, "Be careful Len you don't become prideful!"

RA   The "Catholic guilt"?

LS   I know! "I'm Catholic, and I'm sorry!"

RA   Well, you don't have to worry; not everybody likes you, and people who like you don't think you're a saint.

LS   [*laughs*] I know, that's true. It's interesting, of course, but it's also disappointing. You know, what I think of as my coming into a certain modicum of wisdom is simply to recognize the obvious: This is where you are, and that's okay. To be really able to say to myself: You are not a saint, you're really just trying, and it's okay. It's okay to be where you are.

RA   It *is* okay.

LS   Hey, I'm eighty-four! I've been working for a long time, and I'm really very lucky! I've got lots of good friends.

RA   . . . who like you.

LS Yeah, I can feel that. I really have to love persons. Like, all persons, you know?

RA What do you mean?

LS I love my students, especially the ones who come and have some little concern—or a big concern. I guess especially I love those who are somehow speaking or reaching out to me, so that it's person-to-person. It's why I love you.

RA You love the ones you encounter.

LS Yes. Right.

CHAPTER 13

"One Man in His Time": Hans Küng, the global ethic, and the founding of ARCC

To live honestly, we must strive, confuse, mistake, begin, and quit—and always fight and sacrifice. Contentment is turpitude of the soul.

—Leo Tolstoy, *War and Peace*

Professor Küng and Len Swidler almost missed each other at Tübingen University. A Swiss priest and theologian educated in Rome and the Sorbonne, Küng was invited to Tübingen in 1958 to replace Len's Doktorvater Fries, so they corresponded then only briefly about publishing Len's dissertation, but it was enough to create a connection, and a connection would lead to a friendship that has endured through decades, distance, and occasional discord.

It really began a few years later, in the early sixties. Len had started teaching at Duquesne University in Pittsburgh and was busy developing a theology department there, looking to bring in exciting people, looking for an inspiring start. Küng's first major book had just come out, *The Council, Reform and Reunion*, in response to Pope John XIII's announced intention to convene the Second Vatican Council, and so Len sent him a letter: *Come to Pennsylvania for a year. Change the scenery. Teach.* Küng wasn't opposed, but by 1963 the book's popularity was growing so quickly that his trip to America became a speaking tour of theology's new rising star.

He started with Harvard and went everywhere, drawing mobs and selling out venues. At the White House, he shook John F. Kennedy's hand; in St. Louis, he received an honorary doctorate. At Duquesne, Prof. Swidler set up his lecture in the biggest hall they had—the one that seated 1,500 people—and added chairs onstage, behind the speaker, but two weeks in advance of the date, the ticket supply ran out well before the demand did. The organizers sent out notices: *Do not come if you don't have a ticket!* All, of course, was in vain. On the day, hundreds showed up to storm the auditorium doors, and there could have been trouble if the Duquesne techies hadn't piped the microphone sound to the outside.

It was an exciting time, 1963—Vatican II in full swing, Hans Küng's lecture called "The Church and Freedom." He was thirty-two years old.

Yet, not everyone was so enthusiastic. Hans Küng declared himself from the outset and would remain for the rest of his life a voice of criticism in the church—full of loving concern but also ruthlessly frank. Reading *The Council, Reform and Reunion,* many Catholics took his analysis of the church's worldliness and sin as an attack; many found his insistence on decentralization disturbing; other complaints abounded. A number of dioceses—Philadelphia, DC, Los Angeles—banned the speaking tour from their territories. The book was making waves, and the adventure had just begun.

Vatican II swept through the early sixties like an ocean wave, leaving the Catholic world woken up and drenched, and Hans Küng, one of the principal writers of the Council, seemed to be riding the wave high—stirring up controversy and changing minds. But the climate changed with the passing of John Paul I in 1978, and so did Küng's life. Bold moves would soon bring consequences.

Several years after Vatican II, in 1971, Küng would come out publicly against the doctrine of papal infallibility in his *Infallible? An Inquiry,* and, though not until 1979, it would lead him into an interrogation by the department in Rome known in the vernacular as the Holy Office. Until about a century ago, it was officially called the Supreme Sacred Congregation of the Roman and Universal Inquisition. Today we call it CDF: the Congregation for the Doctrine of the Faith. Of course, *by any other name . . .*

In December 1979, the Holy Office stripped Hans Küng of his license to teach Catholic theology, but Tübingen kept him on as a professor of ecumenical theology. This was after his enormous, groundbreaking volume *On Being a Christian* and just before *Does God Exist? An Answer for Today.* He wrote on world religions and dialogue; on a global, unifying ethic that gives all humanity a common moral ground; on the church and its reform—tirelessly, stubbornly, dozens of books. He received awards and wrote again.

In 1998 he published *On Dying with Dignity*, a Catholic scholar's argument for euthanasia. A new tornado of controversy whipped itself into a frenzy, but the Holy Office couldn't do much more to him short of excommunication, and they didn't go there. He is eighty-six years old now and has Parkinson's disease; he is not hiding the thought that keeps him up at night: that maybe he, too, would want help one day to end his life with dignity, when it is emptied of the things that make it meaningful—writing, seeing, self-expression.

One of Küng's later books, from 2006, that caught a lot of attention from the general readership is *Why I Am Still a Christian.* It isn't scholarly as much as personal, and unlike his usual issue of intimidating monographs, it is slim, even short. It's a reflection—maybe a confession—and it asks this question: In the face of the painfully apparent ugliness of the church, its corruption, its cowardice, its conceit and hypocrisy, its abuse of its own and rejection of the neighbor, after all the suffering the church has inflicted on its faithful son Hans—what is the value in being a Christian? What is the difference between the tradition and the institution? Can the church's battered child persevere in his faith?

Küng's answer is, "Yes." He talks about the values Christianity has to offer humanity, and he stands vulnerable and hopeful, but I find hope in this book mixed with the melancholy of its title. That Hans Küng feels he must justify his Christianity—to us or to himself—is by itself a thought that keeps me up at night.

RA   Len, to most of the world, Hans Küng is a larger-than-life figure, but to you he is a friend and colleague. When you founded the *Journal of Ecumenical Studies*, Hans became a member of the board, and your first issue in 1964 featured his editorial alongside Joseph Ratzinger's article. What is he like in real life?

LS   He always had a very good political sensibility—in the best sense, that is. When he met people, he looked them in the eye and listened to them, even if only for thirty seconds. I remember that first time in 1963 at Duquesne. Andie and I arranged to have a lunch on the day of the lecture, and as we walked in, there was a group of Sisters in habits, and they saw Hans and clearly got very excited. We got seated, but Hans excused himself and went and chatted with them. I thought it was so typical of him; he had a real sense of how important it was to talk to people one-on-one. I observed that time and time again. He'd be very attentive to you, right now, nobody else—and then the next person.

RA   You've visited Prof. Küng in Germany throughout the years, too, haven't you? You, Arlene, and the girls lived in Tübingen on your sabbatical in '72, and you went there alone as well.

LS   Oh, yes. One summer I was there alone, I remember going with Hans and his institute on an outing, and we were walking up hills, and Hans was talking at length about how at that time he was working on a small book: what it means to be a Christian.

RA   *On Being a Christian*? Oh, it turned out to be a very big book! Both in size and in impact.

LS   Exactly, and it caused him all kinds of problems. I think his problems with the Vatican can all be summed up in this condemnatory statement by Hermann Volk, who was the bishop of Mainz and a cardinal when *On Being a Christian* came out. You know the book became popular and was being attacked by conservatives, and they called a colloquium with some bishops and a professor of canon law—and Hans. Anyway, there was a three-day-long conversation, all recorded, and at one point Prof. Volk says in exasperation, "Mr. Küng, your book for me is too plausible!"

It must have stunned Hans. He knocked himself out to be as clear in his writing as he could, always. I remember publishing an article by his assistant Karl-Josef "Kajo" Kuschel, which described the process Küng went through to produce a book. First, he would hand-write something. Then, his secretary would type it up. They'd go through several versions. If it bordered on philosophy or physics or biology, he'd have colleagues in those fields give him feedback, and so on it would go. The last stage was that they'd sit next to each other and read each chapter out loud. One read, one listened: Is it absolutely clear? The whole point was to make it as plausible as possible, and he obviously succeeded. But for Volk, plausible in that direction was not good.

You know, one of Hans's assistants before Kajo described him as a Swiss clock. Everything had to be regular and on time. He took a nap at a certain time, and one day it didn't happen, and he was driving and fell asleep, almost drifted off the road.

RA   Prof. Küng had strained relations with the Vatican for most of his career, long before 1979. *On Being a Christian* didn't go over well. So what about the official censure in 1979, the loss of his *missio canonica*? He couldn't teach Catholic theology at Tübingen, but he could still teach. What was the impact of the censure? What changed?

LS   Sometimes, before he was so viciously attacked, I'd go and sit in on his lectures. There'd be 150 students taking his course. Then, when Hans was condemned by the Vatican, in the following spring or summer semester he didn't have 150 students—he had 1,500 students! He taught in the biggest auditorium, and the next room was filled up with the sound piped in. People would go to the lecture course before Hans's—or two courses—sit through whatever it was, drive from as far as Munich, just to keep the seat for his course. So the decree that declared he could no longer be considered a Catholic theologian totally backfired. It did not diminish his effectiveness; it made him more effective.

historical interlude

Len refers to 1979 as a "bad year." After Pope Paul VI passed away in August 1978, Pope John Paul I died in September, suddenly, after only thirty-three days of papacy. John Paul II was elected his successor and brought with him a vast and quickly moving cloud of strict moral conservatism and Cold War mentality, which meant immediate prosecution of theological dissent. The "watchdogs" at the Holy Office pulled on their weakening chains.

A French Dominican Jacques Pohier was an early example. The CDF had accused him of "clear and certain" errors of faith in his 1977 book *Quand Je Dis Dieu* (*When I Speak of God*) before the death of Paul VI, but condemnation and extraordinary personal sanctions did not come until April 1979. He was forbidden to preach, to celebrate the Eucharist publicly, to teach theology publicly in any form, and was effectively run out both of the priesthood and of the Dominican order.

Later in the summer, the all-seeing eye of the CDF turned to the U.S., where a group of theologians, which included Charles Curran, Anthony Kosnik, and Küng's doctoral student Ronald Modras, published their explorative *Human Sexuality: New Directions in American Catholic Thought.* The hammer came down, and the book was condemned.

A similar fate would have befallen Edward Schillebeeckx's writings on Christology and ministry, but, lucky for him, it seems he was already too preeminent. One might guess that the scandal caused by the condemnation of Schillebeeckx would have exploded the world of theology: Edward Schillebeeckx was more than a heavy-weight; he was one of the world's leading scholars, an author of Vatican II, maybe the foremost authority on the nature of Christ, who offered resurrection to the people as conversion and approached sacrament from the direction of experience. Censuring him for his scholarship would be like saying that Leonard Bernstein employed incorrect imagery in his music, or that Dr. King's dream, while well intentioned, deviated from proper doctrine. When it came to Schillebeeckx, the Holy Office had to be satisfied with a series of interrogations and a list of clarifications, precisions, and rectifications.

Others were not so lucky, and the CDF implemented more and more sweeping measures to keep, if not minds, at least tongues under control. In September, Pope John Paul II pressed the Jesuit Superior-General Pedro Arrupe to bring his Society into greater "fidelity to the magisterium of the church."[26] About the same time, attacks began to focus on Latin America's liberation theology, and they would soon increase with the arrival at the CDF of Cardinal Joseph Ratzinger.

Propelled by the plight of the disadvantaged in the climate of radical economic inequality, liberation theology stood as an affront to those church leaders with vested interests, to the chaplains to the rich, and to highly conservative organizations such as Opus Dei. Writes Paul Collins in *From Inquisition to Freedom*, "Liberation theology is not so much a specific theological interpretation of revelation, as a way of actually *doing* theology. The living experience of the poor is its absolute starting point. . . . Thus liberation theology is subversive of hierarchical approaches to

---

26 Find quote, e.g., in Hebblethwaite, "Don Pedro in History."

faith and the Church, and it reflects the different cultures that character-ize Third World countries."[27]

Gustavo Gutiérrez, a Peruvian theologian acknowledged to be the father of liberation theology, called the church to the "preferential option for the poor" back in 1971 and pointed out that Jesus himself chose to live with the poor and marginalized, that Jesus would not serve both God and money. This, however, sounded too leftist to the Vatican. Equating libera-tion theologians' call to a struggle for social justice with Marxism and communism, the CDF dismissed their theology as "ideology," objected to "secularization," and went after the most notable proponents of the movement. After decades of the Cold War, neither Marxism nor com-munism had to be proved evil in the First World.

Although Gustavo Gutiérrez himself was never condemned, the Holy Office reached for notorious others. They started with the writings of a Brazilian Franciscan, Leonardo Boff, an early supporter and brilliant theologian, in the "bad year" 1979 and silenced him for a year in 1985. Because he would not be completely silenced, after another run-in with church authorities in 1992, he finally left the Order and the priestly min-istry. Jon Sobrino was censured as recently as 2007.

Of course, Boff and Sobrino were not the only ones in the CDF's cross-hairs. John Paul II and Benedict XVI kept up the effort to stamp out liberation theology throughout their pontificates, and, as the head of the Vatican's doctrinal office, Cardinal Ratzinger issued a broad con-demnation of liberation theology for its "serious ideological deviations." Though he had praise for the movement's concern with the poor, what concerned him, he later said, were "rebellion, division, dissent, offense, (and) anarchy," not to mention "politization of the faith."[28] Every signal shone brightly: In the Vatican of the time, rank-and-file that fed its power trumped concern for the poor by a large margin.

Only with the advent of Pope Francis's era of "a poor church for the poor" has the situation begun looking like it's changing. On September 11, 2013, after a series of strikingly favorable articles in the Vatican news-paper, the Rev. Gustavo Gutiérrez was invited to meet with Pope Fran-cis, privately, informally, at the pope's residence. This unofficial meeting made all the news in the Catholic world because it may be change; it

27 Collins, *From Inquisition to Freedom*, 24 (*emphasis* in the original). See this book also for a general history of the CDF and for Hans Küng's more in-depth story of censure.

28 Rocca, "Under Pope Francis . . . "

may be hope; it may be policy. But in truth, it may not be the first sign of change. Several months before stepping down, Pope Benedict XVI had appointed a new prefect of the CDF: Archbishop Gerhard Müller, who is well known to be not only an admirer of Father Gutiérrez but a co-author with him of a book on liberation theology.

It may be that the tide is turning, and the bishop of Rome, the most influential man in the Catholic Church, will not be wanting for help in making it once again "a poor church for the poor."

end interlude

On December 18, 1979, Len's telephone began to ring at three in the morning, piercingly, insistently, as telephones do when sleep doesn't matter, when something has happened that supersedes manners and propriety, something that demands worry, or rescue, or grief. Middle-of-the-night telephone calls are adrenaline shots: before a word is spoken, they announce trouble. They are the town criers of nervous action.

Len picked it up still only half-present to the voice on the other end of the line but feeling bad news pumped through his body with every heartbeat. The voice belonged to Ed Grace, an American theologian and journalist in Rome, and it was breathless. It said, "The Vatican just condemned Hans Küng!"

Morning had only had enough time to settle in and Len's adrenaline enough time to translate into enraged resolve when he got back on the phone, with his first phone call to Charles Curran of the banned *Human Sexuality* fame. Curran, by the way, would soon join Küng among the ranks of "no longer Catholic theologians" alongside our other giants like Roger Haight, Peter Phan, and Jon Sobrino. Listing their names, Len shakes his head and says with a crooked kind of smirk, "What do *I* have to do to get condemned?"

In the meantime, the morning of December 18, 1979, rolled on at a frantic pace. Prof. Len Swidler of Temple University, Father Charles Curran of the Catholic University of America, and Father David Tracy of the University of Chicago, three voices on a phone line, were cooking up a plan. They had to do something. They couldn't do much against the Vatican's statement except issue their own statement. After all, a condemnation is essentially talk, so they would talk back. They would gather signatures and issue a press release from the U.S. Catholic theologians. What would it say? That Prof. Hans Küng was a Catholic theologian indeed, and no one could convince them otherwise!

"We decided to fight Rome with Roman tactics, and we took a leaf from Caesar: *Omnis America in tres partes divisa est!*" Len's eyes are tiny fireworks of triumph. He's just combined, if for a second, his two favorite things: telling a good story and dropping a Latin phrase onto an unsuspecting head.

They each took a third of the country and twenty-four hours and called everyone. Catholic theologians from coast to coast pledged their signatures in support of Hans Küng and then added, one after another, in a refrain-like, surreal similarity, "This cannot go on. We have got to organize."

And so they did. The condemnation of Küng was the last thing that notably happened in the "bad" year 1979 to Catholic theology, it was really only the beginning of the reactionary era of the next thirty years, but it prompted the creation of the Association for the Rights of Catholics in the Church—far away from the Swiss dissident and from Rome, across the ocean, in America.

Len sent his proposal for what became ARCC all over the country, and in March 1980, the founding convention came together in Alaska Hotel in Milwaukee, Wisconsin, and formulated the mission of the nascent organization: to "institutionalize a collegial and egalitarian understanding of Church in which decision-making is shared and accountability is realized among Catholics of every kind." Soon they put together a board of laity and clergy, women and men from every corner of the nation and got to work.

Len with a few others began to write the *Charter of the Rights of Catholics in the Church*, a document that now, in its fifth edition, is endorsed by fifteen renewal-minded organizations such as Call To Action, Women's Ordination Conference, and Dignity/USA. They are definitely not alone.

The *Charter* enumerates thirty-two rights of all Catholics that ARCC considers inalienable, some by virtue of our humanity, others by virtue of baptism. After all, justice, in the words of Paul VI, is "love's absolute minimum." "Christ has destroyed all divisions," the Preamble to the *Charter* continues and calls for the renewal of the church structures, the elimination of authoritarian and patriarchal order, and radical equality with no regard for gender, sexual orientation, or state of life—"because all are equally beloved by God."

The rights range from such basic freedoms as free speech and dissent to particular Catholic matters, and they clearly signal ARCC's positions: Catholics have the right to ministry relevant in the contemporary world; to end a broken marriage; to receive sacraments in any state of life, even if divorced and remarried; to plan a family with the same or opposite sex or to be celibate. The work of the church is not to judge this conscience but to help every faithful person fulfill his or her vocation to its full potential, including a call to the priesthood. The work of the church is to start eliminating sexist language from its documents.[29]

Armed with the *Charter* and the later proposed *Constitution for the Catholic Church*, ARCC has spent the last thirty-four years fighting for the fringe, the invisible, and the unheard—sometimes the very silenced few, sometimes the enormous silent majority. It puts out a newsletter, helps parishes write their own constitutions, encourages letter-writing to the bishops, promotes causes of church democracy, and provides information and resources, defending victims with open letters. But, as many grand undertakings, it started with a phone call on the night Hans Küng was in trouble. This is often how it works: A boy tinkers in a garage, a friend drops a word in a conversation, and an idea is born that becomes a world-embracing reality. All it takes is someone to make it happen.

RA   Len, what is your relationship with Hans like now?

LS   I think, on the mend.

RA   What is it mending from?

LS   This whole business about a global ethic.

RA   Tell me what happened.

LS   Well, Hans wrote this book in 1990: *Welt-ethos* in German. Something like *Global Ethic*. The gist of the book was a lot of statistics, but the conclusion he was pushing was: We the world need to develop a global ethic. I thought, *Yes, great idea!* And I thought we would spell out in writing a universal declaration of global ethic, more or less an analogy to the United Nations Declaration of Human Rights. So I drafted a *JES* editorial making that argument and we got some prominent signatures from

29 For full text, see "Charter."

around the world and launched it with Hans's lecture at UNES-CO in '91.

Then. I'd been involved in Trialogue—this Jewish-Muslim-Christian scholars' dialogue—since 1978, meeting every January at that time. I brought up the global ethic at the '92 meeting, and the group asked me to work on putting together an initial draft from the editorial we already had. So I got on that track.

Now, the people who were planning the Parliament of the World Religions meeting for 1993 contacted Hans and asked him to write the declaration. So we both were doing it, sharing stuff, faxing back and forth and tweaking. By early '93 we got his draft done and sent it off to this guy who was the executive secretary of the Parliament's preparatory committee in Chicago, who was to distribute it to them for revisions and what not, but we never heard, and never heard.

Finally it got to be the latter part of August, the blooming Parliament was starting in September, and Hans was talking about withdrawing when we got a letter from this guy blaming his secretary for this disaster. We had to go with what we got. I wasn't there on the last day of the Parliament, when they publicly announced it, but a big fight occurred. The committee was furious, since they were presented with this *fait accompli* with no time to debate. So instead of a Universal Declaration of Global Ethic, they approved it with the word "toward" in front. And it still hasn't changed since.

It was like an elephant giving birth to a mouse. And practically no one knows about delinquency on the part of this guy Gomez!

RA   Why did this damage your relationship with Hans?

LS   This didn't; this was September '93. But I had also produced my own version and submitted it to the Trialogue in January '94, and there were lots of other places people invited me: to a conference for Religion and Peace (ACRP) and to Italy and Poland.

    Anyway, there were these two versions. And I was arguing from the beginning that it was a great start, and what we needed to do was have lots of groups go through the same process: to articulate their ethical principles in a way that others could sign up also. We should tell them: don't include anything controversial but only universals, such as "no hurting of innocent people." And we should ask: What's *de facto* in human cultures across the globe? Whether you are Hindu, Christian, or atheist, these are our ethical principles. And various groups go through the same process, they think about it and make these principles active in themselves rather than attacking or despising others.

RA   This became a problem, your second version?

LS   Well, Hans thinks that his document has been signed onto by all these different people from all these religions, and we should just use that, like a UN declaration. There's a certain plausibility in that. He obviously thinks that my promoting the idea of multiple groups going through the process is distracting. I, of course, think it's exactly what needs to be done. So he is very unhappy.

RA   But this didn't kill your friendship. It's on the mend after all?

LS   On the mend.

PART IV

Toward the Ocean—Teaching

CHAPTER 14

Minds and Hearts: Pittsburgh

. . . but Hope

Smiles from the threshold of the year to come

Whispering "it will be happier," and old faces

Press round us, and warm hands close with warm hands . . .

—Alfred Lord Tennyson, *The Foresters*

Len and Arlene came to Duquesne University right out of Germany, in 1960, as Len was about to get his PhD from the University of Wisconsin, and stayed there for six years. He taught full time in the History Department; she, part time in English. They lived in a second-floor apartment over a concert pianist from China. Every day they heard her practice for hours on end and breathed in the sounds of music like habitual smells of home. Len didn't know it yet, but after twenty-seven years in Wisconsin and three years in Germany, Pennsylvania would become his home for at least the next fifty-three years—probably for the rest of his life.

He was young and full of fire and passion, and he had an ally in his department chair—the "fighting Irish" liturgist and medievalist Bill Story, who'd worked on Catholic reform for decades before Vatican II. Together they rolled up their sleeves, spit on their hands, and happily bumped shoulders. A major program in history got started; a professor in a new field—History of Science—was hired, despite a tiny budget. He was another young scholar, the sharp-minded and mild-mannered Al Costa.

"Mild-mannered?" Len seems to taste the expression. "He was so quiet that he made mice sound garrulous!"

The department was on its way, and someone whispered to Len that female teaching assistants were calling him "Cutie Swidler." It stroked his ego.

Their "bread-and-butter" course was American History. A hundred students in a section, urban corruption themes, a chapter on Pittsburgh. "Cutie" Prof. Swidler gushed fire and passion in front of his students. They looked back at him, gloomy, cast-over eyes.

He remembers imploring the class, "Just imagine if over a ten-year period a hundred honest people—all of you—went into business, there would be one thousand honest business people in the city!"

He remembers someone's answer: "You can't fight the system." Others were nodding in the room.

Then a tragedy struck. One nauseous day they came to work to be told that one of the teaching assistants had shot himself. In the head. With a shot gun.

He had been a silent type, not to be much noticed. They usually are. And nobody had noticed.

We usually don't.

LS   It was awful. And we had no idea something had been amiss with him beforehand.

RA   What was the reaction?

LS   I just remember horror and shock.

RA   Did you guys get together, talk? Feel like you could learn for the future from this?

LS   We came up totally empty. Nobody had any idea. We talked about what we could have missed, but, as I said, we came up empty. There seemed to be no handle. It's the sort of thing where you think later, "He said this or did that"—but here, nothing. Beyond the horrible tragedy, we were just totally surprised, so when we tried to reflect afterwards, we could come up with no missed cues. Seemed like a blank. Maybe today one would think there was an extraordinary chemical imbalance . . .

Yes, today one would. We, school teachers and college faculty, are now trained to pay attention to students who might be giving clues not only to suicidal but also to homicidal thoughts, because we live in the world where teenage suicide and school shootings are no longer news but a crushing, accumulating emotional burden of "Oh, no, not another one!" We have rules now and laws about what to do if we notice warning signs, whom to talk to, whom not to talk to. We have rules about what to do if a student comes in with a gun. We treat it all as mental illness, emotional disturbance, and we understand much more, though far from everything, about chemical imbalance.

Does our awareness save lives? I hope so. I hope it has saved at least some.

I had a student many years ago—brilliant, talented. Quiet. One day he stopped turning in his papers, wouldn't come to me, and it took a persistent and meddlesome effort for me to find out that he was devastated by depression. Suicidal. It took more effort, a trusted friend, time, and therapy, but I know that he's doing well and that his gift, his exquisite gift, is shining. And so I hope.

Yet, nothing can console us in our grief for those we've lost to the exploding silence. Len Swidler's face grows long and a shade of morbid gray when he says, "Wasted life." It's not just about the quiet TA at Duquesne. It's about every kind of loss he thinks to be a waste: the unfulfilled human potential.

A ubiquitous truism is that life does not move forward without setbacks, and Len, of course, had his share in Pittsburgh: student apathy he faced in the classroom, misogyny Arlene faced in and out of faculty meetings. Loss of life. Still, six years at Duquesne were good to him. The city was a hot bed of intellectualism, and the university, founded by the Holy Ghost Fathers, didn't lag behind.

Powered by the steam of Vatican II, the Catholic circles of Pittsburgh revved up their engines, and every day something was happening: discussion, innovation, development. Bill Story was known in the literary world, and Father Henry Koren, who doubled as the chair of Philosophy and Theology, directed Duquesne University Press. There was never a shortage of thoughtful, provocative voices on campus. The Psychology and Philosophy departments, both at the vanguards of their fields, invited lecturers from near and far, and temperatures rose, debates boiled, perspectives softened and cleared new paths into promising futures.

Together with Father Koren, Len started work to create a Department of Theology that was real, rigorous, and academic out of what he calls, with a note of disdain, "a souped-up catechism." A radio program followed on Duquesne's FM radio station with interviews and analysis.

"It's hard to describe how exciting those days were." Len's nostalgia is tangible. "Everything not humming but roaring along: Go, go, go!"

Just as the Council was getting off the ground, Arlene turned to Len with a notion: Not in the whole of North America was there a scholarly journal devoted to ecumenical dialogue—and at such a crucial time! Maybe they should start one. "Thus," he'd write later, "as happened frequently in our fifty-one years together, Andie again had one of my best ideas!"[30]

Like-thinking minds brimmed with designs everywhere they looked; finding allies was easy. Several of them put together an ecumenical discussion team, began tossing about a plan, and soon there emerged a board of associate editors, with Len as the Founding Editor and Elwyn Smith, a Protestant, as Co-Editor. Arlene took on the role of Managing Editor. Two years later, the first issue of the *Journal of Ecumenical Studies* would come from Duquesne University Press. It celebrates its fiftieth birthday in 2014, the flagship journal of its field.

Len's ecumenical group met at the home of the Catholic chaplains at the University of Pittsburgh—four ordained Oratorians who became the center of the assembly—and bonded into a sort of mind brotherhood with the Oratory for a beating heart, and they planned, they talked, they made things happen. Oratorians of St. Philip Neri are not an Order bound by formal vows but a number of communities of priests and lay brothers in a bond of charity: a rather unique arrangement, to which Len refers as a "loose kind of religious life." Oratorians work their ministries and come together to eat and to pray as they decide, perhaps, once a day or twice. They don't have to, but they do. It's "loose" compared to monastic life, but by its very charism, this life is built on welcoming, listening, preaching, and changing—a perfect kernel of reform.

St. Philip was a reformer. In the turbulent time of the 1530s and to the end of the century, in the aftermath of the Protestant schism,

---

30 Swidler, "'In the Beginning,'" 7.

he brought sense and renewal through compassion into his embattled church. He was a reluctant priest, for whom serving the laity always remained first order. He was a son of the Republic of Florence and infused its breath of democracy into the Roman, imperial Catholicism. He was an irrepressible spirit—four hundred years after his death, we call him "the saint of joy"—and the Oratory he founded still gathers people as if to a warm hearth, still radiates the feeling of home and hope.

The Pittsburgh oratory still exists. It's one of seventy or so around the world, one of ten in North America. It shelters new people now, new topics of discussion, and new concerns, but when I think of the names that gathered together inside those walls in the 1960s, my heart quiets for a brief repose of hushed reverence—an assembly of giants.

Father George Tavard was teaching at Mount Mercy College then and flying back and forth to Rome to serve as a *peritus conciliaris* for Vatican II and as a member of the Pontifical Secretariat for Christian Unity— a living, ongoing report from the Council sessions. The Secretariat was a critical battleground for the church's ecumenism, make or break, and Tavard, its fragile turning point.

"It was as though we lived an account of the French revolution," Len says. "A daily sense of freedom and unlimited possibilities."

Gregory Baum helped the Secretariat as an advisor. A son of a Jewish mother, born in Berlin, he was seventeen in 1940, when he boarded a boat on its way to Canada and became a war refugee. His perspective on unity had extended far beyond Christian ecumenism long before the Council, and we owe much of the *Nostra aetate*'s conciliatory spirit to his wisdom. From the time he first spoke up, Baum has been defending Jews against the Christian urge to convert. "After Auschwitz the Christian churches no longer wish to convert the Jews," he wrote in 1977. " . . . asking the Jews to become Christians is a spiritual way of blotting them out of existence and thus only reinforces the effects of the Holocaust."[31]

Frank Littell. A young Methodist minister in 1939, he had attended a Nazi rally in Nuremberg on his way through Germany and was so appalled by its raging, religious racism that it propelled him into his life's cause, and the question of the Christian conscience complicit in the Holocaust occupied him till his dying breath. He was the father of the Holocaust Studies field in American academia: organized the first course on the Holocaust, one of the first annual conferences, and the first ever

31 Baum, "Rethinking," 113.

doctoral program, in 1976, at Temple, where he came at Len's invitation. A world-stage supporter of Israel and opponent of religious extremism, he was an early, booming voice calling Christians to look inward for ancient prejudices rooted in Nicaea, to recognize the fundamental Jewishness of Christianity. And he reminded us of what should have been an obvious, if uncomfortable, truth: Jesus, Paul, and Peter would have been executed at Auschwitz.

H. A. Reinhold, one of the Oratorians, had been a diocesan priest in Germany and worked with sailors in Hamburg and Bremen before he had to flee from Nazism in the mid-thirties. He was a writer and an anti-fascist, a singular fighter for social justice, the threads of which he always found interwoven with liturgy. We remember him as the "liturgical prophet." After he developed Parkinson's disease, mundane things of everyday living were difficult—the things most humans between five and sixty-five take quite for granted. Buttoning a shirt. Holding a bar of soap.

"I sometimes helped H.A.R. with showers and clothing and stuff," Len remembers, "and students did, too. Bishop Wright was his patron: supported him financially, had him stay at the Oratory. Bishop Wright was an extraordinary kind of guy. Lots of bishops did crazy things with diocesan money, but he did good stuff. All this quiet patronage."

John J. Wright, who'd come to Pittsburgh from his earlier see in Worcester, Massachusetts, was indeed a distinguished servant of the church—he'd go on to be elevated to Cardinal, the prefect of the Congregation for the Clergy, and the highest-ranking American priest—but he was well loved in Pittsburgh, it seems, for the qualities of the heart. His theology was, in fact, rather conservative, and I doubt the members of our group would come to agreement with their bishop on many an issue, considering that some of them loudly advocated women's ordination and at least one explicitly called for recognition of same-sex unions already in the sixties and seventies. Yet it didn't seem to matter. Bishop Wright was a sincere cleric with open arms and open eyes, a proponent of civil rights and peaceful solutions. From Vatican II, he brought home a fiery enthusiasm for dialogue, ready to see united efforts between Catholics and Protestants in every undertaking of "good works and charity." And, above all, he was an intellectual. Agreement or not, he was the fosterer of a climate of free-thinking, supporter of growth and debate, patron of need. In Pittsburgh, you didn't have to agree with your bishop. Not every see was so lucky.

historical interlude

On a diverting note, quite a few of the guest faculty at Duquesne in the early 1960s hailed from Holland, maybe because the Philosophy chair, Henry Koren, was himself Dutch. A most vivid story that had stuck in Len's mind came from one of them and concerned, no less, the Holy House of Loreto. This is well-known Catholic lore: *Basilica della Santa Casa* in Loreto, Italy, contains what the popular tradition holds, reverently if against logic, to be the house that had stood originally in Nazareth, in which Mary grew up and lived at the time of the Annunciation, gave birth to her first son, and continued with her Holy Family. The legend has it that just before the end of the Crusades, in 1291, saving the House from impending destruction, God's angels carried it through the air, from Palestine to Illyria in the Balkans, and then three years later to Loreto.

Of course, the authenticity of the house has been more or less thoroughly debunked by historians—all other arguments aside, there doesn't appear to have existed any holy house in Nazareth before its "translation" to Europe—but so beloved is this myth that Loreto is one of our most visited pilgrimage sites. Numerous saints have worshiped at the shrine's doors, numerous popes affirmed the tradition. December 10 was designated the feast commemorating the translation of the Holy House to Loreto, and, in 1920, Pope Benedict XV declared Our Lady of Loreto the patron saint of aviation. Her statuette crossed the Atlantic aboard the Spirit of St. Louis in 1927 and hovered over the North Pole aboard the Norge and the Italia in '26 and '28. James McDivitt took her medallion with him on the Apollo 9 lunar mission in March 1969.

Ironically, the age of the house inside the basilica is less relevant to Our Lady of Loreto's patronage of air travelers than the angels' carrying it over the Mediterranean, and that was the part of the story a Dutch lecturer took up with Len one day at Duquesne. He had heard, the visitor said, from a scholar working in Rome that a bill of lading had been found in the Vatican archives dating back to the thirteenth century, for a shipping company that had carried some sort of masonry materials to Loreto. Here's the best part: it was paid for by the Angeli family.

Len was stunned and delighted. He still remembers the feeling, the sparkle of recognition—finding himself, as though brand new, for a moment, at the root of the making of a myth. Who of us is not familiar with that feeling? It is one of those exhilarating rewards of education: a burst of knowing and realization that rains down pieces of information previously disjointed into a flawless mosaic—*click, click*—into clarity and comprehension and discovery. Bits of reality coming together and—suddenly, finally—making sense. *Click.*

end interlude

CHAPTER 15

For Living Well: Temple University

What a misfortune it is that we should . . . let our boys' schooling interfere with their education!

—GRANT ALLEN, *POST-PRANDIAL PHILOSOPHY*

RA   So, Len, why did you leave Pittsburgh for Temple? You seem to have been having a knock-out of a good time.

LS   Well, it was 1965. Temple University had been organized around a Baptist Temple and used to have a School of Theology, but it just got affiliated with the Commonwealth of Pennsylvania, so the new Religion faculty was founded. Separation of church and state. It was one of the first in the country. This young fellow Lowell Striker from Temple was passing through Pittsburgh. I interviewed him on my radio program, and I asked if he wanted to come teach at Duquesne. Three or four days later, he calls me back and says, instead, that his department chair, Bernard Phillips, would like me, my co-editor Elwyn Smith, and *JES* to join them at Temple.

RA   Flattering.

LS   Yes, except I really was having every kind of fun at DU, but Elwyn . . . He was frothing at the mouth to go. So I decided I'd go for an interview at Temple and tell Dr. Phillips that I wouldn't even consider the offer unless he committed to hiring several Catholics—and also Jews and Hindus and so on.

RA   Did you plan this as a dare?

LS   I thought it would kill it right there, because universities were *not* doing that. So anyhow, Elwyn and I went to Temple and Phillips wined and dined us. I gave the whole "several Catholics" spiel, and suddenly Phillips says, "Great idea! I'll offer you full professor, a nine-month schedule, and $13,000 a year." I was then an associate professor at DU. My twelve-month salary was $9,500. Quite an offer, of course.

RA   Couldn't turn it down?

LS   I thought Duquesne might match something, at least give me a raise, but they didn't. Plus, Temple provided a $50,000 subsidy for the *Journal*. You know, $13,000 then is almost $90,000 now.

RA   Was Dr. Phillips true to his word?

LS   Absolutely. Next year we hired Patrick Burke, and Patrick gave him Gerry Sloyan's name. And the fourth Catholic was a former Benedictine monk, Rod Hindery.

Bernard Phillips didn't stop with the Catholics. At the time when it was still the predominant practice for Protestants to teach every religion at Protestant schools, for Catholics at Catholic schools, and for Jews at Jewish schools, Temple began to hire practitioners to present their traditions from inside. When Len came to Philadelphia in '66, the Religion faculty went from six to ten. The next year, it was twenty-one strong and growing, heavyweights of their disciplines making their home there: Franklin Littell to found the Holocaust Studies program and explore church-state relations; Isma'il al-Faruqi to found Islamic Studies; Seyyed Hossein Nasr, who would become the first Muslim to deliver the Gifford lectures, in 1981; Richard DeMartino, a practitioner of Zen, an apprentice to D.T. Suzuki and Shin'ichi Hisamatsu, a co-author with Suzuki and Erich Fromm.

Late sixties, early seventies—it was the time of political, social, spiritual turmoil, but turmoil is involvement, boiling life, and college campuses bucked and rioted, sang and hollered, inside, outside, spit out the lava of generational change into the heated, debate-rich air, looking for something and never stopped.

"Giddy," Len says. "Alive and heady and giddy."

They'd go to demonstrate with their students: civil rights, the Vietnam War. They would take buses down to Washington to protest. Len remembers a whiff of tear gas and getting little Carmel out of the way, quickly. He marvels now at taking for granted how involved in political action all his students were then, how spiritually curious—it appeared, everyone was. He was teaching an introductory two-credit course with a generic title, something like "Religion in Life," and it seemed to him that every two weeks, as they moved to a new religion in their class, the students had a religious conversion.

"The '68 national election was such a horrendous one, with Gene McCarthy!" Len shakes his head. "He drew young people like honey. Such riots at the Chicago Democrat convention!"

Eugene McCarthy, a U.S. Senator from Minnesota, challenged President Lyndon Johnson in the primaries in 1968 on an anti-war platform and did so unexpectedly well at first that he forced Johnson to withdraw from the campaign. It proved in the end to be a bitter and tumultuous political year that, above all, took the life of Bobby Kennedy, and Sen. McCarthy never did win the nomination, though he tried again and again. Still, his cultural impact on 1968 is hard to overestimate: the young people he drew "like honey" used to be the long-haired, hippie-looking, counter-cultural sort who craved a stand against the Vietnam War. To go door-to-door for McCarthy's campaign, they cut their locks and shaved their beards. *Get clean for Gene*, the slogan sounded—and they did.

RA   Len, didn't you get Bernard Häring to lecture at Temple about that time?

LS   Yes, Andie and I knew him. She translated a couple of his books from German into English, and in '67 we taught in DC at the same time. Now in the summer of '68 he said he'd be teaching at Union Theological Seminary in New York, and I said, "You can catch a train from NYC to Philly, one hour twenty minutes. Would you come down once a week and give a course in the evening at Temple?" He said, "Yes."

Our chair agreed, so then I sent out notes to various places in the archdiocese, and suddenly the word spread like wildfire, especially among the Sisters, that Frater Bernard Häring would be lecturing on Vatican II! A hundred and fifty nuns and a hundred priests signed up for the course! Six hundred people altogether. There was no hall big enough, so we held it at the Baptist Temple. And the Sisters would bring their tape recorders and then play the lectures back home for hundreds of others. That was the experience.

historical interlude

Bernard Häring never aspired to become the most important moral theologian of the twentieth century. Even worse, he didn't want to be a theologian at all. The son of a German peasant, when he entered the Redemptorist Order in the 1930s, he wanted to be a missionary, but then the war hit, and the young priest found himself conscripted into the army as a medic, under instructions not to exercise any priestly duties. He gave out Communion anyway and got into repeated and predictable trouble for it.

Deployed to Poland with his unit in 1941, he held Bible classes, baptized, and ministered to all that he could reach—Polish, Russian, Jewish, German—and at the inevitable court martial defended himself: How was he more offensive to military order than the soldiers who fraternized with Polish women? The Wehrmacht officer in charge shook his head and let the frater go. He worked to save the lives of prisoners of war and Polish Jews and convinced his fellow soldiers to help. So beloved did he become among the people that, when the time came for his own life to be in danger, the villagers banded around him, named him their pastor, and kept him safe.

Bernard Häring emerged from the war with a wounded heart—one among unspeakable many. He would talk of his wartime experience in his autobiography, *My Witness for the Church*, a lifetime after the war, still boggled and horrified. He emerged with no certainties, but, devastated by the atrocities committed in the name of following orders, he knew that his morality would never be premised on obedience, but on responsibility, courage, and love.

Asked to teach moral theology, Häring buckled much in the way of the biblical prophets tapped on the shoulder by the Almighty for missions frightening, revolting, and abrasive to every nerve fiber trying to pass on the thought. Moses, Isaiah, and Jeremiah pled with the Lord for mercy. Jonah cut the cord and took off in the opposite direction. Bernard wrote in *My Witness for the Church*, "I told my superior that this was my very last choice because I found the teaching of moral theology an absolute crushing bore. He mollified me with the answer, 'We are asking you to prepare yourself for this task with a doctorate from a German university so that it can be different in the future.'"[32]

He did—and it was. After centuries of busywork cataloguing types of sins, describing and discussing the origin of sin, the meaning of sin, the punishment for sins, and the nuances of sinful behavior, Catholic moral theology finally took a deep breath with the publication of Bernard Häring's *The Law of Christ* in 1954.

Having been through an abundance of sin in the meat grinder of the war, he was not so concerned with stepping around sin as leaving it behind. Commonplace now in thinking of Catholic morality, this was a revolutionary change in approach: focus on positive rather than negative, on how to lead a truly Christian life, how to find the very heart of the Gospels' message and fan its fire in our hearts. Häring's law of Christ was about love.

He studied Protestant theology and overwhelmed his teaching auditoria with students flocking to hear his fluid and ecumenical ideas. When Pope Paul VI stirred up the church with the prohibition of birth control use in his *Humanae vitae*, Häring took a decidedly prominent stand against it, then later, through the years, raised issues of sexual morality again and again. He was investigated by the CDF, interrogated, hassled, but no censure came of it, and in 1998 Bernard Häring died at his monastery in Germany as he lived: a priest, a Redemptorist Father, and a moral theologian in every sense of the word.

end interlude

---

32 Häring, *My Witness for the Church*, cited in Stewart, "Bernard Häring, 85, Is Dead."

LS   Häring was a real Hebrew prophet. He spoke the truth. We got to know each other quite well eventually, and when Andie and I were teaching in Tokyo, we both took up translation projects— partly because we just couldn't make any headway with Japanese neighbors or friends. I took up his *My Witness for the Church*, and it was much about church reform and how badly it was needed. And it was all about his experience with the Holy Office. It was terrible. Here this guy was suffering from throat cancer, he'd had several operations, and they insisted on him coming in for an interrogation! Cardinal Šeper was the prefect of the CDF then, and Häring said something like, "I was called before two Nazi courts, and I was not ashamed. I am ashamed to be called in front of this court for this charge." I thought when I heard this, *Man, if I were Šeper, I would look for the nearest chair to crawl under.*

RA   When did you see him last?

LS   I visited him one last time with Ingrid Shafer, not long before he died. We were working at Oberammergau, and he was living in Gars at the Redemptorist house. He was very frail already. Asked about my "holy wife"—he always referred to Andie like that—and said she'd been his best translator. She never "moderated" what he'd written.

Only days after their last good-bye, Ingrid Shafer would describe it in an almost visibly tear-stained online tribute to the prophet of Catholic morality:

> I will always remember his slight figure in black, with a cane, standing in the sun, waving goodbye to us. He was surrounded by a glow, and I will never be quite sure if it was only the sun playing tricks with my eyes.[33]

Meanwhile, the turbulent sixties with their student riots, weekly conversions, and the Baptist Temple overflowing beyond standing room for a visionary's lectures, became history—at Temple and in America. The country, its economy and culture, even its education have all been changing. Concern for political apathy among the youth now occupies our minds more than worry over civic unrest. The Religion Department, too,

33 Shafer, *Bernard Häring*, para. 7.

has changed. It has shrunk, and the league of proverbial superheroes Len remembers as the golden years is largely gone. Al-Faruqi was murdered in his home in 1986. Hossein Nasr and Gerald Sloyan left the university. Pat Burke retired, and many others. Some passed away. There are new people at the department and a couple of the "old guard," but it's much smaller now. Administrative shifts brought changes in teaching loads and policies, and a faculty that once offered a selection of sixteen to eighteen graduate seminars a semester to a cohort of 150 doctoral students, now barely offers six courses by fourteen professors, and its students, between PhD and MA, number maybe in the fifties.

Len doesn't hide disappointment when he talks about it. Change is hard, more so the change that brings the background of your life from boil to simmer, but Len is more than a sunny spirit: He's an entrepreneurial one.

"We are allowed only one graduate seminar a year," he says. "The difficulty, of course, is that what you can offer as a seminar then is very limited. I end up doing independent studies for students all the time. Sometimes there are several students who want to do the same study, so it's a *de facto* seminar. I am giving one this semester on mysticism with four students, and it's a very stimulating academic experience for all five of us."

And so, more often than not, one evening a week a graduate seminar of three to ten students gathers in a classroom or in Len's living room for anything from a discussion of a global ethic to Catholic mysticism. I've taken part in more than one, led a couple sessions when Len was away on one of his whirlwind globetrotter trips, and observed a few others. No surprise, Professor Swidler's seminars fall at the "*in-*" extreme of the formal-*in*formal spectrum of such events. They are essentially student-run, with the Professor seeing himself as an unobtrusive guide to the seekers of knowledge gathered around him—sometimes, around a selection of steaming dishes from cuisines around the world prepared by the students' hands. Len offers up reading materials—though the reading list, too, can be amended through discussion—and he offers up opinion, provocative questions, and insight into the theological greats they study, virtually all of whom he seems to have known personally. Conversation is started by students and flows where it may. Len interlocks his fingers behind his head, crosses his ankles in a dreamy pose, and "hangs out." He is the wise man.

Many thrive in the free-flowing waters of Len's seminars, and some wither. Some carry a kind of reverence for his wealth of experience, his international status, and the scale of his reflective statements; others—the challengers and provocateurs—poke and trouble and never let well enough alone, knit-picking practice out of theory and theory out of practice, making a local spectacle out of an occasional meeting. I tended to fall in with those. But, big group or modest, loud or quiet, Len always has a small yet devoted following around him: graduate students who pursue his ideas in grassroots movements, develop his initiatives, intern at the Dialogue Institute and for the *Journal*, and use the terminology he's created in their everyday speech. They are his Temple.

Temple's main campus sits in the heart of North Philadelphia—yet another neighborhood of Philly, what newcomers tend to refer to as "the rough part of town" until they learn that it is by far not the only one. Besides Olde City, North Philly is my favorite neighborhood. Much of it is depressed, gray, and dangerous. Once a bustling area of a production-rich city, it was pushed to devastation and urban blight by the industrial collapse of the mid-twentieth century that got only progressively worse decade after decade. Here, driving must be done with care, and walking, more so. Here, robbery is common, guns abound, and hooded figures loiter at street corners, fidgeting with something in their pockets. It is also here that moms and pops sit outside in sunny weather, chatting lazily, as if the days were still old and the new had never happened. Here, window signs for African braiding are as common as fried chicken and old, glorious Philadelphia jazz. Mosques and churches share the same corners. It is the home of the best halal foods I've ever had.

If you walk or drive in North Philly, you will feel the ache of an abandoned hope. And then you'll turn a corner, and in the midst of trash and ruin, between boarded-up windows of crumbling buildings, in the middle of a post-apocalyptic horror, beauty will blossom—a mural on what would have been a blind wall—in full and unexpected glory, more stunning and more alive for its surroundings. A miracle of human spirit pushes its way up through despair, unconquered and unashamed.

The Philadelphia Mural Project is all over the city. It has been an effort to bring together neighborhoods in common labor to help artists transform empty walls and bring breath to empty streets. They picture faces of meaning, symbols of hope, flowers and suns, messages and books, clasped hands . . . Heritage and future. They are everywhere, but nowhere more than in North Philadelphia are they triumphant. Poignant. Like conversion. Like a spiritual, rising in the silence.

North Philadelphia is murals and tiny lot parks with sculptures and greens and sudden, touching, almost out-of-place little blocks of homes immaculately tended, fence to fence with the scarred and decomposing corpse of a city. Temple University has no buffer from it all: It is an urban campus, much like a cell unto itself but with a permeable membrane that mixes the city into its swirling space. It is flooded at night with the light of the mightiest, wall-mounted projectors, and during the day with the din of student mobs, churning and moving, like ear-splitting lava, from building to building, along the Liacouras Walk, over crosswalks and between cars, curling around the Bell Tower, pooling in front of Anderson Hall—arguing, loitering, running, smoking, reading, talking, laughing, tanning, pushing, eating . . . And the mingling aromas of every type of food one can possibly sell from a truck or kiosk. Len comes here to work at the offices of *JES* and the DI and to teach his undergraduate courses in World Religions.

Talking to Len

(On undergrads, free will, knowledge and belief, limit questions, and our notion of God)

RA   Len, how do you feel about teaching undergraduate courses? Some scholars at research universities find it a burden.

LS   I did part-time teaching ever since I was a grad student at the University of Wisconsin, and my recollection of teaching was always positive, but I have to say that now, first of all in terms of undergraduates, I find it much more interesting and rewarding than I remember it being in those earlier decades. I think it probably is because what I'm trying to do with my undergrads now is not so much content or information but to get them to think and to get to basic human issues, for which teaching religion is a perfect context. So I find teaching undergrads not at all a tiresome job, but rather an exciting challenge.

        I also find working with my grad students exciting, but that has been so for a long time, whereas the excitement of teaching undergrads has emerged in the last twenty years. And I think that it goes together with the fundamentally dialogic nature of the world and my need to move in that direction. That's what I am doing—or trying, at least. It fits with my worldview in a perfect hand clasp.

RA   How are Temple students?

LS   Undergrad? Interesting. I really enjoy teaching them. I find a lot of human, intellectual payback working with them. I know you will oftentimes hear among academics that students can't write or read, as if they used to be paragons of intellectual virtue. But now I find them as a group much more polite. Almost "aggressively polite"—sensitive. I find emails from students saying they're sorry they're going to miss class because there's been a death in the family or they have surgery or something. Even a year and a half ago, I ran late from a doctor's appointment and got to class fifteen minutes late and saw three students there lingering. But in my office several emails were waiting from students who were worried about my health and if something had happened, if I was all right. I'd never had that before; it was really very touching and sincere.

What's very interesting, when I think about it, is that almost all of those students were foreign students. One was from Kuwait, another from Southeast Asia. These are obviously students who "stretched," as it were, to come to the university, at least to an American university. A high value they place on study, I guess, translates onto me as professor. In my classes I try to engage them in intellectual conversation. I hear them say they haven't had this kind of experience before and find it stimulating. Good. That's partly how I explain it to myself.

RA   I recently attended your World Religions class, and more than once I noticed that you didn't exactly answer their questions but said those were "limit questions." What did you mean?

LS   Limit questions are essentially questions without answers. Substantially, it's about free will, and for me it goes back to Augustine.

RA   You once said that Augustine of Hippo "painted himself into a corner with free will" arguing against Pelagius. Would you speak to that?

LS   Oh, I spent so much time praying about it in the novitiate! Talk about head-breakers: predestination and free will! I finally decided: If it's free will, you can't conceptualize it. A relationship between an unknown factor (a) and an unknown factor (b) is unknown. Category mistake. How far is yellow? Not a profound analysis.

RA   I appreciate theology's willingness to leave a blank space. We call it "mystery." But we wouldn't have theology if we didn't dig into mystery with reason.

LS   The problem is the theologian who says, "The answer is such." We don't grasp the mystery. If anything, the mystery grasps us. A Buddhist friend kept saying, "This is beyond" and "That is beyond" and so on. Finally I said, "If you want to assert that experience cannot be expressed in words or concepts, fine. But then stop talking and don't try to describe it!"

The dilemma that Augustine and others found themselves in was that, on the one hand, he was obviously convinced of radical monotheism, that there was one source of being for everything that exists in the universe. And that therefore everything that comes into or out of existence ultimately has to rely on this ultimate source called "God." On the other hand, he wanted to claim that humans are radically free, meaning they choose to do something or not and are responsible for the choice and are to be recompensed accordingly. But that sets up a diametrical contradiction: a free human being who claims he did this for good or ill and would be rewarded or punished, but nothing happens except that God makes it happen or not.

Augustine felt he had to come to a solution of that dilemma and therefore decided in favor of God, so human beings somehow were transformed into automatons. He doesn't want to say that, but in fact that's what he does with his notion of predestination: that I, allegedly a free person, can do the right thing only if God moves me to do it—this theology of grace as the gift from God that moves us to make the right choice. Poor Thomas Aquinas ended up saying that God moves us to choose "freely," but that's literal nonsense. Either you are unmoved by an outside force and can freely choose—or you are not.

The stupidity, in my judgment, was to attempt to resolve the equivalent of a math equation when you have only two unknowns. You can't solve it that way. So they all set themselves up for failure by asking questions that are fundamentally category mistakes. You can't come up with an explanation of radical freedom with God as the ultimate source.

RA   So what's your answer?

LS   The answer is, this is another one of what I call "limit questions": questions that force themselves on our intellects, and we ask them willy-nilly, but they are the kinds of questions that for our intellects, given the way we think through analysis and synthesis, are impossible to answer. Limit questions are precisely the kinds of experiences that force humans to create what we call "religions."

Religions are our attempts to provide answers that are not knowledge but are based on trust, meaning they are an act of the will. A decision is made; I choose this position against another position because it seems more persuasive, although the alternative cannot be completely excluded. "Trust" is English for "faith." We create our religions, which come up with the answers we find helpful but cannot by the nature of reality and by our mode of knowing possibly produce pure knowledge.

RA   And pure knowledge is . . . ?

LS   That there is no thinkable alternative by way of investigation. Logically.

RA   Pure knowledge is rational knowledge.

LS   It wouldn't contradict it. We come up in many instances with solutions for ourselves, but we don't give them the title of "knowledge." It's belief. Belief can be based on a range of kinds of knowledge, including emotional and experiential. These do the job when rational intellect faces a blank wall. And the questions often don't go away. They keep asking themselves. Most people avoid them, but . . .

RA   Is there a hierarchy of knowledge? Is rational superior to emotional or experiential?

LS   I am persuaded that we cannot end up literally contradicting our rationality, but in the area of these limit questions it's become very obvious that rational intellect is not adequate to come up with solutions. There will often be "either-or" positions. God exists or not. We are free or not. And our rationality cannot give totally definitive answers. So then we are pushed in the direction of having to make decisions, by an act of will, that position (a) or (b) is the one we want to affirm. Or maybe not; maybe we're stuck. But we do so positively or negatively with the totality of our knowing facilities, which include experience, emotional intelligence—all together. And we sometimes then make a choice. We believe such is the case. That's always, it seems to me, a position that can change in a way that a purely rational position should not—unless we are recognized at a later point to have involved ourselves in a rational flaw.

RA   Rational positions change all the time, don't they? With new evidence, for example.

LS   Then what you have is a new question. Additional information brings new questions.

RA   Then, your problem with Augustine is not so much his position as that he calls it "knowledge"?

LS   Well, no. As I understand his conclusion, I disagree. I disagree with predestination. And then I ask myself how such a smart person can make such a dumb conclusion. And I think he wasn't sufficiently observant of the way we think. He attempts to come up with a rational answer.

RA   You think he goes about a limit question in the wrong way.

LS   Right. I mean, I am not at all an expert on Augustinian thought, but from what I read, I think he has somehow misunderstood human epistemology. That doesn't surprise me given that he was enamored of Manichaeism.

RA   Yet he rejected it.

LS   But subterraneously. He brought it with him. He was totally un-Jewish in that way. But then, pretty much the whole of the Hellenistic Christian world was naïve with regard to epistemology.

RA   We probably still are. Understanding develops.

LS   You know, as grade school students in Catholic school, we were told if we went into a church and said this prayer with plenary indulgence attached to it . . . You know. And I just accepted all of that growing up, never said, "It makes no sense, I reject it."

I didn't think about it as I was maturing. It just slowly kind of faded in my thinking. But more recently, I guess, I've been seeing that this is an understandable and necessary way that humans have developed, and our explaining to ourselves the meaning of things, which we call religions, had to go through a process of maturation. And when I look at many of our various scriptures and the traditions interpreting and applying them through thousands of years, it's clear that much of it has to be very radically rethought. And this is going to be a painful and very long process both for individual persons and for larger communities—and eventually for humankind in general.

Take the notion of prayer, for example. We pray that my cancer abate or for a loved one. But when you think about it, it really is quite blasphemous to the notion of God that God is going to be like some stereotypical potentate lying on cushions, deciding that he'll let this poor slob not suffer and the other billion suffer. The whole idea of individual miracles projects a horrible image of God, and we do it quite unthinkingly. It's just a tiny example.

Our whole notion of God . . . I mean, first of all, the affirmation of the existence of God means we have some concept of what we are affirming. And everything we are learning about what ultimate reality must be like is belied by everything we learn about it. It's either positive or negative deficit. One becomes mentally tongue-tied—which is doubtless a good thing. Nevertheless, I find myself, when I do my meditations on my stationary bike, saying to myself (and it comes out in German best), "*Du muss ein Du sein.*"

RA   And in English?

LS   "*There must be YOU.*"

CHAPTER 16

"Beyond This Flood a Frozen Continent": Japan

There are no foreign lands. It is the traveler only who is foreign.
—Robert Louis Stevenson, *The Silverado Squatters*

During World War II, the American government commissioned a study of the Japanese culture from a leading anthropologist of the day, Ruth Benedict. She released it in 1946 and called it *The Chrysanthemum and the Sword*. The book has been criticized both for its methodology and for its conclusions, but, for better or for worse, it has since remained the source of our ideas about the mysterious Japanese mentality and created a pervasive, persisting, now-standard way of thinking about the difference between Japan and the West: They are a "shame culture," we are a "guilt culture."

By "shame," Benedict meant "an external sanction for self-respect." An identity-shaping pattern of "good" behavior driven by the judgment of society—real, perceived, imagined . . . Shame is external. Guilt is internal.

> A society that inculcates absolute standards of morality and relies on men's developing a conscience is a guilt culture by definition, but a man in such a society may, as in the United States, suffer in addition from shame when he accuses himself of gaucheries which are in no way sins. He may be exceedingly

chagrined about not dressing appropriately for the occasion or about a slip of the tongue. In a culture where shame is a major sanction, people are chagrined about acts which we expect people to feel guilty about.[34]

Benedict does not leave the Japanese without the sense of guilt, and this is by far not the only observation she makes. Her study is complex and even today as praised as it is maligned—a sign, perhaps, of a thought-provoking work. In Japan after the war, during the period of painful self-examination, it became a long-standing bestseller. Still, the notion of shame and guilt cultures grew to be one of her most noted contributions to anthropology, and many Americans, when they encounter Japan—in person, in the news, or on the big screen—explain it to themselves in terms of this singular paradigm.

Leonard Swidler is one of those people. He was reading *The Chrysanthemum and the Sword* in 1987, when he spent a summer session working at Temple University Japan in Tokyo. He so loved the adventure that both he and Arlene signed up to go back for a full twelve months from September 1990 to August 1991, to teach English-speaking Japanese students. He taught Religion and Intellectual Heritage, and Andie, English.

They lived in an apartment near the Meguro metro station on the Yamanote line, which circles the center city. Today, it connects more than a dozen of Tokyo's subway lines into a dense, convoluted web with two or three lines converging on almost every one of its stations. Twenty-four years ago, the metro was less developed, but Len's memories of it are indelible. His eyes still widen when he recalls torrential throngs pouring through the hallways, in an awesome orderliness of a mudslide, flowing around obstacles and separating in the directions known only to nature, settling to fill every space to capacity. He remembers a railroad worker packing people into the train cars with a long pole so the doors could close.

LS I'd never seen it anywhere else in the world that people could sleep standing up in a train. That's how packed it was in there. Whoever wasn't sleeping, though, seemed to have their nose stuck in a comic book. It was so orderly! Streams of people, like looking into infinity where all blends together. Like a waterfall. I remember standing there looking, listening, and nobody said anything to anybody. Children in uniform would be chattering together, but that's all: it was very impersonal. Not "excuse

34 Benedict, *Chrysanthemum*, 222.

me," nothing. It had to be that way, or it all would come to a screeching halt.

RA   Because of the numbers?

LS   Right. Through Shinjuku station, a million and a half people would go on a daily basis! This one time, coming out of the Meguro station, at the busy intersection, I was approaching the curb—mobs of people going all directions—and out of the corner of my eye I saw a Japanese man trip and fall forward, and I automatically grabbed him by his shoulders, and he said in English, "Thank you." I was stunned: how did he know I was a foreigner? He hadn't even looked at me. Then eventually I figured it out, I think. A Japanese man wouldn't have done that.

RA   A Japanese man would have let him fall?

LS   This is my judgment. It's how I experienced the Japanese *en masse*: It was very impersonal and in many regards had to work that way.

They started out riding to Meguro and walking fifteen minutes to their apartment, then gave up on the subway and walked all the way from Temple Japan at the end of the day, about an hour's walk, getting to know the city and wondering about its idiosyncrasies, observing, solving for *J.* Soothing their sizzling bafflement with the shadow of Ruth Benedict.

They'd pass by a Kentucky Fried Chicken near the metro, where a life-sized Colonel presided over the entrance. Every Christmas, the KFC employees dressed up the Colonel in a Santa suit.

They'd walk by the Meguro River, known to Western tourists for its marvelous views of cherry blossoms. Outside of *sakura* time, though, it was rather unimpressive: full of muck and encased in cement, and it attracted the attention of the American professors mainly with little inns spaced along its banks and labeled "Love Hotels." Despite the label's questionable taste, love hotels all across the East no longer have to do with prostitution. They are the products of urban overcrowding and offer, via hourly "rest rates" and multiple discreet entrances, a chance for an uninterrupted romp mostly to couples embattled by the burdens of responsibility and lack of privacy.

The Swidlers would go to museums, the chrysanthemum gardens and parks, an occasional Shakespeare play. Out of sheer curiosity, they saw a kabuki version of *Jesus Christ Superstar*. Sitting in the balcony filled with high-school girls, Len thought, *What are they doing here? What could they think of this play, so entirely foreign?* He did not understand kabuki—stylized, mind-boggling, in Japanese. He parsed only three words: "Jesus Christ Superstar." And Jesus—completely androgynous in build and voice. Len and Andie argued whether it was deliberate and decided it was. They liked it.

There weren't many contacts for them: mostly American colleagues, friends, Westerners. With Steve Antonoff, a Temple PhD student writing his dissertation on Zen, they'd go to picnic in cherry orchards and to a Shinto shrine. Filo Hirota arranged for some lectures, mostly to Catholics on Catholic reform. They'd go for Mass at a Catholic church staffed by Benedictines from Collegeville, Minnesota. All those were good and pleasant things, but the deeper hope—the very connection for which they had come—the crux of the matter never did happen: Japanese neighbors, Japanese friends, Japanese students. Japanese people remained a torrential throng of mystery, flooding all spaces and speaking in tongues and pouring past, close and unknown.

They didn't speak the language. It is against this wall that every swell of effort to understand would naturally break. Without the language, nothing Len saw about him ever meant what it was intended to mean. Out of order and out of context, his Japan remained a phonetic and visual jumble, and he, its observer—at best entertained, at worst perplexed, but always, always foreign.

In fairness, Len and Andie both wanted to learn Japanese, tried to read, and memorized a number of kanji. Years later back home, in the early stages of Alzheimer's, Andie would pass a Honda in the street and draw with her finger in the air the two kanji that make up the word: Hon and Da, "source" and "rice field." She would do it compulsively, time after time.

Still, Japanese is a difficult language, and the timid carrying around of some written characters ended up the extent of Len's success: With the students he had to speak English—after all, they came to Temple for that; with his wife and his friends he spoke English or German. His neighbors' etiquette didn't seem to make them chatty with the Americans, and people on the subway didn't even speak to each other. He turned on the TV and stared into familiar images overlain by incomprehensible voices. In the end, only the ghost of Ruth Benedict offered him some consolation in the familiar shape of scholarly, thoughtful, and preconceived notions, skin-deep and filtered in his Latin-lettered enclave, but the best thing a tongue-deficient academic could hope for: an explanation.

Talking to Len

(On shame, mutual awareness, impasse in dialogue, and having to choose—and on teaching and failing in Japan)

RA   Len, you said your Japanese students and you suffered from cultural misunderstanding. How bad was it?

LS   It was frustrating. The students didn't seem to understand what I called "religious questions": questions of the meaning of life. I'd get blank stares when I asked if life had meaning. I asked ethical questions and got blank stares. The only ones who understood the questions turned out to be those who'd gone to Christian high schools and one from a Buddhist high school. It seems those questions were so foreign, like a foreign language.

You know, this matches what Ruth Benedict wrote about Japanese culture: that it's not one of guilt but one of shame. It struck me as being on the mark. I tried jokes, stories, being angry—nothing seemed to get them to respond. I even kicked them, but they would not answer. Just "yes" and "no."

I said, "Let's have a conversation!" Nothing. So I had them sign up to see me individually for fifteen minutes. I asked them about brothers and sisters and stuff, and we had perfectly human conversations, but in group they wouldn't speak. I would make a pact with them: "Promise you would ask a question in class." I did this thirty, forty times. Then in class: nothing, torpor.

RA   Have you considered the fault may have lain with your teaching, your lack of comprehension of them? Why, for you, does this support Benedict's thesis about shame cultures?

LS   Andie had the same experience in her English classes, but she finally struck on the method. Instead of asking, "What do you think about X?" she said, "What would your Aunt Mary think about X?" Then they went on and on! They'd talk about other people's thoughts, not their own. That revelation was too late for me to use, but fundamentally, it's an "other-directed" culture.

RA   I see.

LS   This helps me understand the horrible atrocities the Japanese committed.

RA   You mean in war. Don't we find that all parties commit horrible atrocities in war—guilt, shame, and all?

LS   Yes, but I'm referring to events like the contests the Japanese had on how many beheadings they could do in one swipe of a sword. There was no one there to shame them. Today, when Japanese politicians get caught, they are publicly shamed—that's the origin of *hara-kiri*. It's really disturbing—tells us how much we humans make ourselves whatever we are.

RA   I'm not sure I know what you mean by that.

LS   Well . . . just this morning someone sent me a copy of "Why should I do good rather than evil?"—and it's a deep question.

RA   It's an old and common question, with many familiar answers. What is yours?

LS   One way I've dealt with it is this: It's in the very nature of being human that we somehow see ourselves and other people—at least *an*-other person. The mother is the obvious first one. And we tend to identify more or less with this person's goodness when we discern him or her as a person. That's the birth of the Golden Rule. When you love somebody, it seems almost inevitable that you develop a sense of being more in the *alter ego* than in the *primus ego*. Every father would give the one remaining life jacket to his daughter rather than keep it, no questions asked. I am more "there" than "here." That, it seems to me, is rock-bottom what makes us human rather than a tree or an ant.

RA   Animals sacrifice for their children.

LS   For us it's conscious.

RA   How do you know animals are not?

LS   We don't; we infer from behavior. It strikes me that, when you get to the human, there is a qualitative jump in self-awareness and the ability for mutual self-awareness.

RA   What is that?

LS   I'm sitting here and thinking and talking, and I'm also capable of noticing that I'm thinking these thoughts, and I know that you are understanding these thoughts. You and I can be aware of each other thinking these thoughts.

RA   Self-aware and aware of another's self?

LS   Mutually so. I'm aware of "we," you're aware of "we," so we can be mutually aware of us. I believe this to be at the core of freedom and responsibility, at the core of what it means to be human.

RA   So what is the good for a human?

LS   The good for anything is to attain that toward which it is directed, oriented.

RA   This is very Thomistic.

LS   I'm a rock-bottom Aristotelian Thomist. So my greatest good is to expand myself, my ego. I love you, I love others. It doesn't stop with persons, but it's a peak with persons. That's the line of thought I would try to articulate. It's not easy to put into words that are clear and persuasive.

RA   Love is in the human nature, so to love is to fulfill ourselves?

LS   Yes. Love is the source and goal. We talked before about my per-
        sonality, which is sort of automatic on my part, but that's also
        what I try to do consciously.

I have trouble imagining Prof. Len Swidler, the consummate nice
guy, puffing himself up to get angry at his class, yelling and hollering,
raining fake fury upon their heads, jumping from one to another and
kicking them. I believe the story, but my imagination fails me.

I have a much easier time picturing rows of Japanese students,
hands folded, combed-haired heads bowed under the six-foot-tall, spit-
spraying fountain of American passion, their lips barely trembling:

"Yes, Swidler-sensei."

"No, Swidler-sensei."

What does he possibly want?

Our dear Ruth Benedict, may she rest in peace, wrote thus in the
famed *The Chrysanthemum and the Sword*:

> [The Japanese] have been brought up to trust in a security
> which depends on others' recognition of the nuances of their
> observance of a code. When foreigners are oblivious of all these
> proprieties, the Japanese are at a loss. They cast about to find
> similar meticulous proprieties according to which Westerners
> live and when they do not find them, some speak of the anger
> they feel and some of how frightened they are.[35]

To a degree, we can all identify with the sentiment, though it may
be more extreme for Japan. Having been such an enthusiast of Benedict's
at the time, Len had to have read this passage—only a couple of pages
away from her exposition of shame and guilt cultures—and a host of others like it, but I wonder if he took her message to heart. For sure, the
renowned anthropologist would have told him that neither kicking nor
screaming could dislodge the permeating heredity of an ancient culture,
change in a semester the way people interacted.

The question I keep asking is: Why try?

RA   Was all of your teaching in Tokyo so unsuccessful?

LS   I wouldn't say it was unsuccessful. Andie and I really enjoyed
        our time in Tokyo. I taught this one graduate seminar in Inter-
        religious Dialogue, and we had a particular argument there that

---

35 Benedict, *Chrysanthemum*, 225.

I remember. This is not as much so now, but especially years ago, when liberal-minded people came to talk about dialogue, some figured that anybody's religion, whatever they do, you know, it's okay. It's their religion, so you may not touch it.

I think I may have used my book *After the Absolute* that was just forming at the time. One section is on extremes and how to deal with them. Are there times and places when further dialogue is not appropriate? And I argued, "Yes." My example was: When I find out that somebody gives religious sanction to clitorectomy, I don't say, "Great, let me find out more about it." I know all about it. I'm against it, and here's why, and then we can discuss whether my standards are acceptable and irrefutable or not.

In a sense, philosophically, rationally, you have to come with a starting point you can't get behind. You have to make an argument for yourself, and it's accepted or it's not. For example, you accept that human beings are to be always treated as ends not means—the Kantian rule of ethics. You accept it or don't. This one Jewish American woman was all, "No, no!" I tried to convince her: "Wouldn't you say, 'No' to the Nazi equivalent in religion of killing all Jews even if you weren't a German or a Nazi?" That made her stop and hesitate. That sticks in my mind. I must have had a rather strenuous conversation with her.

RA   If you come to a point in dialogue when you and your partner are down to these rock-bottom positions and can't accept them, what happens?

LS   I wrote about it in the book. Some differences that seem contradictory in truth can be complementary: like, I say it's brown and you say it's blue. But what do you do if really contradictory positions are arrived at? Well, if it doesn't violate human persons just to stay there, then my position is that we can agree to disagree. But if it in fact in my judgment seriously injures human persons, then, I feel I am morally obliged to oppose it in what seem to be appropriate ways.

RA   How do you judge propriety of opposition?

LS   If I am sitting in England in 1857, during the rebellion in India, I might write letters to *The London Times*, but if I'm in Delhi, I'd do something about it.

RA   How far would you go in "doing something about it"?

LS   I guess I'd say proportionate to the damage and circumstances. Let me put it this way: If there were something physically damaging going on, on my block where I lived, maybe I'd go down and be part of a protest at City Hall, talk to people about donating money. An American citizen nowadays. It's quite different if you are a Chinese citizen in 1989. One of my former students was in the Tiananmen Square and had to escape for his life, smuggled out and over here. I later helped get his wife out of Hainan. Wrote letters, that sort of thing.

RA   Would you ever pick up a weapon to defend the powerless?

LS   Absolutely. I am not a pacifist. It seems to me logical that in some instances you don't have a choice between good and evil, only between evils. Sometimes not to choose is to choose, and you have to choose the lesser of the evils. You must act in a violent way because the only other choice is to have worse violence occur.

When I talk to complete pacifists, sometimes I tell them about one of the documents from the Nuremberg Trials I read at Marquette. It was a detailed report of a German engineer who had worked in Eastern Poland. He once saw busloads of Jews brought from a local city, and they were told to disrobe and walk to a huge pit already dug by others, walk over dead bodies in the pit, some still moving, then told to lie down by an SS trooper, who was sitting on the edge of the pit with a machine gun in his lap, smoking a cigarette.

Question: You see this, and you have a pistol. Do you look the other way? Go peacefully and protest? I hope I'd have the courage to take out my forty-five and shoot the bastard. Not to shoot him would implicate me in the shooting of these twenty innocent people.

RA   What did the engineer do?

LS   Reported it. He didn't say if he had a forty-five or not, plus it's a complicated situation. It's easy to be very brave when you're not there, but when you're there, your life . . . And you ask, "Will I make a difference? Will these people be shot anyway, and me too?" I set it up in the class in such a way that I have a choice to make a difference, but from the document I suspect he may not have. There could be six other guards. But maybe he did; maybe he reported it years later because his conscience had been eating at him all those years.

There is a debate about peaceful disobedience, and what it amounts to is that people have to make a choice, an act of the will—not of intellect. Because there are limit questions, because you can't prove rationally one side or the other. You have to choose. Can't get away from it. If you're honest, you have chosen. If you do your best to marshal the rational arguments in the broadest sense—including experience and intuition—you choose.

Take a typical one: Is there in fact a first cause? An uncaused cause? You can't prove it by the very nature of things. You look at the whole range of things and end up choosing.

RA   So you don't believe in honest agnosticism?

LS   Agnosticism, to use an analogy from physics, is an unstable position. We are driven to know, we want to know. Driven to choose. No one wants to be an agnostic. We want to be in a "yes" or a "no" position. Maybe, it's a question of timing. Maybe, as Hinduism would suggest, you need several lifetimes to outgrow the agnostic position.

Of course, it doesn't mean that, if you choose one side or the other, you have proved it. You may be so overwhelmingly impressed with an argument that it leaves precious little room for the opposite decision, but if you're honest with yourself, you recognize a possibility: Okay, you got a 99 percent position, but 1 percent of opposition exists. [*smiles*] Me, I go with the 99 percent rather than the 1 percent, but I always know the 1 percent is there.

PART V

Toward the Ocean—Dialogue

CHAPTER 17

Around the World in 280 Days: the life-changing sabbatical

"Whosoever, madam, did not in his youth have the skill of faith, will not acquire it in the old age. . . . I reckon, faith is an aptitude of the spirit. It is like a talent: one must be born with it."

—ANTON CHEKHOV, *ON THE ROAD*

IN THE FALL OF 1983, Len took a sabbatical that would turn out to be his last and—by leaps and bounds—the most important. He speaks of the academic year '83–'84 with a kind of wistful reverence we reserve for spiritual apprenticeships, with an ecstatic passion we hear in stories of conversion. In the nine months between fall and spring, Len circled the world, place after place, and stayed and spoke with people—Middle East, Europe, Africa, and Asia—and found his eyes opened in ways he had never thought real before. Having for decades devoted himself to dialogue, he found away from home some truths within and about the world, some truths within and about himself that made him a dialogical man—anew, deeper, and better. They made him what he is now.

The wise cynic Qoheleth wrote long ago that there is a time for everything: a time to be silent and a time to speak, a right time to embrace, to love, and to mourn. We must be ready to see what life has to show us. I have spent hours listening to the stories of Len's trip around the world, watching his face change from wonder to exhilaration. He has thought much about the nature of the insights he brought home from his last sabbatical, and he doesn't understand every reason for its life-changing impact upon his heart, but he knows one thing: It was the right time for him to see.

Hamburg

Before embarking on the journey itself, Len worked out his research plan—this was, after all, a sabbatical, not a vacation. He'd written ahead of time to a long list of religious practitioners around the world—friends of friends and those twice removed—and planned to meet them, see their religions in their home environments, and ask them questions from a list he composed for each tradition: *Do Muslims really think God speaks Arabic?* The list went on from there. He got himself a little voice recorder and set out for Hamburg, where the welcoming home of Dr. Khalid Duran was waiting for him.

Khalid Duran might not have been a classic case for Len's study of religious practice *in situ*, but he was probably a perfect starting point. Born to a Spanish Catholic mother and a Moroccan Muslim father, he was raised Muslim, learned Spanish and Arabic from his parents, German when he studied in Germany, and spoke also Urdu, Bengali, and the languages of Afghanistan. In the late sixties, he worked in Islamabad with the controversy-raising reformer Prof. Fazlur Rahman, eventually chased out of his Pakistan all the way to the University of Chicago for arguing, among other things, that we cannot understand the Qur'an unless we read it historically, in the context of its seventh-century Arabian setting.

At the time Len stepped through the doors of Duran's house in '83, Duran was working for the Middle East Institute in Hamburg and served as a sort of liaison between the West German government and the Afghan immigrants, which accounted for a veritable cornucopia of people milling about the rooms—what an astounded Len formulated as "a big party." A churning mass of men dressed in traditional garb, they seemed to the American onlooker "the Afghan versions of country bumpkins"—noisy, disordered, gesticulating, and talking over each other in every corner—but the host mixed with the crowd at perfect ease, and they, with him.

It took a while before the two managed to find an empty room, closed the door, and turned on the tape recorder, but then, a conversation ensued greater than anything Len had counted on.

LS   I must say, I was happily astonished. He took what I'd call a very modern, critical-thinking approach to Islam and the Qur'an, like I do to Christianity and the Bible. So we just had this fantastic conversation. I asked him questions. For example, did he think a pious Muslim would believe the Arabic in the Qur'an was actually dictated by God, that God spoke Arabic? And his response was much more nuanced than that. He'd worked in Pakistan at the Islamics Institute with Rahman, whose approach was historical contextualization, which meant in essence, "No." These words were not somehow uttered by God but, whatever else one believes, were uttered by Muhammad. And, in general, his understanding of religion was one that I found very sympathetic. He clearly was a person who lived in the mental world of what I call "modernity," critical thinking: Western Enlightenment forward, historicism, and dialogue—what Western humanity is all about.

RA   You keep using the word "Western" when you positively characterize thinking. Do you consider it a good and necessary thing for practitioners and scholars of all religions, including non-Western traditions, to have the approach of the Western world?

LS   Well, true, in a certain sense it's a misnomer to call critical thinking "Western," as if that implied that nobody else ever went down this path. On the other hand, historically, what we call "modernity" that dominates the world today comes from the Western Enlightenment and forward. And if you go back and look at the four civilizations of the Axial Period, the understanding that we are talking about is something that was shaped in the Western world, starting with Greece.

You have these axial shifts in the other three primal civilizations—Chinese, Indic, and Semitic—but the peculiar way of modern thinking, which has led to the creation of the scientific method in physical analysis and assumption-and-proof in the human world, it was not so developed by the other three civilizations. They had their own special contributions to make, but you don't find the Greek philosophical approach matched in the other three. The Chinese development, for example, was much more focused on practical living, not on abstract reasoning. That seems to me peculiar to the Greek world.

RA   What about the abstract that's not like the Aristotelian logic? Say, Advaita Hinduism, the hub of Indian pantheism? Or the Buddhist Prajnaparamita literature, which reasoned out the concept of Emptiness through a twelve-step cycle of dependent co-origination? Those are about the time of Greek philosophy, and they are highly abstract and require much reasoning; they're just different. Try something like the Diamond Sutra, our best example of the Neither-Nor logic.

LS   Those don't seem to have moved nearly so fundamentally as the Greek world to develop epistemology: thinking about thinking. It was a special development in the Greek world that had subsequently a massive kind of effect, and once seen and understood, no matter where you come from mentally, once you grasp it, it's transformative. You can't ignore it. I'd use an analogy in growth to puberty: You can't go back and make believe that you're not an adult, as if puberty hadn't occurred.

The Semitic contribution—say, Israelite prophets—was the emphasis on ethics, morality, the personal, especially for the outsider. Universalized, this is as incredible a contribution as what you get from the pre-Socratics and Greek thought. It's become part surely of Christendom and Islam, and by sheer numbers you've got close to half of the world population in these two religion-cultures. And as people living in the twenty-first century become aware of what's going on globally, everybody wants it. It's like freedom: another fantastic discovery that's at the core of being human. Once people understand this claim, every human being wants it.

RA   So, the two core aspects of being human that everybody wants are freedom and critical thinking?

LS   Right. Add to that, I would say, this whole sense of historicity: that reality is change. Of course, it's at the heart of the Buddha's philosophy that all reality is fleeting, changing. It's the foundation of his Four Noble Truths, but he doesn't go from that notion to social change or evolution, to social growth.

RA   You mean, Buddhism is mostly escapism?

LS   Buddhism is personal. You get saved, and another, one by one. It's atomistic in that sense. The fusion of freedom and critical thinking from the Greeks and the Semitic ethical responsibility for others provide the setting for the sense of historicity in communities. It's not just Len Swidler who develops and grows over eighty-four years. It's communities that Len Swidler lives in that also grow and change. And that has all kinds of fall-out in the way we act in the world. How we see the world changes how we act in it, gets our heads straight—or, let's say, straighter.

RA   What's the fall-out? What does a straighter head look like?

LS   Let's take the fundamental meaning of the Golden Rule, which weaves through all these ancient cultures. Its implications involved are the exact opposite of selfishness and also of any destructive asceticism. Growing up Catholic, we were told to mortify the flesh, diminish the ego, obedience—religious fascism at its worst. Seems to me that the aim of the Golden Rule is not to diminish my ego but to expand it limitlessly so that I draw the Good to myself and want to unite with it through Love. You know? Hear the music. Eat the ice cream cone. You have a friend, and you want to be one together: do things, write letters, think about them.

And so we get to the point where the highest Good that we know, we humans, is persons. And what you want to do then is be one with this Good, this person, this *alter ego.* Jesus articulated this: "No greater love than to give up his life for his friend." If I'm in a boat that's sinking with only one life jacket, I'll give it to my granddaughter. No question.

RA   You seem to imply that the traditions not grounded in your definition of critical-thinking-based historicity would suffer from lack of impetus for action for social change. What about Buddhism's well-known activism in social change?

LS   I have not yet come to know it, except in these new-age versions like Engaged Buddhism. From what I can see, it started by way of sympathetic vibrations from encounter with Christian social justice sensibilities. Ask yourself: Why have there not been great efforts on the part of Hinduism or Buddhism to create schools or hospitals to change society? They've always been focused on trying to change the individual. I don't think the cyclical sense of time helps—it's the cause and the result of this mentality of powerlessness on the large scale. But the Greek/Semitic society is linear in its thought, so you *can* change things.

RA   I don't know. Compassion is one of the two great virtues of Buddhism, and the Boddhisattva vow in Mahayana Buddhism seems like an expression of a mentality that would underlie social rather than just individual outreach, no? After all, a Boddhisattva vows to help the world "until grass itself is enlightened."

LS   One would think so, but empirically it has not been the case. It seems to be a one-to-one. "Me and Amida Buddha."

After a day with Khalid Duran, Len boarded an airplane to Tunis. He looked out the window and thought about the first encounter of his trip, *Wow! What a way to begin, with a peak experience!*

The concept of peak experience that we use so colloquially now belongs to a twentieth-century psychologist, Abraham Maslow, but flows remarkably freely between psychology and religious mysticism. Maslow believed that all of us—ordinary people in ordinary circumstances, with or without practice or intent—can undergo epiphanies, times of out-of-the-ordinary awareness in commonplace, daily lives: waiting for a bus, gazing at a loved one's face, picking up a flower. He heard people describe these peak experiences in the rapturous language so reminiscent of the mystics' confessions East and West that he became convinced: One need not meditate in a Buddhist monastery or embark on exotic travel to unfold the depths of self, and he wrote that "the sacred is in the ordinary."[36]

This is a very old truth in mysticism, but it appears to have been a new bridge between spirituality and psychology. "[P]eak-experiences," Maslow wrote, "can be considered a transient self-actualization of the

---

36 Maslow, *Religions, Values, and Peak-Experiences*, x.

person."[37] They are rare emotional and spiritual heights, and if we are wise, as we age they become rarer still and plateau into a life of serenity. A peak experience is a precious memory, and on his plane ride from Hamburg, Len Swidler marveled at the auspicious start to his journey and planned to treasure the memory fully. It could only go downhill from here, but what a ride it would be!

Tunis

In Tunis, Len had the name of Mohamed Talbi, a Muslim historian already involved in Christian-Muslim dialogue. He met Len at the airport and brought him home—unobtrusive, soft-spoken, fluent in English. They drank chai and ate fresh pitted dates, and they talked for the first time of many, for this was just the beginning of a thirty-year-long collaboration. Talbi would become a member of Len's Trialogue effort, and his articles would appear in *JES*. He would come to Philadelphia, and together they'd go to the Academy of the Vocal Arts to hear the opera they both love so much.

In April 2011, Mohamed Talbi gave an interview to *Ibraaz* on his long-standing fight for pluralism and flexible interpretation of the qur'anic text. "God does not only speak to the dead but also to the living," he said. "The Quran is not politics. . . . It is Light and the Source of Inspiration that is viable at every moment of time and life." The term "democracy," understandably, does not exist in it, but the term *Shu'ra* does: a word that means "consultation" or "dialogue" and refers to life as a whole, ensuring freedoms for all—of body, of expression, of justice—and social cohesion. He believes that "Quran is modernity. The Muslim world or *Ummah* needs to free itself from the historical and ossified magma of narrowly defined dogma. Free itself from the fear of the future."

As he spoke in the wake of the sweeping political changes in Tunisia in January 2011, his hopes were grounded in the new aspirations simmering all around his country: "Freedom in the context of egalitarianism, fairness and empathy is in my view the most important promise made by the Arab world today."[38]

Len met this man thirty years ago, but he already was the voice of change, peace, and justice that we recognize today. They spent three days

37 Ibid., 80.
38 Talbi, interview for *Ibraaz*.

together—talking at home over tea, talking with others in Talbi's dialogue group. And Len thought to himself, *How can this be, again, so much more incredible than I have thought? Another peak experience?*

LS   Mohamed took me to a meeting of his dialogue group, and it was so positive—not just mentally stimulating but mutually confirming! Maybe I'd even go so far as to say there was a loving atmosphere among these intellectuals. These Muslim and Christian thinkers were each deep in their own traditions and drilling down, as it were, finding a common well. Amazing.

RA   Was it a surprise for you?

LS   Yeah! I mean, I had begun the Trialogue meetings five years before, and had moving experiences with Muslim thinkers there, in a positive way, but those were people coming from all around the world—and Mohamed's group was right in one locality, clearly a highly developed gathering of sensitive thought in the city of Tunis.

RA   Why the surprise?

LS   Partly, the level of intensity in one place was surprising. I guess, I just felt once again, it was another peak experience.

Cairo and Jerusalem

And so it began. Reality peeled its layers under Len's feet like a mind-boggling onion, and on this quest, guide after guide turned the marble of the world before his eyes, each precious face shining its light more deeply into him, finding hidden crevices where Self meets Other.

In Cairo, he was welcomed by George Anawati, an Egyptian Dominican, and lived at the Dominican monastery with the Fathers, shared meals with them, spent time with George and the chief justice of the Egyptian supreme court, who'd just come back from a conference in Spain on the golden age of Iberia, when Jews and Muslims lived in harmony. He returned to Cairo talking of three-way dialogue, all aglow with possibilities of a better future.

"George was a personification of walking on the golden path." Len's face is affection and serenity. "He treated me like a brother he hadn't seen for ten years. I felt like I was home."

In Israel Len had friends, yet the encounter that sparkles on his memory involved somebody new: the director of a Swedish Christian institute in Jerusalem, whose name Len can no longer recall. He was a young man, very Norse in appearance—blonde, blue-eyed, a palette antithesis of the Middle East—and he exuded a magnetic, hypnotic spirituality. An aura of profound and grounded connection with That Which Is. Some people call it "faith." Others, "wisdom." Yet others, "zen."

LS   He had a very intense spiritual life, which was just . . . deeply Christian. Not at all new-age-ish.

RA   What does that mean?

LS   Deeply solid. Not spooky. "New-age-ish" is somebody you'd take with several grains of salt.

RA   But why? What would be the symptoms of a "new-age-ish" spirituality?

LS   For one, they see what I'd say would be projected connections—taped on by them from the outside.

RA   Like what?

LS   Saying, "The Holy Spirit was leading me to do that." Blaming the Holy Spirit for all kinds of stuff, which, it seems to me, is saying too much. It's the assumption that things happen in the world because God makes them happen. Okay, I understand the metaphysics of it: God is the unmoved mover; all things are sustained by God, the source of everything. But that's true of everything, so how do you say you are led to one thing or another? That ends up being just pure pious pap.

      And he was not that type. I even hesitate to use the term "spiritual." He had a very intense interior life that expressed itself in loving ways of friendship. There was an immediate person-to-person connection that you don't always sense. We have extra skins on the outside, by which we protect ourselves from becoming intimate, and then we can't be sorry. He didn't have it, he was very present to you—which led me to say once more, "Oh, my God, a fourth peak experience!" And I thought to myself, *What is going on here?* I began to wonder if spooky thoughts were to be totally waved aside.

RA Spooky new-age-ish thoughts?

LS Well, upon thinking about it more, I decided that's not what was going on.

RA What was?

LS I think about it now, and I believe that over the years I had reached a sort of ridge, a tipping point in my life, if you will. That somehow I was giving out the energy that was calling forth these responses—from Duran and Talbi and Anawati, and now my unremembered Swedish director. They were responding to the signals I was giving out.

You see, this continued through the rest of the trip—and, less repetitively and with less intensity, it continued throughout my life, but very overtly during the trip. Of course, the people I'd written to were committed to a life of interreligious and cultural dialogue, an in-depth kind of life. But, as it turned out, this connection didn't just happen with the people I'd written to. One of those I met quite accidentally in Delhi became one of my closest friends to this very day: Filo Hirota. But first, I went to Pakistan.

Pakistan and India

Pakistan was a disaster. For the first time in the weeks since Len had left home he hit a low, but it was a real Mariana Trench. All this time he'd been eating local fair in every place, accepting with open hands whatever he'd been given, with an open mind, new tastes of the Old World, congratulating himself on never having gotten sick. Then he arrived in Lahore.

Len doesn't know what he had. Food poisoning? A particularly hostile virus? The scourge of tropical climates: amoebic dysentery? Splayed out on the bed soaked in cold sweat, he had not enough in him to care, barely enough to writhe in pain, to take shallow, laborious breaths—slowly in and quickly out. For three days he knew nothing else, only pain and the one all-consuming desire of a tortured animal: for the pain to stop.

It was October—Lahore's beautiful autumn. Outside, sunshine infused warm air with subtle aromas, and one could see for miles over the intricate cityscape of roofs and minarets. Outside lay adventure and churning life. Len didn't know any of it. If he had the presence of mind to be grateful for the caring hands of a friend, he doesn't remember. He is grateful now.

Riffat Hassan was a member of Len's Trialogue group, a Lahore native and a good acquaintance. Whatever plans she had made for his visit never came to fruition, but she didn't leave his side. In a few days, with the help of a doctor and some medicine, she put him back on his feet, weak as a weed, quite a bit lighter, and having missed everything about Pakistan but a brush with death. For the rest of the trip, Len couldn't hold down much food and ate very little, very mild foodstuffs, and tried to hold to the familiar, losing by Christmas just about twenty pounds.

"I remember in Kuala Lumpur I saw two blocks from the hotel an A&W Root Beer stand, and I went there for all my food in Malaysia. It wasn't all a bad thing." He chuckles, but I can hear a nervous memory surfacing in his voice. He is making light. "I lost lots of weight, but then, I was somewhat stocky when I started out."

He got out of bed in Lahore just in time to leave for India.

RA   Len, what happened on the border with India?

LS   Security. I went to cross over, and they asked me, "Why do you want to go to India?" I explained that I had this sabbatical and the whole thing, and they go, "Rejected."

RA   Why?

LS   Apparently, I should have said, "I just want to be a tourist and see all the wonderful things in India!" Then, *stamp!* I learned this later. As it was, I had to go back to Islamabad, go to the embassy to get a visa, and then proceed.

RA   What was the problem with your reason for visiting?

LS   It's that I was going to interview people. These border guards were being protective, and you know: a little power is a dangerous thing. They thought it was a risk their country should not take, and I dropped right into it.

New Delhi greeted Len with soaring skies, cooling evenings, and unfamiliar challenges: Finding tolerable food was now an effort, and an admittedly board-like bed where he was staying immediately did a number on his newly protruding hip bones. Excitement, however, was not lacking. He quickly found a conference on Catholicism in non-Catholic countries about to begin—a gathering, as he put it, of "Catholic theology types, all religious"—and joined in on the action.

Still, the meetings weren't starting until dinner, and this was morning. Only two members had arrived: a young Vietnamese man living in Germany, representing the German Misereor organization, and a Japanese nun working with the Justice and Peace Division at the Asian Federation of Bishops Conference, headquartered in Manila. At the building where they stayed, Len found the young man, with nothing else to do and agreeable for an adventure, and Sister Filo Hirota even more so: being the only woman, she had the whole empty upper story to herself.

For a tour of the city, the sundry trio piled into a *tuk-tuk*: a little three-wheeler with a doorless, one-bench cabin and a driver's seat up front. These zippy "auto rickshaws" are the most common means of public transport in much of the world, and their sunny yellow tops speckle the streets of India to this day. They don't offer much room, but Len's companions were rather compact, and he was smaller than he'd been, so they squeezed into the back and took off without a plan.

Delhi assaults the senses of a newcomer. Buildings crowd together, climb upon each other without end, varying heights, roofs and overhanging balconies, every space in between filled with a motley mix of colors: cars, buses, *tuk-tuks*, people whooshing among them with no conception of driving and walking surfaces, here and there an elephant towering over the mobs. The mind-bending chaos of Delhi's aerial view is surpassed only by being plunged into the thick of its street-level life, into the din and mingling aromas of markets and gasoline, shirts and saris and prime-colored billboards, beggars, and shops—blinding, deafening, whizzing by. The speed of it all . . . Every second a near-miss.

"It's very scary in the New Delhi traffic, you know?" Len giggles. It's funny now. "The three of us sort of bonded in all kinds of screams and squeals."

After a day or two, they rode a train to Agra, 127 miles from Delhi, where the great wonder Taj Mahal stands a monument to undying love and unthinkable luxury. It is probably the best known mausoleum in the world. Who doesn't recognize the contours of its soaring dome; who doesn't know the story of Shah Jahan's adoration of his Mumtāz Mahal? Who has not imagined the palace in its celebrated change of colors through the day: rosy hue in the mornings, snowy white in the evenings, golden in the moonlight? Who hasn't dreamed of walking down the path by the reflecting pool?

And yet for Len the overnight train ride to Agra yielded something more precious: a life-long friend. Kept awake by the cold, he wandered up and down the hallways and came upon the car where Sister Filo had an upper bunk, and they sat and looked out the window into the dark and talked quietly of many trifling things, and of many important things, and of the meaning of life. And they listened to the knocking of the wheels against the rail seams together.

RA   Was this the end of India?

LS   Almost. I was on my way to Malaysia and stopped in Bangalore first. I just remember I got there at night and went to bed, and in the morning I looked out the window and, *Oh my God: I'm in a different country!* Cars got to a light and stopped! It was all very orderly. A different civilization. Of course, it was. They also had a different language, a different alphabet and script. Only people looked the same. Then I stopped in Madras.

RA   Modern-day Chennai?

LS   Yes, and what I recall about it is strange: going to the shore. It's on the Indian Ocean—I think called the Bay of Bengal on that side. And on the shore, looking past all the isles, past the Pacific, toward the United States, stood a gigantic statue of Lord Cornwallis. My sole knowledge of him was that he'd surrendered his sword to General Washington in the Revolutionary War. What he was doing there, I have no idea. How did he get from Yorktown to Madras?

historical interlude

Charles Cornwallis was born on December 31, 1738, in London and is best known indeed for his spectacular defeat in the last significant campaign of the American Revolution, but his career did not end in Yorktown. In 1786, five years after his surrender in Virginia, Earl Cornwallis was knighted and appointed Governor General and Commander-in-Chief in India, where he would spend the next eight years engaged in reforms and military action, and where he would return in 1805, soon to die. He is buried in what is now Uttar Pradesh.

Although India in the mid-eighteenth century was quite fractured, with a variety of European colonial outposts dotting both coasts and a few kingdoms like Mysore and Travancore still holding together, by far the largest presence was British. From 1757 and exactly for a century— until the rebellion of 1857 forced the Crown to assume control—the British interests in the Subcontinent were effectively managed by the East India Company, an enormous private trading conglomerate with its own, very complicated administrative structure and its own hired armies that governed either directly or through its presidencies. By the 1780s, the Company was struggling financially and slowly sinking into the quicksand of its own regulations that mixed with a mish-mash of native policies in the huge territories under its rule. Lord Cornwallis arrived to clean up the mess.

Out of his Fort William residence in Calcutta, the Governor General altered the system of compensation within the Company to reduce corruption, reformed the taxation of landowners, and moved on to the justice system. The local rulers' judicial powers were taken away. With the help of a linguist, Cornwallis had Hindu and Muslim legal codes translated into English and consolidated them into a single system still known as the Cornwallis Code, which would be administered from then on by the Company's European employees through a network of circuit courts, with a superior court hearing appeals in Calcutta.

Unsurprisingly, the common biases of his time and culture are prominent in Cornwallis's reforms. With the same benevolent condescension, he introduced living wages for Indian weavers, restricted all Company employment to persons of pure European descent, outlawed child slavery, and established a school for Hindus that still exists as the Government Sanskrit College in Benares. For better or worse, his governorship left an indelible mark on Indian history, and some of what he did is still visible in the country's penal system, tax and administrative codes, and memorials.

Though one of his goals was to keep peace in the Company's territories, this Commander-in-Chief did get drawn into a war in India. To be fair, Tipu Sultan of Mysore's hostilities with the British had been brewing before Lord Cornwallis ever got to Asia, which is why this final conflict between them is called the Third Anglo-Mysore War. For bringing the problem to a successful end, Earl Cornwallis was created Marquis Cornwallis shortly before leaving for England and his next adventure, in Ireland.

He is hardly a hero to all. Few commanders are, especially in the after-throes of colonial history. Still, a mausoleum was erected over Marquis Cornwallis's grave and is kept up by the Indian government. His statue stands in Bombay, and another, on the shores of Chennai, gazing seaward—saying good-bye to his defeat in America, maybe, or hello to Fort Cornwallis, named after him on the island of Penang. The fort is still there, in Malaysia, its ten-foot-high walls never having seen battle. It is looking back at its namesake, five thousand miles from home.

end interlude

Malaysia

By the time Len got to Malaysia, it was December, and the air was filled with celebration and electricity. A majority-Muslim city, Kuala Lumpur astonished him with its exorbitant Christmas decorations, but really, it shouldn't have. The country is indeed predominantly Muslim and yet quite multiconfessional, and Christmas, Chinese New Year, and Deepavali are official holidays in the presence of the state religion of Islam. Len didn't know it, but Kuala Lumpur is famous among savvy travelers for its Christmastime lavishness: Stylized Christmas trees tower in the squares, brilliant snowflakes line the streets. Nutcrackers, bows, and still fireworks overwhelm the shopping malls. Huge Christmas-tree balls greet visitors at the Pavilion. A cornucopia of lights. He was so impressed that all other experiences there paled next to this ecstatic dance of holiday anticipation.

RA   Len, did you have any interesting encounters in Malaysia?

LS   Well, I went to this one relatively new Islamic university. The president was an Arab Muslim scholar, whose son is very well known now: he's the imam of the Cordoba Project mosque.

RA   Feisal Abdul Rauf? He's a very interesting, very progressive Muslim thinker.

LS   Right, so this was his father, Muhammad Abdul Rauf. He'd been the director of the Islamic Institute in Washington, DC, then president of this university, and I'd written to him there. He clearly was a very traditional Muslim thinker, quite unlike his son, even an antithesis. I remember meeting him and talking, and with a number of Muslim professors.

RA   What do you mean by a "very traditional" thinker?

LS   Let me tell you how we met originally. Muhammad Abdul Rauf was at the 1976 Catholic-Muslim "dialogue" in Tripoli, which turned out to be a total disaster, by the way, and we had an interesting conversation.

      At the dialogue, there were maybe four hundred people together for five days, at a big hotel. One of the evenings after the sessions, we were sitting around in a lobby, and Muhammad began to say how he was writing a book on women in Islam.

      I said, "Wow, hey, tell us about it!" I'd just finished publishing a book on the status of women in formative Judaism, so I was very interested.

      He said, "All right," and began talking about the whole business of sexuality. And he thought it was absolutely shameful and disgusting that people in the West sometimes would have sex in the light. It's supposed to be in the dark! Then he went on to say that women, of course, did not enjoy sex.

RA   Did you have a reply for him?

LS   Didn't have to. There was this silence, and a French Tunisian woman journalist happened to be sitting next to him. She reached over and touched him on the arm and said, "Darling, I'm sorry to disappoint you!"

Hong Kong and Shanghai

Hong Kong served partly as a gateway for Len from Malaysia into China, and he spent only a short while there, but every minute counted. It is a special place in itself.

Ceded by China to the British Crown in 1842—an arrangement that had become a century-long land lease in 1898—these 235 little islands and the New Territories have a complicated history. They'd been through prosperity and war, hunger and revival. Population swelled and fell as refugees poured one way or the other between Hong Kong and the mainland during the Japanese occupation of the thirties and forties, the Chinese civil war between Communists and Nationalists, and the terror of the Cultural Revolution in the late sixties. They made their living with light industry like textiles and had their share of poverty, problems, and labor disputes, but by the 1970s Hong Kong seemed to have found its economic niche in the new, high-tech industries and blossomed rapidly, dramatically, unrelentingly.

There are other such gems in the region: Singapore, Taiwan, South Korea—tiny powerhouses of technology, wealth, and controversy, without which we can hardly imagine our economic map. We call them "Asian Tigers." Hong Kong is the fourth.

Confined to a morsel of land tucked in next to the immensity of China, Hong Kong is a bamboo shoot that pushes its way up from under the belly of a sleeping elephant: tiny, odd, and triumphant, almost perceptibly fast, and just as vertical. One after another slender skyscrapers grew up like a gigantic motley bamboo forest among its waterways. Hong Kong boils. Hong Kong lives. Its light pollution is a maddening nightly firework.

"Hong Kong for the first time—it is wild!" Len's arms are flying about, failing to show just how wild it was there, that first time, in 1983. "You see it in movies. There were thousands of shops selling billions of things—it's astonishing! Unbelievable. I can't imagine how they can live. Who eats, who buys all that? It was like shop land for the whole blooming world."

The early 1980s were a crucial time. The land lease to Britain would run out in 1997, and both sides began to worry about the hand-over: What would happen to the rampantly capitalist Hong Kong governed by a Western democracy when it found itself very suddenly bound by the rules of a socialist economy, answerable to communist ideologues? As the elephant rolls over in its sleep, will it crush the young bamboo into powder?

But, then, China itself was in flux. Only a few years before, in 1976, Mao Zedong had died, and the Gang of Four, led by his wife and blamed for the worst of the Cultural Revolution's mayhem, had just been tried and imprisoned. Len came to China just when Margaret Thatcher and the new "paramount leader" Deng Xiaoping were meeting to negotiate the terms of the famous "One Country, Two Systems" compromise. Under this agreement, when Hong Kong became Chinese in 1997, it would keep its capitalist economy and partial democracy—not forever, but for fifty years.

Whether "One Country, Two Systems" is working well for Hong Kong is a difficult question. The years since the hand-over have seen plenty of protests over freedoms, elections, and legislation. There've been scandals and political arrests and a proposal for "Article 23": an anti-subversion law so frightening that a near-riotous wave of outrage forced the State to shelf the bill. Yet, there are those, like Len, who believe that the timetable has a chance.

LS   When I was there, it was the very beginning of the opening of China. Deng Xiaoping is an alumnus of Temple University: We gave him an honorary doctorate.

RA   How do you feel about that?

LS   I think it was good. This was part of the whole move to open up China, and Deng wanted the same sort of thing. He was the key figure to move China away from this murderous Maoism that killed over a hundred million of his people. Of course, Hong Kong was still independent then.

RA   It was Deng who set up Hong Kong as part of China but a separate system.

LS   It will run to 2048. Hopefully, by then China will become truly democratic so Hong Kong is not ripped apart by its maw.

Whether the People's Republic of China is moving toward what we call "democracy"—or will get there by 2048—is another difficult question, but its economy has changed since the time of Mao, changed drastically and without question. We know this remarkable blend of communist ideology and market economy with private ownership as "socialism with

Chinese characteristics." The term was coined by Deng Xiaoping, its architect and theorist.

historical interlude

Deng Xiaoping was always brilliant. Born in 1904, he finished secondary school at fifteen, studied in France, and pledged his life to communism there. Back in China, he agitated insurrections in rural areas and joined with Mao's movement in the civil war against the Nationalists. When the forces of the Republic of China overwhelmed the Communists in Jiangxi in October 1934, Deng was there, with ten thousand others, for the deathly year of the Long March, through the mountains to Shaanxi, by the side of the Party's new leader, Mao Zedong. When the Communists finally won and the People's Republic of China was proclaimed in Beijing on October 1, 1949, Deng was there, Mao's strategist and political commissar of unequaled depth. By 1956, he was a member of the Standing Committee, at the very top of the pyramid of power in the country, right under Mao himself. Yet, it seems, this is when his path began to diverge from the Chairman's.

By 1958, private ownership of land had been gradually abolished in China, and, with the beginning of the second five-year plan, Mao unveiled a sweeping campaign of collectivization and industrialization: the Great Leap Forward. He planned to outperform the U.K. in steel production within fifteen years, and he planned to do it without investing in technology, by using China's most available resource: manual labor. What financing industrialization did require would come from grain exports, the grain the State would get cheaply from its uncompensated countryside.

There is a degree of abhorrent similarity between what happened next and the catastrophe of the early thirties in the Soviet Ukraine, except that China is a larger crowd. Everything in China happens on a larger scale.

The Great Leap began. Mass mobilization of workers to the cities accompanied forced collectivization of peasants into enormous, five-thousand-family communes. Mao's faith in a grassroots effort of the masses was infinite, so he had backyard furnaces built all around the country—in cities and villages—and forests, furniture, doors disappeared in their tiny maws to fuel the fires that melted scrap metal, pots, and pans, leaving people destitute. But, of course, backyard furnaces could produce nothing but pig iron.

Meanwhile, so much human power had been taken for steel production that crops were rotting in the fields. A past year's campaign against sparrows caused a locust infestation, which made things worse in '59. Botched irrigation projects, crop experiments, and construction devastated agriculture. Grain production was falling, but the State demanded more, raising quotas for export and to feed the previously unheard-of numbers of urban population. Regional party officials inflated their harvests so not to admit failure; villages could not make the quotas; local authorities, forced to deliver on promises, took away everything there was; and starvation set in. Famine began.

The irony of the name "the Great Leap Forward" pales before the tens of millions of lives it took—maybe as many as forty-two million. It took the Chinese economy backward an unknown number of years before the policy was reversed in 1962. And it brought about so much suffering and so much hatred that no numbers can measure them. It is remembered in China with horror and disdain.

We rarely learn from history. Chairman Mao had an example before him only twenty-five years old of forced mass collectivization and the murderous famine it had caused, but he leaped all the same. And, just as in Ukraine, the worst disaster subsumed China's gorgeous, green bread basket: Sichuan province. And, just as in Ukraine, not all deaths were from starvation: More than two million people died at the hands of their local functionaries when, too weak or defiant, they refused to work. Some died in armed uprisings against the regime when shipping grain to the cities and eating leaves no longer seemed like a good enough reason to live. Maybe a million committed suicide.

Just as in Ukraine, militias tortured and murdered peasants, outlawed traditional observances—funerals, weddings—because they were religious, lost humanity, lost dignity, lost sense. And we ask the same questions when we look back at our human-caused famines: can anything so evil not be deliberate? And, when the evil is this great, does the degree of intent really matter?

Deng Xiaoping helped reverse the Leap and likely cemented his moderate economic perspective then, realizing the failure of the extreme left. While Mao, criticized and suffering a blow to his influence, brewed and resented the intellectuals, Deng became less his right-hand man and more his enemy, so when the time came in '66 for the Chairman's triumphant rise to cultic status, Deng didn't stand a chance.

Mao Zedong orchestrated the Great Proletarian Cultural Revolution very carefully, starting from inside the party with accusations and replacements of key positions, cementing his support in the Politburo, only then spilling a flood of alarm bells onto crowded city streets, slogans of paranoia waving high and wide: The party, the society had been infiltrated by the bourgeois elements, "capitalist roaders" and "counter-revolutionary revisionists"! Only a renewed class struggle could purge these corrupting influences and preserve the dictatorship of the proletariat.

The language of the Central Committee's documents didn't need clarification: The subversive enemy was "academic," "intellectual," and used "old culture" to "capture people's minds." Inside the party elite, the message aimed squarely at Mao's learned opposition, which prominently included Liu Shaoqi and Deng Xiaoping. Outside, frenzied youth in explosive fervor, worshiping Mao's every word, banded into loose formations they called the Red Guard—squads of fanatical children who measured their revolutionary zeal by the desire to kill. They wreaked havoc, but havoc appeared to suit Mao's goals of rapid cleansing of the leadership ranks, and he egged them on with slogans and big-character posters and the *Little Red Book* of quotations, and by giving them unprecedented power even over the military—and no earthly reckoning.

Freed by Mao's directive from police interference, the Red Guard ran rampant over the country. Violence swept through China and left behind thousands of mutilated corpses of teachers and cadres—uncounted numbers beaten, tortured, publicly humiliated, and dead by their own hands. It left behind looted Buddhist temples and razed cemeteries; places of worship—destroyed; art, architecture, books, and historical artifacts—lost forever; a halted economy; and railways in disarray.

After about three years, the State began to rein in the Red Guard, and much of the physical violence subsided, but not the Cultural Revolution. Any potential opposition within the Party—anyone of independent thought-pattern or of anything but staunchly orthodox Maoist background—was purged, sent out to the rural labor camps. Toward the end of 1968, Mao extended the move to the general population. "Down to the Countryside Movement" rounded up urban intellectuals and shipped them out of the cities to work in the villages, though the term "intellectual" now included students barely out of high school, many of them former Red Guard. With teachers, the educated vanguard, and anyone skilled above the average dead or rotting in labor camps, the Chinese intelligentsia lost a generation of potential, a generation who would not go to college and would not return home until the late seventies, after the public declaration of the end of the Cultural Revolution by Deng Xiaoping, himself only then rehabilitated.

Deng was purged twice in the ten years of Mao's Great Terror and endured everything but death. He was paraded through the streets of Beijing in a ritual of disgrace with a dunce cap on his head, worked manual labor in a tractor factory, served meals at a party training camp. He was purged, brought back when no one competent seemed to be left to run the country, then purged again—writing and surviving through it all, bending and straightening up. Not until after Mao's death in 1976 was Deng pardoned by the Chairman's successor and regained influence and positions of importance.

Though he never held top posts in the state, quickly he became the unquestioned "paramount leader," denounced the Cultural Revolution and declared its policies void, started the work of moderating the Chinese economy and of opening up the country to the rest of the world. By 1980, the guiding star of Deng Xiaoping shone brightly in the sky over China. Only one wound could never be healed from the time of the Great Terror: In 1968, during an interrogation by the Red Guard, Deng's son Pufang was thrown—or jumped—from a fourth-story window, to be paralyzed for life.

In 1983, Deng Xiaoping was a compact elder of seventy-nine. He packed so much paradox into his tiny, five-foot-tall body that *Time Magazine* called him "half elf, half gunman."[39] In the same article he was dubbed "China's foremost pragmatist," and that pragmatism wasn't new. Already in 1961, arguing for an end to the Great Leap Forward, Deng had uttered what might be one of his best known aphorisms: "Doesn't matter whether a cat is white or black, so long as it catches the mice."

Returning to the helm, this captain found his gigantic ship devastated by violent internal crusades and resentment, famished, illiteracy at 40 percent, so devoid of intelligentsia that in some places students were teaching students how to read. Ruins of relics and treasures, book fires

---

39 "China: Six Who Rule," para. 2.

still smoldering. Hundreds of thousands of fresh graves. A nation in mourning for its dead living god. Deng gathered up allies and rolled up his sleeves, and he let his pragmatism as loose as he possibly could.

It is somewhat remarkable that the groundbreaking Deng Xiaoping Theory, which is now written into the Chinese constitution and taught at every university, breaks no substantial ground. "Socialism with Chinese characteristics," the theory that in only a few years made China self-sufficient in food and created the fastest-growing economy in the world, invented nothing essentially new. Rather, it stated the obvious—what should have been obvious. Genius is often simple. So is, really, the concept of Deng's market socialism; all it takes is an erasure of pre-drawn boundaries.

Deng Xiaoping Theory starts with a refusal of exclusivity: Planning does not define socialism, it says. Capitalist economies plan. Market forces do not define capitalism. Market exists in socialist systems. The conclusion is startlingly simple: Why not utilize the best practices of capitalism for the benefit of a socialist economy? "Socialism does not have to mean shared poverty," he is reported to have said.

And so it was. Under Deng's direction, rural communes were dissolved and peasants permitted to control their plots and sell product; city dwellers could open small private enterprises; trade began with the outside world; people started buying consumer goods. He received heads of state and visited others, worked out Hong Kong's and Macau's "One Country, Two Systems" arrangements to the laud of the West. The educational system was reformed, with students encouraged to learn English and go abroad to college. Deng once said that the Cultural Revolution had produced an "entire generation of mental cripples,"[40] but soon enough some of them would be returning home with knowledge and skills and innovative foreign techniques.

Of course, not everyone shares this paradisiacal vision of Deng's China, and its critics come from both sides of the aisle. Sober advocates of democracy remind us that, alongside economic liberalization, the iron fist of the one-party system continues to rule in Beijing. Deng was no Western flunky and never, not a day in his life, betrayed his Marxist-Leninist philosophical ideals. Until the day he died, he promoted Mao Zedong Thought as the only guiding, if interpretable, ideology; he mercilessly incarcerated and exiled dissidents and created and enforced the infamous "one child" policy of population control, complete with forced

---

40 See, e.g., Ebrey and Walthall, *East Asia*, 525.

abortions and the unprecedented spike in female infanticide. The degree of his support for the 1989 massacre in the Tiananmen Square is debated, but his responsibility is not. He was, after all, the paramount leader. The market economy of Deng would stabilize China on its way to the communism of Mao, and anyone who said differently paid a dear price.

This is the worry of those who say Deng Xiaoping didn't go far enough in opening up China, that he just offered a market economy without democracy. Others are worried he's gone too far—they are core, to-the-bone communists who hear the rhetoric of compromise as a cop-out. They say that a train of socialism, shabby as it is and late to the station, is better than a capitalist train, even a posh one running on time, and their reason is simple: The ends do not justify the means. The country must be brought to stability; standards of living must be increased, but not at the cost of reintroducing the very original sin of economy against which the Revolution was fought: exploitation of workers by management, growing the inequality that breeds class struggle. Look, they say, that's exactly what's happening: Inequality is growing rapidly in China. It's a passing phase, Deng was hoping. "Some must get rich first," he said. But look at the wealth gap in the United States. Core, to-the-bone communists are worried that every dark chapter of the last sixty years, every lesson and sacrifice will have been for nothing if socialism erodes in China.

Time will tell what happens. Deng Xiaoping passed away in 1997, just as Hong Kong was passing from British control. He was ninety-two. Did he leave behind an increasingly prosperous, newly entrepreneurial nation guided by higher ideals toward communism? An oppressed nation without the prospects either for Western democratic freedoms or for the equality and security of planned socialism? A nation ultimately on its way toward democracy? The debate is still on, and time will tell, but a miniscule piece of the puzzle among many is in place: one Leonard Swidler comes to help. Through his father's grief he inherited the aftermath of Ukraine's horror, and he comes now to China in the aftermath of its own, similar tragedy, but this time he is no helpless bystander from overseas. He is part of the solution.

end interlude

RA   Len, you were in China the first time in 1983, but then you went back many times.

LS   I went to teach every summer from then on, and Andie went with me, until 1995. By then Andie was deep into Alzheimer's, and I didn't go again until 2004. It was an extraordinary experience. What happened to China between '95 and '04 was like a miracle. It was magic!

RA   What kind of changes?

LS   Concrete example: In Shanghai in '95 there were maybe ten high-rise buildings all together on the Bund, this waterfront business district. Across the river, there were abandoned wharfs. In '04, there were four thousand high-rises of twenty stories or more.

Before, whenever the Chinese built buildings by themselves, it was junk. I mean it literally. I used to joke that China was the only country I knew that built brand-new archeological ruins. I remember a bathroom where walls didn't meet in the corner. It's hard to describe.

Well, now, here you have it in 2004: gorgeous buildings by the thousands. And people utterly changed. In 1995, walking down Nanjing Road in Shanghai it was wall-to-wall people, and it was rude and crowded, people bumping into you. In 2004, as though the population of Hong Kong was transplanted in Shanghai: modern people, polite, going about their business. Extraordinary!

And, of course, one of the deficits in China has always been that, relatively speaking, there is not very much historical aesthetic value preserved there for the size and population. They just didn't have a very strong sense of the importance of history and retaining things of the past. It's very different from Europe, even from the U.S., but it's clear now that that sense is growing, and it comes with a certain kind of mentality.

In 1983, from Hong Kong Len flew straight to Shanghai, where an American philosopher Henry Rosemont had a Fulbright fellowship at Fudan University. Len didn't speak a lick of Wu or Mandarin, but a desk clerk at the hotel helped him dial the number for Rosemont's home. Rosemont wasn't there; with some other visiting Americans he was out on the town, later to go to a concert on the Bund.

Shanghai's Bund is the heart of the city, where its lifeblood of noise, lights, and skyscrapers is churning deals and diversions along the

Huangpu River. It was famous already then for its "high-rises"—Len smirks and puts the word in air quotes. The buildings were maybe ten or twelve stories high in 1983, built by European and American companies in the twenties and thirties. It looks very different now—a mini-Hong-Kong. So there, to the Bund, Len ventured his first evening in China.

LS   Damn, I was really ambitious and willing to take on anything on my own. I knew no language, and nothing was printed anywhere, and there were no taxies, just buses. I remember going to this concert hall, built by the French—old and shabby-looking on the outside. I was looking for something to eat first, and there was a restaurant nearby. Of course, the menu was in Chinese, and no one spoke anything but Chinese. I looked around, and at a table were five or six guys, all wearing Mao jackets, looking the same. I looked at what they were eating and what looked harmless, and somehow communicated to a waitress that I would try some of that and that. By that time the Chinese guys were very interested in me. Who knows if they'd seen a Westerner in their lives, so I was invited to their table.

　　　　Finally, the concert hall was opened, and I went in. There was nothing to pay, I think: It was communism; everything was free. It was pretty filled up, but everyone looked exactly the same except for this one group on the ground floor in the middle, who stuck out like a sore thumb.

RA   The Americans?

LS   Yep. They weren't wearing Mao jackets. We arranged to meet the next day, and I went to my seat on the balcony.

RA   How was the concert?

LS   You know, some of the local Chinese had been let out of detention camps only a couple years earlier, and they played, I thought, not badly. What struck me was that they'd finish a piece, and there were a thousand people there, but they made about as much noise clapping as ten people. I thought, *Oh, those poor people on stage, playing their hearts out!* Obviously, they had no tradition of going to concerts. That's what stuck in my mind. The Cultural Revolution was a terrible scourge.

Len met with Henry the next day, met several other people through him, young Chinese scholars. And then, it was time for Christmas, time for a break. He went home for the holidays as though stepping back into the familiar out of the looking glass, just for a little while. In January, China would wait for his return.

Tianjin

The beginning of 1984 saw Len back in China. A brief stop in Beijing, a few conversations, and he was off to Tianjin: a major center of seven-and-a-half-million people, a large seaport on the Bohai Gulf, and, since 1980, a sister city to Philadelphia.

LS   Flying in China was an adventure in those days. The airports were tiny, and to say they were ill-equipped would be to praise them unwarrantedly. It would be a crush to try to get into the plane because all the Chinese wanted to get on at the same time. I flew many times after, when I taught in the summers, but this was my first time. So we get into the plane, and overhead bins are just open shelves. Then getting ready for take-off, half the plane is up in the aisle. I thought, *Oh my God, all these human cannonballs! All we need is one big bump!* Fortunately, we didn't hit any such bump. Obviously, the crew didn't know anything or felt totally helpless.

RA   Was it a Chinese airplane?

LS   Ha! Walking across the tarmac, I was looking for bullet holes in the fuselage: it was obviously an old Russian WWII war plane.

On the ground in Tianjin, the head of the Philosophy Department at Nankai University greeted Len with the help of a graduate student who spoke some English. The pleasant young man—Len still knows him because he now lives in New Jersey with his wife—introduced himself as Kang Bowen and pointed to the car they brought to pick up the American celebrity.

LS   It was something from the middle of the 1930s: a Packard, I think. I remember so vividly riding in this car because we were one car in the city of seven million, among ten thousand bicycles, like we were surrounded by swarms of insects.

RA   How long did you stay?

LS   Well, they invited me to come for weeks and weeks later, and I would, but that time I was there for only a short period. I remember lecturing in their biggest hall, maybe it held three hundred people normally, and they squeezed in—on the floor, in the aisles, down the hallway—450, maybe, plus those in the hallways. I lectured on modern Western thought and, of course, got to religion.

RA   Did they understand you?

LS   Ah! I already started on the path of what turned out to be a very good habit from then on: to speak in short statements, intellectual capsules. So I had a reasonably good hope that the interpreter could understand and repeat what I said, not what he thought I said. It turned out to be a really good technique. I would say twelve to fifteen words, and then, while he or she was doing the interpreting, I was thinking what I wanted to say next: something that would hook up with what I'd just said and would lead the way to the point immediately afterwards. I was doing all this thinking about the connections between images and syllogistic lines. So, you know, I was creating new thought.

So we proceeded like that, and about half way through I got a bright idea to check how many people in the audience understood English and to check how accurate the interpretation was. So I told a joke.

RA   Not a play on words, I hope.

LS   Now the rule was, supposedly, to get into the university, English was a requirement. This audience was crème de la crème.

RA   What happened?

LS   Half the people laughed at the joke. Then he interpreted, and the other half laughed. Now in a way it's a comedian's paradise: two laughs.

RA   What if some people didn't laugh because you weren't funny?

LS   I was funny.

RA   What was the joke?

LS   I don't remember. I was funny. Because they laughed.

RA   Did you get to talk to the students?

LS   Indeed. After the presentation, I asked, "Any questions?" Very often from the undergraduates in this country you get silence, and it's not the silence of the Buddha. But these kids were asked to write the questions, and there were scads of them. And it wasn't just the quantity that was impressive but the quality, too. They were obviously not used to reading or thinking about the meaning of life other than food, shelter, or clothing. Period. So here they were asking the "meaning of life/religious questions"—which is a very interesting contrast to Japanese students.

      And that was in the morning. In the afternoon, I was invited to talk to the interested faculty and graduate students. There, it wasn't a presentation—presumably, most of them had heard my lecture. It was a discussion.

RA   What stayed with you the most?

LS   You know, I remember it really struck me that the kinds of questions these more sophisticated people asked were less sophisticated. Straight out of the stuff I was very familiar with from my study of Marxism and the Christian-Marxist dialogue I was involved with. To use an image from baseball, they were feeding high outside pitches: How do you answer such-and-such criticism of religion? How do you deny such-and-such accusation? Easy to put over the fence for a good batter. And when I did, they stood there gaping, in utter astonishment, as if they had never thought of a possible retort for what should have been a squelcher for religion.

      They had a very naïve understanding of religion and dismissed it, but they dismissed a straw figure. See, keep in mind: I can think of very serious questions to pose to religion—but they didn't think of them. They just had these pseudo-questions, as if they were learning their Marxism from textbooks rather than serious Marxism.

RA   So it seems you felt kind of triumphant.

LS   That's a good way of putting it.

RA   You have gone back many times to Tianjin since, to teach, haven't you?

LS   Oh, yeah, starting with the following summer. Andie came with me, and Kang was our interpreter—I later got him a scholarship to Temple.

Funny story. There was an opening banquet the next summer: a typical Chinese setting, with a round table and a lazy Susan. On my left was the rector—officially the deputy rector because the President of China was always rector—and on the right, an older Chinese guy in charge of international affairs. We're all sitting there, food in the middle, and no one is taking any. I thought I was the guest of honor, so maybe they were waiting for me to start, so I took my chop sticks and took some food. The rector pokes me in the side and, through Kang, asks me, "How come you didn't start with a prayer?"

Well, I was embarrassed! Mumbled something embarrassed. Suddenly, the old ones at the table go in unison reciting the whole Hail Mary, in English! Andie and I are looking at each other astonished. Later we learned that both of them had been students before 1949 at a Catholic school, and it was still with them! Not the right prayer at meal time but, still, pretty impressive.

We habitually malign the Chinese regime for narrow-mindedness, for the rigidity of views that accompanies a one-party system, for anti-religious propaganda that's cost the nation so much suffering and so many cultural treasures—and we are right to do so, not that a host of planks in our own eyes couldn't use some taking out. Len's impression from 1984 falls mostly in line with our ideas of the communist China: paper-depth conceptions thrown in line behind the slogans of Marxism, nothing more. And, yet, one must pause at the very fact of an American professor of religion welcomed with such passion by an authoritarian, atheist establishment, with open arms, with a hunger for discussion—they didn't want to make a show of destroying him, but wanted him to teach! And they wanted him to come back, again and again, to do more of it.

And he did. Len's first visit was the beginning of a lifelong friendship with Nankai University. He would come back the next summer with Arlene, and almost every summer afterwards, except for a few years—the worst years when she was in a bad way, deep into Alzheimer's. He still goes there to hold his courses at a sister city, a city-friend. A city-student.

In the spring of 1984, though, having knocked pitches out of the park and created a home away from home, Len packed up and moved on: to Nagoya, Japan, and then to Manila and Taiwan before returning home for good.

Japan

Nanzan University sits nestled into the rolling hills of Nagoya, almost half-way between Kyoto and Tokyo. It is named after forest-covered mountains—a word from the poetry of Li Bai, a celebration of endurance and well-being. Founded by the Divine Word Fathers, it was an early site of the Christian-Buddhist dialogue, presided over by the fluid curves of the Divine Word Seminary Chapel, its bell tower rising out of the shells of poured concrete.

Len went to Nanzan and held a dialogue there. He went to Kyoto, the birthplace of the Kyoto school of Zen Buddhism, and roamed in its temple forest in the footsteps of Nishida, Hisamatsu, and Nishitani. Keiji Nishitani, he met face to face, and they had tea together in his tiny, traditional Japanese house—sliding doors, tatami mats. A tiny wisp of a man with a wry sense of humor and perfect English.

"He smoked like a smoke stack," Len says. "And we had mostly philosophical discussions, but at one point he asked if he could smoke in front of me, and I said, 'Of course. It's your house. But you realize you're going to stunt your growth!' He thought it was very funny. He giggled a good deal."

Talking to Len

(On self-realization and skating on thin ice)

RA   Len, you say this sabbatical changed your life. What is it that this trip so profoundly did for you, and why?

LS   I think in many ways it goes from the end all the way back to the fall—from Nishitani to Filo Hirota to Talbi and Duran—and this series of peak experiences that somehow created a new level of self-awareness in me. I've said this before: I believe I had gotten to a certain point in my self-realization to send out invitational signals, I suppose, to enter into safe friendships: intellectual, spiritual, personal relationships. It seemed like a corner had been gone around and a new vista opened up for me that I hadn't been aware existed before.

RA   What was the vista?

LS   Well . . . Experiencing kindred spirits. Finding them and opening myself to them. It became a habit, something intuitively done—a virtue in that sense. And in a way it sort of changed my perception of the world, of reality—the way falling in love does. Everything looks different.

RA   Did you fall in love with the world and discover it was in love with you?

LS   It was mainly persons, but the world tugged on the skirts and coattails of the persons—the rest of the world, the animate and inanimate and the transcendent. A growing, deepening love affair with reality.

RA   Did this change your approach to the unknown? Your expectations of acceptance or rejection?

LS   I became a lot more sensitive, though, of course, it's hit or miss even now. I have not gotten to the point where I could really be like Augustine and say, "Love and do what you will." Profound spiritual experiences become less tangible with time, then on occasion you revisit it and recall it and say to yourself, "Wow, I've let slip something terribly important!" And it re-deepens and intensifies. It's been like that with me since. So, yes, it makes me more sensitive and in a sense, more vulnerable—unfortunately, not venerable!

RA   This is interesting. When I first heard about this trip that changed your life, I was expecting, I suppose, to hear of some substantive discovery on your part: perhaps, that you learned the world was kinder than you'd thought, or that people were better than you'd hoped. Or that the religions of the world had profound transcendent commonalities. But what I'm hearing is that the life-changing aspect of that year had to do with the discovery of self and its relationship to reality more than anything that can be relayed as information. Yes?

LS   In German, *Jein.* Meaning, "yes and no." I'll use an image I've used before: that somehow I came to a point of critical mass, and now my growth would no longer be arithmetic but geometric. That year I stumbled on the events that made me *see* that. Self-awareness was somewhat inevitable, assuming I didn't crash in my development, but it might have been years otherwise.

RA   So the trip was a catalyst?

LS   I guess you could say that. And it helped me be much more relaxed, dropped the angst level pretty close to the point of disappearance. That's self-awareness at work. And I often think that all of this could be skating on very thin ice, you know.

RA   What do you mean?

LS   I haven't had really bad challenges. Many of the things I want to do in the area of dialogue are just exploding around me, as if the world is saying, "You were on the right track fifty years ago!" I have good health, wonderful friends, no financial problems.

RA   You've had some profound challenges.

LS   I know. But no dark night of the soul.

RA   John of the Cross said: No dark night, no blessed sunrise. The darker the night, the more full and ecstatic the emergence into the light. The mystic who coined the term considered it essential.

LS   I'm fine right here, thank you. I am having such a good time! We have this mentality: if you notice you're having a good time, you'll jinx it. I'm past that. Right now I feel that I have so many good things showered on me, it would be a betrayal of the Good not to enjoy them for what they are. They are going to go away, some time, one way or another, but I'm not anxious about being anxious.

CHAPTER 18

Dialogue Decalogue and Other Astute Alliterations

He attacked everything in life with a mix of extraordinary genius and naive incompetence, and it was often difficult to tell which was which.

—DOUGLAS ADAMS, *HITCHHIKER'S GUIDE TO THE GALAXY*

I WROTE ABOUT LEN'S "Dialogue Decalogue" in an early chapter. I talked about his coming to formulate what dialogue meant and what it was, coming to a persuasive argument for its burning need: a long, slow road. Not till the whirlwind year of round-the-world encounters did he feel ready to dig into the core of the matter: Why dialogue? How dialogue? But once he dug into it, the Dialogue Decalogue was only the beginning of the debate.

Let me remind you of the 10 "commandments"—ground rules—of Len's dialogue, in my own paraphrase:

1. *Come with a desire to learn, not just to teach.*

2. *Dialogue both within your group and with those outside it.*

3. *Be sincere in your desire to seek truth together, and start out believing in others' sincerity.*

4. *Start with the points of agreement, then engage controversy.*

5. *No tradition is perfect. Be careful not to compare ideals with practice but practice with practice and ideals with ideals.*

6. *Self-identify for mutual recognition. Describe your experience of your tradition for other participants, and let them do the same.*

7. *Do not let your preconceptions obscure the other's points. Keep reconsidering.*

8. *Be conscious of power dynamics in your encounter. Value everyone's contribution.*

9. *Be willing to critique yourself and your own tradition as you seek the truth.*

10. *Try to see your dialogue partner's point of view, even for a moment.*

Of course, no theory is without its critics—especially an applied theory, especially a major one. For the past ten years, from his Teape lecture in India in 2004 to his article in *JES* in 2012, Ian Markham has offered a perfect example when he disassembled the Dialogue Decalogue. His criticism had some good points and others that were, in all honesty, unfair. It might be interesting to discuss what Markham called Len's "predominantly western" account of personhood in how it translates to dialogue in more communal cultures, as well as his charge that dialogue, though not termed exactly this, had been practiced in fact since ancient times. However, a thoughtful critic can see that Len's ground rules never consider an individual's "family, community, and religious identifications" to be "virtually irrelevant," nor—though dialogue requires some degree of open-mindedness—do the rules say that "real believers are not invited."[41]

A more nuanced and thought-provoking critique of each "commandment" was offered by the Rev. Francis Tiso in a 2008 volume of essays, *Interactive Faith*. Fully supporting Len's exhortation not to compare ideals with practice, as well as the core of some other principles, Tiso questions the wisdom of relying fully on self-identification by representatives of large religions, given our growing micro-sectarianism, and he questions the feasibility of truly seeing through the eyes of another—a call to a kind of temporary micro-conversion that has often been misunderstood.

41 Markham, "Identity."

Along with Ian Markham, Tiso wonders if the Decalogue needs revision to work for the corporate nature of large-scale interreligious dialogue and on behalf of communally minded cultures.[42]

Len finds none of this valid or interesting. He can get rather defensive about his work and angry at the "jerks" who attack it. Yet, he is not upset by the fact of attacks.

LS   You can tell you have arrived when the next generation begins to attack you, even if attacks are nonsensical. When a Catholic (the head of ecumenical affairs in DC) and an Anglican priest both deliberately attack the Dialogue Decalogue as deficient, it's a mark of having arrived.

RA   Could it be deficient?

LS   Not as they described.

RA   How so?

LS   They both started from the beginning and attacked every single item from it by presenting it in a most grossly distorted way, unrecognizable—and proceeded to destroy it. It wasn't seriously dealing with it. So, I wondered what was underneath it: why such agitated anger, why such foaming at the mouth? I responded, pointing out they'd misconstrued my position, and asked why they felt so necessary to distort it, it seemed to me. No answer.

RA   The Decalogue is pretty old. Why attack it now?

LS   The essay is in a book on dialogue that just came out. That's one of the chapters.

Leonard Swidler's theory of dialogue took root by 1990 and has been growing branches since then and leaves, blossoming here and there, and bearing occasional fruit—Len's favorite part. Back in 1978, out of *JES* grew an outreach arm, the Dialogue Institute: Interreligious, Intercultural, International. Len established the Institute to start putting dialogue into practice.

42 Tiso, "A Closer Look."

TALKING TO PAUL MOJZES

(On Len's organizations, magnetic presence, and jazzy titles)

RA   Paul, how did you encounter Len Swidler?

PM   I was teaching at Lycoming College in Williamsport, PA. Vatican II was taking place. I got a job there in the fall of '64—so, already into the Council—and we were all enthused at the department by the totally new and exciting possibilities. The five of us were thinking, *Why don't we do something on the Council and invite some clergy?* Because there was no contact at that time between Catholics and Protestants.

We invited a Catholic expert on the council from Boston, but the local bishop in Scranton was anti-ecumenical and gave him a resounding, "No." Then a bishop from Washington was willing to come, but when we told him what our bishop had done, he politely declined coming into this hornets' nest. We were ready to give up when we heard of this Swidler: He was a lay person, didn't need permission, and was ready to say, "Yes" to every occasion. He came for two or three days, and it was wonderful. We were sold. We got in touch with King's College, and before long we had department-to-department visits and cooperated across ecumenical lines.

RA   Is that when you got drafted to help with *JES*?

PM   Len is always on the lookout to snatch someone to do something along his lines. He heard I was from Yugoslavia and asked me to screen periodicals from that part of the world. Then about 1970, I was looking to leave Lycoming, and he put me in touch with Rosemont College, near Philly, where I am still teaching. So, indirectly, he is responsible for my being here. He may have made a call for me.

RA   You never asked him if he had?

PM   In some sense, I assumed that he had. He is the kind of person who goes to bat for you. Always, if you ask him something, he starts thinking hard and has practical suggestions. He has an uncanny ability to see a problem and not let it stymie him.

Sometimes they are pretty wild ideas; not everything works, but that's the kind of mind he has: a very bold, imaginative perception of what can be done. I haven't yet heard him say, "It can't be done."

So now I was here, and of course I could do more for the *Journal*. Eventually I became Len's Co-Editor and have been ever since.

RA   Is *JES* Len's favorite baby?

PM   Len has a bit of Taoism in him. *Wei-wu-wei*: "action through inaction." "Let it be, and the right things will happen." He has produced an enormous number of organizations, not all of which come to fruition, but for almost every project of his he's come up with a jazzy title, so there are things out there semi-organized. Sometimes there are check books.

RA   And plaques with the projects' names!

PM   Yeah, and it's all hanging there, some ideas dying. Others work. Still, besides the *Journal*, one thing that certainly didn't die was the Dialogue Institute.

RA   It was called IIID when it was founded in 1978, wasn't it? Institute for Interreligious, Intercultural Dialogue?

PM   It went through various modifications, but he is 100 percent behind it. He spends all his time trying to promote it. In some ways he still puts effort into ecumenism, but more and more he perceives the challenge of changing those parts of the world that are utterly hostile to interreligious communities, and so he goes to China and Pakistan and Iraq and Jordan—you name it, he's there.

RA   Is he effective?

PM   His presence is a magnetic presence. He's got this unbelievably magnetic way of persuading people that this is the future, and, if we don't do it, we will harm the future. He is also down to earth. He doesn't use big words, except sometimes he'll throw down some Latin phrase—and I don't know what it means, and I'm sure almost nobody else does—but he doesn't use this academic, dense language.

I was very impressed that Len does not become defensive. Some guy in Turkey said the word "dialogue" was suspect, and Len said, "Okay, how about another word? How about 'learning together'?" He links people, and they become his followers. There's a bunch of people out there who see themselves pretty much as disciples of Len Swidler. That's the achievement of Len.

RA   How do you see yourself? Are you friends?

PM   Here's something: We met in 1964, and it is now 2013. In all of these years, we've never had a single fight. Not one argument. There've been times when I was mad at him. Partially, it's his tendency not to answer your questions—he would write these thousands of emails to everyone under the sun with not one answer to one practical question I really needed an answer to. Finally, we talked about it, but we still didn't fight. He makes it impossible to fight with him. He is so flexible that he absorbs aggression and hostility.

RA   He is disarming, isn't he? And does the *mea culpa* so sincerely, you can't stay angry.

PM   Yes. I've never had a relationship like that with anybody. Len and I don't socialize much together, but we are best friends in understanding, willingness to work together, sacrifice for a greater goal. This is the core of what I value so much.

DIALOGUE DECALOGUE (CONT'D)

Jazzy titles are indeed Len's particular specialty. Jazzy labels, too. Academics are known for winding, boring titles more akin to abstracts. Not Len. He's authored over eighty books, a number of articles too bothersome to calculate, and seems now to use titles as punch lines, from *Death or Dialogue* to his recent tome on reluctant Christianity, *Club Modernity*. But by far he is most exceedingly fond of alliteration. Since the inception of "deep-dialogue," many a string of like-lettered leads have poured off his stylus: the Dialogue Decalogue, of course, then "Competitive

Cooperation," and, conceivably, his favorite: "the Dialogue of the Head, Hands, and Heart."

As he immerses more and more deeply into the grassroots, daily practice of worldwide dialogue, he writes more and more of our increasingly global village, of the ubiquitous symbiosis between person and society and all things different in this Age of Convergence. He writes of the symbiosis between matter and energy, body and spirit, woman and man—and he calls it all "the Cosmic Dance of Dialogue."

Reality itself, our very existence, is predicated on mutuality—dialogical—and Leonard Swidler formulates humanity's conscious effort to be authentically so with the 3 H's of dialogue: in the Dialogue of the Head we pursue the truth together through conversation with those who think differently; in the Dialogue of the Hands we pursue the good together by working with others to heal the world; in the Dialogue of the Heart we pursue the spirit together by sharing beauty and mystery through the arts, the prayers, and the expressions of self. Not everywhere on Earth do people sit around tables, conducting dialogue, but everywhere on Earth dialogue is going on: head, hands, or heart.

Len always brings up his H's. He's had so much affection for them that over the years three H's have grown into seven: "*the Dialogues of the Head, Hands, Heart in Holistic Harmony of the Holy Human.*" I asked him once if his fondness for alliteration wasn't breaking the boundaries of moderation. Catchy is useful, but will the audience take an idea seriously if it sounds like a game?

He didn't argue but didn't answer. Moved his eyebrows around just a little. Smiled and changed the topic. The cosmic dance of dialogue was turning cartwheels on his face.

I don't know that I understood that smile, but it seemed to say something like this to me: *Nothing wrong with a game, I think. A good game can change the world.*

PART VI

The Ocean of YOU

Talking to Len
(On the dialogical nature of reality)

LS   Fundamentally, the universe is dialogue between energy and matter, positive and negative forces—everything. This is the structure of all reality. When we have "dialogue of the head," we say "Wow, good dialogue!" because we are consciously carrying out this cosmic dance of dialogue. At the peak level of words, we are doing what describes the whole of reality. That's why it feels right: we are aware of being in sync with the whole of reality.

In martial arts, why are effective moves the ones that line up all the forces in synchronicity? It gives them exponentially larger force. That's how I understand dialogue now: down at the physical level, all knowing is dialogic, except most of the time we seem to be unaware of it, and it's only now, in recent times, that some humans are recognizing that it's the very nature of reality and very much so our humanness.

Now that means that all our actions and thinking in all fields need to be fundamentally dialogic. How that is going to look is something we have to work out, but it seems to me this is the major path for the foreseeable future. Even given the rapidity of change, it may be several centuries.

RA   What might it look like? Have you started working it out?

LS   In a sense. There is already an openness among my students on many issues today that just wasn't there when I started teaching. I think the internet has much to do with it. I think we're only at the very beginning of this new wave of student thinking, and, as it progresses, it will transform education. On the flip side of serious dialogue is thinking critically and with emotional intelligence. Eventually it will have to issue into some kind of "competitive cooperation."

RA   What is that?

LS   Cooperation is easy to see: We work together for a win-win. The competitive part is important. First, we compete with ourselves for improvement. That's the meaning of *jihad* in Islam: I compete with my own dark side. And, then, in many circumstances a win-win is really possible, especially if, as we compete with one another, we draw each other into more creative thinking, so there is more beauty, more truth, more goodness—more being than there would be otherwise.

Even if someone must lose a competition, cooperation is possible. For example, students compete for a chance to come to the Dialogue Institute for our State Department-sponsored program—say, from Lebanon—and only one out of fifteen gets to come. Well, I hope the time will come when those who didn't get the spot, maybe from several years, and the bureaucrats involved will come up with creative solutions for what to do with all this wonderful energy and good intention. That's a dialogic solution that will happen more often and in every facet of every dimension of life. Media, travel, engineering, and on and on. All reality is dialogic with competition and cooperation involved, and we need to create ways to maximize the good and minimize destruction.

RA   You've been trying to make this happen, devoting a lot of energy to practical engagement in dialogue over theory.

LS   I must say, there is a level on which I feel quite incomplete because I see my theoretical work needing to be really, substantively institutionalized to flourish—lived out. I'm trying to make the grassroots, practical aspect of dialogue vastly more effective than it is, and it can be done only in that I or someone else can make it institutionalized.

RA   More institutionalized than it is now?

LS   I'd love to have $20 million to put together staff and structure that I know are there with training and experience, to pull them into a dynamically effective network worldwide—maybe through the DI—a really powerful institution promoting dialogue not simply among religions but in all aspects of human society! This is the way to multiply the effect of the idea and all that it entails. In a real sense, this cooperating is on a social level—dialogue in action—while talking is dialogue in theory. If I could get $20 million tomorrow, I would put everything aside and concentrate on doing that.

RA   Are you saying that you've done all you can do where theory is concerned and now wish you could just put that theory into practice?

LS   And then, the theory would expand also exponentially. There are all these areas of life—business, the media, education, all the culture-shaping institutions of society—that need to have dialogic mentality.

RA   Medicine, government?

LS   Yes! Nobody knows how that would look, in media or in medicine. We need all the experienced and experiencing people in these fields to be networked together. Each field would be dramatically transformed and transforming others. That could be a whole other dimension of human life. Like in that town in 1776 that got an idea that "all men" are created equal—this is the idea that all life is fundamentally dialogic.

RA   What does dialogue with a dog look like?

LS   I don't know. It's important for us how we treat others. Dialogue is learning and teaching, and I learned lots from my dog. What I learned from Chubby was this incredible love he had for me. When I was in trouble, he was very disturbed and went to get help, so I learned about love and loyalty.

RA   What did he learn?

LS   Maybe, that he really did love me.

RA   Or . . . we don't know?

LS   Right.

CHAPTER 19

Church Named Dialogue: "Love and do what you will"

*Sure there's different roads from this to Dungarvan—some thinks
one road pleasanter, and some thinks another; wouldn't it be mighty
foolish to quarrel for this?—and sure isn't it twice worse to thry to
interfere with people for choosing the road they like best to heaven?*

—MARGUERITE BLESSINGTON, *THE REPEALERS*

I WAS AMUSED, IN the midst of writing this book, to discover the most
cogent and uncompromising rejection of Len's theory of dialogue in
an email exchange on one of Len's countless listservs. It started when
someone threw off a passing, disparaging comment about him, and Len
responded in his usual manner—trying to connect—and was firmly and
politely rebuffed, but Len is Len. He kept trying, prying, and pushing, and
in the end, I watched unfold a protracted debate on pluralism, dialogue,
and the nature of truth. I later wrote to Len's interlocutor and found out
that he is a Franciscan Brother from Malaysia, with an education in theology. He and his colleagues practice dialogue in their home country, in
their own way, and find the very foundational concepts of Len Swidler's
worldview both archaic and laughable. He wanted to remain anonymous,
so in these pages he will be our Malaysian Brother X.

Mainly, Brother X opposes Len's model of dialogue because he feels it demands a degree of assimilation of traditions and abolishes deep conviction. Danger: relativism. "Such a paradigm of dialogue inevitably breeds a strange form of pluralism that levels everyone's unique view down to an unjustified homogeneity," he wrote in his email. "What starts as an attempt to respect all people's views inevitably ends up disrespecting everyone's views and pleasing no one except the self-appointed arbiter of the newly developed pluralistic framework. I find such dialogue to be illusive, and frankly, quite narcissistic."

Of course, Len disagreed, suspected a misunderstanding, insisted on more detail, and eventually got it. Brother X explained:

> [By positing that "all knowledge is interpreted knowledge"], you have abolished the possibility of absolute truth, so nobody can actually know the reality in a truly objective way. You have, effectively, just informed the reader that your statement itself is your interpreted knowledge and cannot be taken as absolute. The only thing that you can then be sure of is that you cannot be sure of knowing anything for sure at all.

While for Len the idea of interpreted knowledge substantiates the need for dialogue, for Brother X it begs the opposite question: If any statement is a matter of perception, why take it seriously? Why dialogue? How do I know that your opinion is reflective of the reality it claims to represent? "In the end," he writes, "we would all end up just talking much about nothing much." He finds irony in this "tyranny of subjectivism": Since nobody's views are objectively valid, everyone's views are valid. Since "nobody knows everything about anything," nobody's views need be taken too seriously. Then, anything goes but nothing must. In the mind of Brother X, this "brand of 'dialogue' ends up disrespecting everyone in a very respectful way."

But here's the kicker: Len believes absolutely in his "brand" of dialogue, in the need for this dialogue, in the interpreted nature of all knowledge. He believes it so much that, when someone rejects the idea, he blames either a misunderstanding or willful ignorance, and Brother X picks up on that. "In the end," he writes, "you would expect everyone to respect the objectivity of your view that nobody's view is objective."

Brother X doesn't accuse Len explicitly of hypocrisy, only of pseudo-scholarship and of internal contradiction in his views, but, really, hypocrisy is what he sees in Len's stand, and he turns away:

What happened to divinely revealed knowledge? Or has the Objective Divine now been removed from the equation and replaced by the Human Divine as the subjective arbiter of truth and reality? If it is so, then I suppose the most apt definition of dialogue would be, "a community of non-knowers playing the guessing game together and never being able to arrive at any conclusion because nobody can know anything for sure," which makes dialogue a royal waste of time. When I dialogue with my partners, I expect them to be people who are serious about their views and who believe their faith to be good and true and objective. And at the end of the dialogue, even if we cannot agree, we still respect each other as people of conviction.

Again and again, Len's answers started the same way: *Dear friend, you don't seem to understand what I am saying!* And he launched into an explanation of what he meant by "true" with his favorite example of a door. Three people might describe the same door in three different ways: The door is wooden. The door is closed. The door is green. Each observer states the perception that he or she, for some reason, prioritizes. Each statement is true in that it reflects reality, but no statement is exhaustive and, so, no statement is absolute. If we can add to each other's perceptions of such mundane things, how much more so when it comes to the most complex of all things: religion? Len defines religion as an explanation of the ultimate meaning of life and how to live accordingly—based on a notion and experience of the Transcendent.

Len believes that Brother X and he miscommunicated about the term "truth," and I think he is right, but it's not a semantic problem. I think it's bigger than that. Len's "truth" is a human-made series of statements about reality, measured for accuracy and completeness—by us. Brother X's Truth is the Reality itself, looming and permeating and absolute, and we are the ones who are measured in relation to it, by our closeness to it, by our degree of comprehension. And we are defined by the shining light of that which we know of it.

I think also that Len and Brother X miscommunicated about the term "dialogue," and it, too, is not a semantic problem. In the world of Len Swidler, dialogue partners are open-minded, open-hearted seekers of greater knowledge. To make the world better, they come to learn. Dialogue is mutual enrichment. In the world of Brother X, dialogue partners are benevolent, deeply convinced seekers of harmony. To make the world better, they reach out across the divide. Dialogue is persuasion. Neither considers the other's to be, really, dialogue.

RA   Len, what do you say to Brother X and those who point out that you preach incompleteness of all truths, but that you are utterly convinced of your definition of dialogue, that it is inherent in the human condition? You believe it will save the world. In essence, you implore us to dialogue, but not to dialogue *about dialogue*.

LS   I would say that we have not only to engage in dialogue but also to employ critical thinking, which entails being clear about the meaning of terms. There's an understanding of "dialogue" as I and many others are using it now—in the last seventy-five years or so—as the way I spell it out. Others use that term in other ways, and that's fine; language is conventional. But we should note that and not confuse ourselves.

RA   Are you saying that this accusation is equivocal? They're using a different meaning of the term?

LS   Yes. They are using it differently even in their different statements. They are simply confused. One wants to search endlessly for a better grasp of reality. This is what everybody wants to do. When they charge me with hypocrisy, it's either deliberate duplicity on their part or lack of clarity in thinking.

RA   You wanted to exchange personal background information with Brother X, but he declined, repeatedly. Why do you think that interaction on a personal level helps in a discussion of scholarly matters?

LS   He had total resistance. A psychologist might say he is very frightened that what he holds to be the anchor to a meaning of life is embattled all around, and he dare not admit it to himself. And to become even slightly friendly with someone who holds a challenging view will make him vulnerable.

RA   Isn't it possible he was just not interested?

LS   No. Why would he feel it was so irritating and challenging? If he'd answered with ease, it would have made our conversation more human rather than left on the level of abstraction where one tends to move toward debate rather than dialogue, or to score points. When you're personally engaged, it's easier to say, "That's really not what I meant," easier to trust.

Parenthetically, let me say that this response to dialogue emerges almost immediately. People like Ian Markham say that only liberals can engage in dialogue. I answer, "Yes, that's right. Only those who are willing to learn from others." Barest minimum, you will learn what your interlocutor thinks, and your behavior will adjust accordingly. If you are not open to the possibility, you are obviously not engaging in dialogue. Of course, many people still think to engage in dialogue is an evil, sin, and betrayal.

RA   How do you relate to such a person?

LS   Respect, human love, that sort of thing. And in the areas of dialogue . . . Besides the dialogue of the head, you can do things. Dialogue of the hands and heart. That is precisely where one ought to go with those who refuse dialogue of the head. It might move them there. Here is an obvious example: When atheists, Jews, and Christians found themselves in jail together as a result of civil rights marches, they asked each other, "Why are you doing this?" Same happened in Nazi camps. Perhaps, for a vast majority of people dialogue of the head is the last step they reach.

Since I have known Len Swidler, I've pondered his consuming, unwavering passion for dialogue, but only with the help of others have I come to formulate what I now believe to be the meaning of dialogue in his life. It's more than a professional pursuit, more even than a cause. Len has always been a sincere and evolving Christian, but in a certain sense, I think, his religion is Dialogue.

Per Faaland once pointed out to me how easy it is for Len to step out of his Catholicism to propose incompleteness of religious truths. He approaches dialogue as a humanist, and he is the first to admit that Christianity can be wrong. Not so with Dialogue. He appears to feel about Dialogue in the way of those believers who condemn him for what they experience as relativism in religion: His idea of dialogue is *the* idea, and to him it's the only way to exist. Dialogue will save the world. He knows this in the depth of his soul, and he stands no challenge to this knowledge.

Len believes in Dialogue utterly, absolutely. It governs not only his day and his relationships but his cosmology as well: Reality itself is "dialogic." He would like to see all social structures and institutions based on Dialogue explicitly and overtly. Without saying it, he is working for Dialogue to become our state religion, perpetuated by the government into the education system, healthcare, and business structures.

He implores us to dialogue, and he will dialogue, but not about Dialogue. He can respect those who differ from his views, but not to the degree of allowing pluralism when it comes to the concept of Dialogue itself. If they reject his Dialogue, they are wrong. He bears no ill will. He'll try again. He hopes they'll come around. Len's church named Dialogue practices tolerance, but yet he knows that they are wrong.

A long time ago Len Swidler set out to be a saint and an intellectual. He was a devout Catholic. He wanted to be a monk; he wanted to be a priest. And then, the life by which he defined sanctity fell apart and slipped through his fingers, so he went looking for sainthood in the world, and he found his devotion in the realm of intellect.

We've talked a lot about spirituality, Len and I, and it is more than his words that leads me here: It is the aura of this person, the landscape of his soul.

Leonard Swidler's Christianity is kind and reflective. He delivers it to a grateful listener as a pillar of ethical guidance, a source of aesthetic tradition, and an opportunity for sacramental experience. Len's Christianity is loving and friendly and intellectually stimulating. I often get an impression that Jesus to him is a brotherly, somewhat mystical, somewhat scholarly presence, semi-historical and semi-abstract: an epitome of the true human good, more to talk about than to talk to.

Christianity is certainly the philosophical and moral background of his life, but Dialogue—that's an earth-shaking, life-guiding engine: the framework of existence and its purpose, the discovery, the foreground. By Len's own definition of religion—an explanation of the ultimate meaning of life and how to live accordingly—it has all the requisite components: a set of beliefs about reality and a community to share them and to practice the rites. It didn't have a code of rights and wrongs, but Len's taken care of that.

He is calm about Christianity. He is on fire about Dialogue. In many ways, Dialogue is less an academic discipline and more a social movement, but Len set out to be an intellectual and a saint, and he fell in love with a noble cause and was converted. And he created it into an intellectual pursuit. And he became the saint of Dialogue.

Talking to Len

(On YOU and the meaning of sainthood)

RA   Len, what happened to your life goals? Do you feel you've achieved them?

LS   Well, I got started on this whole path back in my college days, which led me to sign up for the religious life with the Norbertines. The goals that I had were to become an intellectual and to become a saint. I think that in a kind of *sotto voce* manner those two ideals have really continued. What it means to be an intellectual is not difficult to grasp, but becoming a saint these days is not so clear and simple, especially as science is finding more answers. It's clear to me and lots of other Christian thinkers that you don't have to have God in the picture to answer everything.

         In other words, we can't prove the existence of the Transcendent. So I continue to grope for that which is beyond reach—which clearly is the nature of human beings.

RA   Is that what a saint is? One who searches for more?

LS   I'm not sure. I think certainly finding myself on this path bespeaks being on the path toward sainthood, whatever that might be. But I am at the point where the angst is gone: *Que será, será*. My thinking about it will not affect the reality of it. Not that I know that.

RA   Modern physics says it might.

LS   That's true. That's why I say I can't know for sure. I'll just do my best. *Satis est*: "That's sufficient."

I like the phrase from Augustine: "Love and do what you will." Interestingly, Confucius had something similar: that at age seventy you can do what you will because you won't drift away from the proper.

RA   It's about wisdom and virtue.

LS   Right. The development of virtue. If you practice enough, the act of courage or prudence becomes second nature. I write about virtue ethics in *Club Modernity*. I wish we would educate ourselves not about what to do in a particular case but about how to be. There's a famous case about telling a lie: If a Nazi knocks on your door and asks if you are hiding Jews, do you lie? Sometimes it's not a choice between good or evil but between greater and lesser evil. When the conflict is between persons and principles, principles are for persons and not the other way around.

RA   Jesus did say, "Sabbath is for man and not man for the Sabbath."

LS   Yes.

RA   Does this help you with the answer on what it means to be a saint?

LS   Okay, on July 9, 2013, I reflect on what it means to be a saint to Len Swidler. I guess a saint I would like to be is someone who takes his, let's say, worldly obligations eminently seriously, whatever they happen to be, tries to carry them all out as thoughtfully as possible. Like consciously driving a car, I am driving my worldly activity at that level, but inwardly I'm aware of myself asking, "Hello? Am I alone? I hope I am not."

So, ultimately, I am looking for Dialogue. I don't expect a dialogue in the customary sense. I went riding my bike this morning and meditating: *Is somebody there or just me?* I don't expect to hear the voice: *YEAH!* I have a sense that this Reality is personal, a whole ocean of YOU out there, but I don't know what to expect. In a sense, I don't expect anything. But I don't *not* expect anything. I am "on the way." *In via.* A seeker, I might say.

RA   Is that part of sainthood?

LS   An integral part. I find that this all much more easily results in loving other persons and other things.

There's an intimate connection that's not easy to explain, but the medieval notion of the True, the Beautiful, and the Good all being different facets of Being, it's a great notion. There is a kind of special blessing we have in English: that word, "Being." In many languages you have to use the infinitive, but this gerund is a kind of magic. It is active, not static, but it means entity and the very state of existence at the same time: life rather than non-life, reality rather than non-reality.

RA   God as a Being. Being as existence. The "ocean of YOU"?

LS   The way we think in the language determines how we perceive reality.

RA   It sounds like you've achieved your goals pretty well. You're an intellectual, no arguing there. By your definition, you're a saint.

LS   Hopefully, on the way. Maybe, a *bodhisattva*?

Bibliography

Baum, Gregory. "Rethinking the Church's Mission after Auschwitz." In *Auschwitz: Beginning of a New Era? Reflections on the Holocaust,* edited by Eva Fleischner. New York: KTAV, 1977.

Benedict, Ruth. *The Chrysanthemum and the Sword: Patterns of Japanese culture.* Houghton Mifflin Harcourt, 1967.

Blet, Pierre. *Pius XII and the Second World War: According to the Archives of the Vatican.* Translated by Lawrence J. Johnson. Paulist, 1999.

"Charter of the Rights of Catholics in the Church." Association for the Rights of Catholics in the Church. http://arcc-catholic-rights.net/arcc_charter.htm.

"China: Six Who Rule—And Remember." *Time Magazine,* September 26, 1983. http://content.time.com/time/subscriber/article/0,33009,949822-1,00.html

Collins, Paul. *From Inquisition to Freedom: Seven prominent Catholics and their struggle with the Vatican.* Continuum International, 2001.

Corley, Kathleen E. Review of *Jesus Was a Feminist: What the Gospels Reveal about His Revolutionary Perspective,* by Leonard Swidler. *RBL* 12/2008. http://www.bookreviews.org/pdf/6342_6909.pdf.

Ebrey, Patricia, and Anne Walthall. *East Asia: A Cultural, Social, and Political History.* Vol. II: From 1600. 3rd ed., illustrated. Cengage Learning, 2013.

Fahey, Rev. Denis., C.C.Sp. *The Kingship of Christ and the Conversion of the Jewish Nation.* Dublin: Holy Ghost Missionary College, 1953. http://www.traditionalcatholic.net/Tradition/Information/Conversion_of_Jewish_Nation.

Folk Tales from Many Lands. Retold by Lilian Gask. New York, NY: Thomas Y. Crowell, 1910. http://digital.library.upenn.edu/women/gask/tales/MOUSE.html.

Häring, Bernard. *My Witness for the Church.* Translated by Leonard Swidler. Paulist, 1992.

Hebblethwaite, Peter. "Don Pedro in History." *America,* February 16, 1991. http://americamagazine.org/issue/100/don-pedro-history-2

Hope-Wallace, Philip. "Michael Redgrave as Lear." *The Guardian,* July 16, 1953. http://www.theguardian.com/theguardian/1953/jul/16/1.

Hopkins, William B. *The Pacific War: The Strategy, Politics, and Players that Won the War.* Minneapolis, MN: Zenith, 2008.

Hurt, Raymond. "Tuberculosis sanatorium regimen in the 1940s: a patient's personal diary." *J R Soc Med* 97 7 (2004 July) 350–53. http://www.ncbi.nlm.nih.gov/pmc/articles/PMC1079536/

Ketchaver, Karen G. "Father Charles E. Coughlin—The 'Radio Priest' of the 1930s." *Theological Librarianship* 2 2 (Dec 2009) 81–88. https://journal.atla.com/ojs/index.php/theolib/article/viewFile/112/372.

Markham, Ian. "Identity, Accountability, Hospitality." *JES* 47 3 (Summer 2012): 385–393.

Maslow, Abraham. *Religions, Values, and Peak-Experiences.* Compass. Penguin, 1994.

Milquet, Mary Kay. "De Pere sesquicentennial 1857–2007." De Pere Historical Society. http://deperehistoricalsociety.org/sesquicentennial.php.

Neigh, Scott. Review of *Jesus Was a Feminist* by Leonard Swidler. April 18, 2008. *A Canadian Lefty in Occupied Land* (blog). http://scottneigh.blogspot.com/2008/04/review-jesus-was-feminist.html.

"Papua." U.S. Army Center of Military History. October 3, 2003 http://www.history.army.mil/brochures/papua/papua.htm.

Phayer, Michael. *Pius XII, the Holocaust, and the Cold War.* Indiana University Press, 2007.

Postanovlenie GD FS RF #262-5 GD, February 04, 2008, "O Zayavlenii Gosudarstvennoy Dumy Federalnogo Sobraniya Rossiyskoy Federatzii 'Pamyati Zhertv Goloda 30-h Godov Na Terrirorii SSSR'." http://duma.consultant.ru/page.aspx?955838.

"Report on the 2010 Oberammergau Passion Play Script." Council of Centers on Jewish-Christian Relations. May 14, 2010. http://www.ccjr.us/news/statements/821-ccjr2010may14

Rocca, Francis X. "Under Pope Francis, liberation theology comes of age." *Catholic News Service*, September 13, 2013. http://www.catholicnews.com/data/stories/cns/1303902.htm.

Saros, Daniel E. *Labor, Industry, and Regulation during the Progressive Era.* Routledge, 2008.

Shafer, Ingrid. "Bernard Häring, CSsR (1912–1998): Celebrating a courageous life dedicated to Love, Faith, Truth, and Human Dignity." August 4, 1998. http://projects.usao.edu/~facshaferi/haring1.htm.

St. John, Vincent. *The I.W.W.—Its History, Structure, and Methods* (University of Arizona Special Collections AZ 114 box 1, folder 1A, exhibit 19). University of Arizona Web Exhibit: The Bisbee Deportation of 1917. August 3, 2013. http://www.library.arizona.edu/exhibits/bisbee/docs/019.html.

Stewart, Barbara. "Bernard Haring, 85, Is Dead; Challenged Catholic Morality." *The New York Times*, July 11, 1998. http://www.nytimes.com/1998/07/11/world/bernard-haring-85-is-dead-challenged-catholic-morality.html.

Swidler, Leonard. *After the Absolute: the dialogical future of religious reflection.* Minneapolis, MN: Fortress, 1990.

———. "'In the Beginning Was the Thought.'" *JES* 49 1 (Winter 2014) 7–12.

———. *Jesus Was a Feminist: What the Gospels Reveal about His Revolutionary Perspective.* Lanham, MD: Sheed & Ward, 2007.

———. "A Life in Dialogue: autobiographical reflections." Personal notes. 2010. Last accessed June 2014, http://astro.temple.edu/~swidler/autobiographical_fragments.htm.

Talbi, Mohamed. Interview by Lina Lazaar. *Ibraaz,* April 10, 2011. http://www.ibraaz.org/interviews/7.

Tiso, Rev. Dr. Francis. "A Closer Look at Swidler's 'Dialogue Decalogue.'" In *Interactive Faith: The Essential Interreligious Community-Building Handbook*, 231–39. Edited by Bud Heckman. Walking Together, Finding the Way. Skylight Paths, 2008.

Warren, Donald. *Radio Priest: Charles Coughlin, the Father of Hate Radio.* Free Press, 1996.

Made in United States
North Haven, CT
26 January 2022

15302118R00166